How to Mother a Successful Daughter

ALSO BY NICKY MARONE

How to Father a Successful Daughter

What's Stopping You? Overcome Learned Helplessness and Do What You Never Dreamed Possible (published in hardcover as *Women and Risk*)

How to Mother a Successful Daughter

A Practical Guide to Empowering Girls from Birth to Eighteen

NICKY MARONE

Three Rivers Press

New York

Published by Three Rivers Press, 201 East 50th Street, New York, New York, 10022. Member of the Crown Publishing Group.

Originally published in hardcover by Harmony Books in 1998. First paperback edition published in 1999.

Random House, Inc. New York, Toronto, London, Sydney, Auckland www.randomhouse.com

Three Rivers Press is a registered trademark of Random House, Inc.

Printed in the United States of America

Design by Susan Hood

Library of Congress Cataloging-in-Publication Data
Marone, Nicky.
How to mother a successful daughter: a practical guide to empowering girls from birth to eighteen / by Nicky Marone.—1st pbk. ed.
Originally published: New York: Harmony Books, © 1998
Includes bibliographical references.
1. Mothers and daughters. 2. Daughters—Psychology.
3. Teenage girls—Psychology. 4. Self-esteem in adolescence.
5. Parenting. 6. Sex role. I. Title.
HQ755.85.M273 1998
649'.133—dc21
97-14587

ISBN 0-609-80276-3

10 9 8 7 6 5 4 3 2 1

First Paperback Edition

To my mother, Maxine, a fierce, funny, difficult, loving, and talented woman whose influence I will never be able to truly measure.

Yet the circle would not be complete without mention of the other adult women who mothered me as a girl and who presented such splendid, diverse, and striking models of femininity. They also happened to be my aunts: Aunt Blanche, Aunt Estelle, and Aunt Anne. No girl ever enjoyed such luck as I did in being exposed to a group of smart and caring female mentors. Their lessons linger with me still.

Acknowledgments

From inception to completion, a book is a collaborative effort. The dedication of the following people made this book what it is.

First, many thanks to my editor, Leslie Meredith, for giving me the opportunity to share this information, for her commitment to girls, and for her professional acumen; to Laura Wood for the close reading and diligent effort she gave to this project; and to my agent, Sandy Dijkstra, for her extraordinary foresight, keen judgment, and loyal support over many years.

I would like to recognize the work of my professional associates Alice Swanson, Lisa Gerstacker, Janet Beardsley, and Suzanne Roser for the many different ways in which they contribute to helping women and girls achieve their goals.

And finally, the deepest gratitude goes to Deana Bennet, Alice Cohen, Kristen Yount, Suzanne Gerleit, Mary Neumann, Rick Losoff, and Dennis Shaver for being there when I needed help through the trying times that accompanied the writing of this book.

Contents

Contents

PART I

Getting the Big Picture

CHAPTER 1

Achievement Behavior

Here Today, Gone Tomorrow?

At puberty, my daughter pulled a Jekyll and Hyde thing, only it was Thelma and Louise. She went from being Louise, strong and levelheaded, to being Thelma, goofy and naive.

*Patty, workshop participant and mother
of a fourteen-year-old girl*

"I swear there was no way to see this coming," said a woman in a blue jogging suit. "Holly always had a strong sense of who she was. She was bright, assertive, got good grades in school. Then, at twelve, it all just seemed to drain out of her." She paused. "I was so sure it wasn't going to happen to her."

"I know what you mean; it happened to my daughter, too," replied a woman in the back row. "Amy went from wanting to be a heart surgeon to dropping out of organic chemistry the minute she got confused."

"My daughter has been a nearly straight-A student," added another. "This year she finally encountered a math class she couldn't breeze through, so she has become convinced that she is stupid."

"My daughter still likes math," said a nurse in uniform, "but she is considering dropping it next year because she doesn't like competing with 'a bunch of obnoxious boys.' She says she doesn't want to act like *them.*"

"I can relate to that," mumbled a woman in the back.

If I had handpicked them myself, I could not have assembled a group of women who more accurately represented the diversity of modern mothers. Baby boomers and Gen-X'ers; working women in dresses, business suits, and jeans; academic types with glasses hanging around their necks; nurses in uniforms and moms in jogging outfits; mothers of daughters from infants to teenagers. What united them, despite their diversity of backgrounds, economic situations, and education, was their concern for their daughters, especially during the crisis of puberty. This was their first session in a six-week seminar for mothers who wished to raise successful daughters.

"I think my story is scarier," said a woman who appeared to be on the verge of tears. "My daughter is in love with a boy that *I* think is a loser. There are so many nice boys in our neighborhood she could pick from, but no, she likes this one who gets bad grades, has an attitude, and verbally abuses her. She sneaks out at night to meet this kid. Remember, this is a girl who used to challenge boys in elementary school."

She paused to sip coffee from a foam cup. "The other night I overheard her talking on the phone. I almost lost it when I heard her say how cool it would be to get married and have his baby! I went ballistic, to use one of her favorite phrases. My God, she's only fourteen!"

"I know what you mean," said the woman whose eyeglasses kept falling off her nose. "My daughter was the star forward on the basketball team, but the minute she got a boyfriend she lost interest and quit. I never thought it would happen to her, either." There was a pause. Then she turned to me and said, "Is there any way to turn this situation around?"

The low self-esteem, lack of persistence, lowered aspirations, and self-doubt that are suddenly (or so it seems) manifested in teenage girls—even in many of the brightest high achievers—have shocked these mothers into seeking help. They feel frustration and pain when they witness this change of behavior in their daughters, and the mothers of younger girls are hoping to take preventative measures.

On a recent episode of *The Oprah Winfrey Show* featuring the authors of some of the latest books on teenage girls, audience members listened attentively to the data on the crisis of confidence that overwhelms many girls at or during adolescence. Then, in tones of desperation, they began to plead, "But what do we *do?*" The standard advice to "raise your daughter's self-esteem" was too bland to be of much help.

Luckily, help is available. Research on resilience and persistence offers information that can be used to help keep daughters hardy in spite of the fact that the culture into which they have been born is not "girl-friendly." This book will offer mothers a fresh perspective from which to view the situation and bring provocative new insights to the discussion of girls and achievement. You will learn concrete strategies based on thirty years of research in the fields of learning theory, gender studies, and self-esteem. The information, advice, and techniques are presented in age-appropriate segments. Let's begin with what we know about girls as they grow up.

My Daughter, the Amazon Warrior

First, the good news. Girls actually have a developmental advantage over boys: they talk earlier, count earlier, read earlier, and get better grades in grade school. Prior to age twelve, many girls are bold, even brazen, willing to challenge boys in a variety of situations and not give a hang what the boys think. Young girls are curious about their environment, eager to explore and try new things. Full of moxie, they may become indignant at inequities, objecting that "boys get to do everything." As a mother in one of my workshops put it, "My daughter Megan is a fourth grader. She goes around acting like an Amazon on a mission from God. Honestly, sometimes I wish she'd tone it down a little."

Even if your daughter is not an Amazon-in-training, if she is under age twelve you probably recognize some of the above qualities in her. Only the degree may be different. In other words, prior to age twelve, most girls exhibit a certain style of behavior that is conducive to healthy risk-taking and high achievement. Professional educators know enough about this style to have given it a name: *mastery-oriented behavior*—a complex and interdependent set of skills that you will read about throughout this book. *Mastery-oriented behavior is the persistent effort over time—not destiny, heredity, or luck—that produces desired outcomes.* Also known as *self-efficacy* or, more popularly, *achievement-related behavior,* it consists of specific attitudes, behavior patterns, and responses. The critical factor in staying resilient in the face of difficulty and confusion is a behavioral style exhibited by all successful adults.

Many girls, however, experience a precipitous fall in confidence, aspirations, and motivation, which affects their performance and achievement. This fall is documented not only in the literature but by distraught parents as well.[1] We know that this phenomenon is partly the result of firmly entrenched patriarchal values in the school system. Schools have catered to males and male learning styles while failing to provide an equitable education to girls.[2] But this is only half the story.

While writing my first book, based on the breakthrough discovery that successful, high-achieving women had encouraging fathers with whom they identified, I realized what the key element was in a father's influence: fathers tend to reinforce and promote the mastery-oriented behavior exhibited by their children. Fathers who were close to their daughters, or who had no sons, mentored their daughters—a service usually reserved for boys. As it turned out, these girls responded as positively to the reinforcement of mastery as boys did. Today's girls need models of mastery and positive risk-taking in their *mothers*. They need to observe how adult women— their mothers, aunts, neighbors, and teachers—triumph over societal forces that see women as weak and passive. In other words, girls need both exemplary modeling and skillful mentoring from their mothers and other women to help them stay hardy and resilient and keep their high aspirations and motivation to succeed.

Accordingly, the purpose of this book is threefold: (1) to raise your awareness of the connections between mastery behavior and achievement; (2) to train you in the responses of mastery-oriented behavior; and (3) to show you how to reinforce types of mastery behavior your daughter already exhibits and to teach her the ones she needs to learn. Your ultimate goal is to maintain and increase the resiliency your daughter exhibits in early childhood, so that she can triumph over the perils of puberty to become a self-sufficient adult who experiences the happiness, fulfillment, creativity, productivity, love, friendship, and family that contemporary mothers wish for their daughters.

This is a big job, to be sure, one that is further complicated by two aspects of modern life that need to be clarified if you are to understand the advice given in the rest of this book. The first of these is *success*. The second is *femininity*. Because social norms are fluctuating rapidly, it behooves us to examine the definitions and uses of these important terms.

Who Is Successful?

Any discussion of success in contemporary culture must take into account the complexities of a diverse, sophisticated, and free society where individual ideas about success come in as many varieties as the people conceiving them. All of us can point to an assortment of individuals and lifestyles and recognize elements of success in all of them. While some are obvious and enjoy near universal consensus, such as winning a gold medal in the Olympics, many more fall into a gray area of ambiguity.

Does landing a prestigious corporate job, bringing home a hefty paycheck, and enjoying the material accoutrements of an upscale lifestyle while putting in sixty hours a week at the office constitute success? How about quitting a professional position and scaling back the material needs of one's family in order to spend more time together? Suppose the children in this last scenario feel deprived? Does that change the perception of success? How about painting watercolors that are beginning to sell at a local gallery, while simultaneously missing the mortgage payment? Is success different for a man than for a woman? If so, why? Some of the mothers in my workshops worry they are not "successful enough." Is this because they are buying into a definition of success created by a materialistic and competitive society, as some of the workshop participants suggest, or is it because they have not reached their own goals, as others assert?

Pinning down a single definition of "success" in an America so full of choices is a nearly impossible task. The *American Heritage Dictionary* solves the problem by presenting a broad, encompassing definition: "The achievement of something desired, planned, or attempted." What may appear to be "success" to someone looking at a life from outside may not necessarily be felt as such by the person experiencing it from within. Thus, the corporate attorney arriving for work in her BMW, who sits at her desk in Manhattan longing to buy an organic farm in the green woods of Oregon, may appear to be a success but may not feel like one or, even if she does, may be unhappy. The mother of three happy, healthy children who returns to the workforce after a twelve-year absence and lands a minimum-wage job as a bank teller may feel like a success while the mother of three happy, healthy children who never wrote her dissertation in organic chemistry may feel like a failure.

Defining success for oneself, then, is one of the most challenging and pressing concerns for young people today. Not only must they refine their personal definition of success, which is likely to change over the years, but they must also begin acting upon it when they are young to make it a reality. For girls, the picture becomes even more complicated.

In our modern society, worldly success and achievement are viewed as individual and competitive. This attitude is a holdover from a value system historically shaped by males. The media have created the impression that all successful people make a lot of money and are mostly men: CEOs, megabuck entrepreneurs and developers, inventors of new technology, professional athletes, celebrities. While there is nothing inherently wrong with a value system that is hierarchical and individualistic, my experience has been that this concept of success tends to be too narrow to satisfy the female population's multifaceted concept of success.

The mothers in my workshops reflect a female value system that encompasses a wide range of options. Some define success in career terms, citing power, responsibility, status, prestige, and authority as indicators. Others define success in material terms: financial independence, security, and consumer power. Many define success in emotional terms such as love, intimacy, friendship, and family. Others prefer to discuss success in spiritual or metaphysical language: service to others, wisdom, awareness, and self-actualization. Still others use the language of artistic creation: originality, creativity, and productivity. A few courageous souls even use the language of testing one's mettle: freedom, adventure, excitement, and risk. Of course, the word "happiness" is uttered frequently by all groups.

Statistics from the U.S. Department of Labor Women's Bureau[3] present an interesting picture with regard to women and the conventional definitions of "success"—that is, those areas of employment rewarded by lucrative material compensation. In medicine, women are more likely to be in pediatrics, family medicine, and geriatrics than in higher-paying fields like cardiovascular medicine and surgery, where the males tend to congregate. Women attorneys congregate in real estate and divorce law while men dominate corporate law. Academic women are concentrated in the less prestigious, lower-paid fields of education and the humanities. In every career requiring math and science, females are underrepresented.

Women constitute only 11 percent of today's en—
force. There continues to be a significant sho—
versity candidates for technical degrees as v—
female applicants for the increasing number—
nical skills.

Statistics show large numbers of women ﹏
oriented fields. A case could be made that these fieﹶ—
interests and concerns. However, women in nontraditional joﹶ—
20 to 30 percent more than women in traditional jobs. Sixty-seven
percent of American women work, 70 percent of mothers with
preschool-age children work full-time, and 60 percent of working
women are either supporting families or are part of a household
where the husband's yearly earnings are less than $15,000. This
makes a compelling argument for increasing female representation
in more-lucrative male-dominated occupations, especially as our
society moves into the high-tech workplace of the twenty-first century where our daughters will be earning a living and competing
for jobs. Although not all girls must aspire to be computer techies
or "quantoids" (one eighth grade girl's label for a computer programmer), the longer we keep our daughters enrolled in math and
science classes, the more options they will have in the future.

I have found that most mothers are reluctant to surrender any of
the concepts of success enumerated above. It's not that they want
their daughters to "have it all." They are too realistic for that.
Rather, they want their daughters to recognize and keep open their
options. In other words, today's mothers are sophisticated in their
understanding of some deep human truths: first, human beings
require different kinds of fulfillment, and a successful life involves
achieving balance between all areas of life; second, since life circumstances are constantly in flux, one's abilities and earning capacity must be competitive and flexible; and third, life is really a work
in progress, and what is fulfilling at one point in life may not be fulfilling at another.

Finally, women have the option to bear and raise children. This
awesome capacity and awareness of this responsibility influences
how girls see their future lives. Certainly the option of children
exists for men, but boys do not typically take children into account
when they fantasize about the future. Most young males do not say,
"Let's see, I need to plan in here somewhere for having children."

hildren is not an "If…then" proposition for men, which
e as interrupting their careers. Girls, on the other hand, are
that childbearing and child-rearing is an issue with which
y must contend.[4]

Femininity: What It Is and Isn't

Add to the already multifaceted concept of success the even more
fluid and hard-to-pin-down concept of "femininity" in today's
world, and a picture of increasing complexity emerges—one that
isn't likely to get any simpler as we move into the twenty-first
century.

First, it must be acknowledged that traditional concepts of femininity have been seriously challenged over the last twenty-five
years. Today's mothers own businesses, supervise employees, serve in
high-powered political offices, lift weights, run marathons, perspire
real sweat, take real risks, make real decisions, and earn real money.
Daughters today can identify with their mothers to learn the
achievement-related life skills that were formerly in the male
domain.

On the other hand, this challenge to traditional femininity has not
been complete. Lurking just below the surface of society's tolerant
acceptance, there exists a deep ambivalence toward female power
and achievement—rewarding it one minute, ignoring it the next,
even vilifying it on occasion. The most visible example of this is
Hillary Rodham Clinton. While many assert that Mrs. Clinton's
troubles were entirely the result of her own actions, an equal number believe that she was targeted for vilification precisely because
she "overstepped" her role as First Lady.

A highly educated Ivy League graduate, an ambitious ultra-
achiever in her own right, Hillary Clinton was never in her husband's shadow. Before Bill Clinton was elected president, she was
the higher wage earner of the two. During her husband's guberna-
torial campaign she generated controversy by having the temerity
to use her maiden name. In order to appease her critics, she acqui-
esced and became Hillary Clinton instead of Hillary Rodham.
Then, during the presidential campaign she made the famous "mis-
statement": "Well, I suppose I could have stayed home and baked

cookies." And for this she was severely chastised. Finally, by taking on the health care establishment during her husband's first term, even though it was at his behest, she came dangerously close to wielding too much power for a political wife and was stopped in her tracks—and remember that this was before any Whitewater investigations. At that point, she turned her focus to the welfare of children, an "acceptable" role for a First Lady, and some of the controversy died down.

To continue to portray presidential wives as merely decorative seems a bit anachronistic, particularly given the intelligence and notable achievements of Hillary Rodham Clinton. Anachronistic though it may be, however, the tendency remains, and women like Mrs. Clinton still take a risk when they wield power and authority.

Thus, one of the greatest challenges facing girls at this time in history is to bring balance to our culture's conflicting definitions of "achievement" and "femininity." Why? Because the traits used by individuals in our society to define an achiever—or a mastery-oriented person, as you will soon see—are the same traits that individuals use to define masculinity.[5]

To illustrate this point, review the lists that follow. They were generated from participants' responses taken for over a decade of conducting "How to Father a Successful Daughter" and "How to Mother Successful Daughters" workshops. Participants were asked to name the traits necessary for success and achievement. The lists of those traits were gathered from the group and written where everyone could see them. Next, participants were asked to name the traits of femininity and masculinity. In order to avoid politically correct responses, I asked participants to think of a specific individual whom they knew personally and thought of as feminine and another whom they thought of as masculine. (You may wish to pause here for a moment yourself and get a person of your own in mind.) Then we listed those adjectives and traits where everyone could see them.

What has emerged from these lists over the last twelve years is interesting for two reasons: first, because the traits are consistent across different geographical regions, and, second, because there has been virtually no change in them over the last twelve years.

Masculine

Feminine

Positive	Negative	Positive	Negative
Adventurous	Violent	Nurturing	Weak
Aggressive	Aggressive	Caring	Helpless
Assertive	Inflexible	Emotional	Emotional
Independent	Stiff	Sensitive	Sensitive
Confident	Hard	Sweet	Talkative
Intelligent	Coarse	Curious	Powerless
Logical	Rigid	Domestic	Defenseless
Objective		Intelligent	Impotent
Reasonable		Understanding	Vacillating
Athletic		Flexible	Conniving
Active		Intuitive	Fickle
Vigorous		Compassionate	Inconsistent
Strong		Playful	
Forceful		Gentle	
Powerful		Sensual	
Firm		Sexy	
Virile		Attractive	
Sexual		Self-sacrificing	
Decisive		Passive	
Rugged		Soft	
Sturdy		Pretty	
Brave		Refined	
Daring		Slight	
Stoic		Dainty	
Courageous		Fragile	
Tough		Frail	
Muscular		Submissive	
Robust		Childlike	

Reprinted from *How to Father a Successful Daughter* by Nicky Marone (New York: Ballantine Books, 1988).

Success and Achievement

External	*Internal*
Power and authority	Belief in self
Money	Willingness to take risks
Responsibility	Independence and autonomy
Status or rank	Willingness to change
Nice clothes, car, house	Willingness to risk failure
Expense account	Willingness to accept success
Freedom to set own schedule	Confidence
Freedom to travel	Intelligence
Stability	Humor
Good mental health (happiness)	Creativity

If you compare the lists, paying particular attention to the internal traits listed under Success and Achievement, you will see that the words used to define an achiever are, for the most part, similar to those used to describe a masculine person. In other words, our society defines "achiever" in masculine terms. Furthermore, the traits that appear on the masculine side of the equation are also the traits of a mastery-oriented risk-taker. These traits will be required in the highly competitive economy of the future—an economy, experts tell us, where workers will be contract employees who must constantly hustle their next job. In contrast, the list of so-called feminine traits contains terms more readily associated with diffidence, helplessness, passivity, and risk aversion.

For example, the first three internal qualities necessary for success—belief in self, willingness to take risks, and independence and autonomy—are all supported by the assertive, confident, and action-oriented qualities of the masculine list, in contrast to the more emotional, passive, and decorative qualities listed on the feminine side. Although there is some overlap between the lists, with adjectives such as "intelligent" making an appearance on both sides, for the most part, the masculine list is more consistent with the action-oriented qualities our culture associates with a successful person. The qualities listed on the feminine side tend to be passive, fearful of risk-taking, in need of protection, or serving a decorative function, with a few exceptions, such as an adjective like "flexible" showing up on the feminine side but being a clear advantage.

Other unspoken messages and assumptions are constantly perpetuated and reinforced by the adults who interact with children. Teachers ask boys to move desks and books, while girls erase the blackboard and enter grades in the record book.[6] Parents rescue girls in situations where they do not rescue boys.[7] Boys are expected to fix things while girls are not.[8] When boys do poorly in math, parents tell them to try harder, while girls are excused because parents say they are not as smart in these subjects.[9] Parents are more likely to discuss past sad events with girls than they are with boys, and they often use more emotional language with girls.[10] Parents buy sports equipment, science tools, and building kits for boys, but they buy dolls, furniture, and kitchen utensils for girls.[11] The list goes on.

This poses a conundrum for girls and takes its toll. Particularly when they reach puberty, both boys and girls want to distance themselves from the traits associated with the opposite sex. They are trying to discover what it means to be a man or a woman. As adults with more life experience, we know that the traits on either list can be exhibited by both males and females, but adolescents oversimplify. With little worldly experience to guide them, they rely on stereotypes and polarize themselves.

Because popularity with the opposite sex becomes paramount during puberty, the last thing a girl wants is to be thought of as masculine. Instead, appealing to boys becomes the raison d'être of many young girls who regard femininity as the most potent weapon in their arsenal. If a girl's perception of femininity has been tainted by helplessness and passivity, she may feel pressure to downplay her achievements in order to appear feminine to boys. Boys, who fear being feminine, are required to be mastery-oriented high achievers to be masculine. And let me add here that some things never change. Even after a decade of doing workshops, I still have adult women raise their hands and say, "What do you mean this is an adolescent's problem? I'm thirty-five years old and I still haven't figured out how to be competent and successful and still appeal to men!"

This perceived link between masculinity and achievement is reflected in research which shows that by middle school, girls' scores decline on standardized tests, especially in math and science.[12] Boys are more likely than girls to enroll in higher-level math and physics courses because they have more confidence.[13] More than 40 percent of girls do not have definite plans for high school course selection.[14] Adolescent girls are more likely than boys to say they are "not smart enough" or "not good enough" to achieve high aspirational career goals.[15] On important standardized tests like the PSAT and the SAT, girls' scores are significantly lower than boys'. Even when the scoring is rigged in favor of girls, the score differences are shocking. In their book, *Failing at Fairness,* educational researchers David and Myra Sadker put it succinctly: "Handicappers would have to spot girls about 60 points to make the SAT an even bet." And later, "The SAT is a clean male sweep."[16] (There will be more discussion about grades and performance in Chapter 2.)

As your daughter attempts to incorporate femininity into her self-image she is likely to experiment with many different aspects of a feminine personality, one which is nice, sweet, passive, small, quiet, polite, deferential to the needs of others, and above all, nonthreatening. She is encouraged to do so by society. "Every time I'm in a bad mood my mother says, 'Jennifer, nobody likes a sad face. Smile!'" volunteered a teenager in one of my workshops for girls. "The thing is, she never says that to my brother, and he's always grouchy." As you already know if you are a woman in this culture, the desire to please, to be polite and inoffensive (feminine), can be the root of many problems women encounter, especially when confronted with the harsher realities of ambition, achievement, and business, not to mention technology, science, and math—in other words, those risky, highly competitive arenas that men have already defined.

Right about now a lot of you are undoubtedly feeling pained indignation at the suggestion that we must train femininity out of our daughters if they are to compete with men in the workplace. Mothers in my seminars constantly voice concern that the traditional feminine traits of consensus-building, consideration, and sensitivity to the needs of others are devalued in our culture; yet they represent our last glimmer of hope for a society in which caring for others is a cultural norm.

I agree wholeheartedly. These feminine traits are the glue that holds together relationships, nurtures self and others, and creates consensus in a divided world. Besides, femininity has a fun side. It's exciting to discover the alluring and sexy aspects of oneself. This, too, is part of the experience of puberty, but girls must learn how to handle the powerful forces of their own youthful femininity.

Because this period of oceanic change with regard to sex roles is still in progress at the cultural level, however, enough of the old feminine stereotype remains alive to cause confusion. When deference to others is not a cultural value for all members of the society, an opportunity exists for exploitation. Suffice it to say that strengthening your daughter's achievement-related behaviors and resiliency responses will achieve the goal of creating a strong, hardy, decisive young woman who gets her needs met.

A couple of girls in one of my intervention groups said it best.

"My boyfriend likes me to act all sweet and nurturing," said an African-American girl, "so I do. But I don't confuse it with other stuff."

"Like what?" inquired another.

"Like if I have to ask for a raise," she continued, "my boss couldn't care less how sweet and nurturing I am."

Another girl, a high school senior, chimed in with her variation on the same theme when she recollected the events around a recent audition. "I went back to find out if I made the cut," she began. "I found out I didn't."

"Ahh," everyone murmured, genuinely sympathetic.

"Thanks," she said, "but my point is, I acted like such a *girl*. I sat down on the steps and cried. There was a bunch of guys around who didn't make the cut either. They must have been as disappointed as I was, but they didn't *cry.*"

"Well, that's all right," I said, in my most nurturing tones. "Your response was probably healthier. They were just holding their feelings inside."

"Yeah, but that can be a good skill to have when you need it," she observed.

Her point is well taken. When traditional feminine responses are inappropriate—when the moment to ace one's physics exam, run for class president, or annihilate the opposing basketball team has arrived—traditionally feminine behavior can be ineffectual. In situations where even more intense action is required, such as defending oneself against physical abuse, an assault, or a hostile environment, it can be downright dangerous.

Reconciling Success and Femininity

If our daughters are to experience the broadest range of success we can envision for them, which means achieving the seemingly dissimilar goals of being self-sufficient *and* attracting a life mate, they must reconcile and bring balance to the shifting, ambiguous, and often conflicting concepts of femininity and achievement. The only reconciliation that makes any sense and gives girls the options they deserve is to teach them how and when to adapt their behavior appropriately so as to do whatever they must do in order to get what they want. That is the only way to prepare them for something even more important than success—*life.*

That old rogue, life, the most demanding of teachers, is supremely indifferent to sex. Life places us in situations that demand great compassion, sensitivity, and the other nurturing qualities associated with femininity. The successful individual, male or female, will respond appropriately. By the same token, life places every individual, male or female, in situations that demand assertiveness and, yes, perhaps even aggression and intimidation—if one is attacked in a dark parking lot in the middle of the night, for example. Again, the successful individual will respond appropriately. For our purposes, then, we shall define the successful individual, male or female, as one who adapts his or her behavior appropriately in each and every circumstance. Such an individual is not hampered by cultural definitions of either femininity (often tainted with helplessness and passivity) or masculinity (competitive and often lacking in compassion).

Successful people are able to modify their behavior and employ a set of responses over the course of a lifetime that enables them to reach desired outcomes—a definition that is synonymous with self-efficacy, achievement, and mastery behavior. Whether they choose to challenge the dominant paradigm or function within it, be employed by a corporate giant or paint watercolors in the garage, enjoy the stimulation of an urban setting or walk the earth in a rural community, raise a family, pursue a career, or none of the above, the common thread is that all successful endeavors, indeed life itself, require a set of skills that remain the same. These skills include taking positive risks; staying resilient and persistent through difficulty, obstacles, and setbacks; and being a creative and strategic problem-solver who copes effectively with change.

The Power of Deep Beliefs

At a still deeper level, there must exist a foundation upon which one's behavior rests. It is the belief that one will achieve one's goals. While to some it may seem that a belief is simply too insubstantial to be effective, the truth is that persistent people are persistent because at the deepest level they believe in their ability to bring about whatever future they may envision, regardless of how long it may take or how difficult it may be.

The women in history we venerate today had this sense of self-efficacy and displayed it for all the world to see. They overcame great obstacles, suffered setbacks, knew hardship, and endured public scorn and ridicule. But they were not deterred from their belief in themselves and their mission. The suffragists, the abolitionists, the prohibitionists, the early labor activists who helped establish child labor laws, the pioneers of birth control and women's reproductive rights, the women of the frontier who scratched out an existence in a hostile land, the garment workers in turn-of-the-century sweatshops, even the southern belles fainting, not from the delicate state of their womanhood, but because they were so tightly corseted that they couldn't breathe—all required belief in themselves, all required self-efficacy to survive in a difficult world.

In the formative and developmental years, girls are immersed in this profound task of building their self-efficacy. The premise of this book is that raising successful daughters is really the challenge to preserve and increase self-efficacy. I will be taking you through these processes step by step, but remember that *in life,* these processes are like a fabric, a tapestry, in which each thread helps to maintain the whole cloth. Your job as a mother is to

- Strengthen and increase your daughter's self-efficacy—that is, the belief in herself that will enable her to see opportunity and bring about desired outcomes.
- Strengthen resiliency so that she can persist through hardships and difficulty.
- Teach and train your daughter in the attitudes and responses that will enable her to adapt her actions and modulate her behavior appropriately to various circumstances.

To raise a successful daughter, every caring mother must ask herself these questions:

- Is my daughter learning the life skills of positive risk-taking, resilience, and persistence? Do I model these skills myself?
- Am I teaching my daughter that success and achievement are a set of behaviors rather than a set of goals, processes rather than products, verbs rather than nouns?
- Am I teaching her how to be strong and capable or how to stay safe and secure?
- Am I preparing my daughter to be economically self-sufficient in the twenty-first century?
- Is she receiving the formal education she will need to be competitive in a highly technological society—is she taking math, science, and computer courses?
- Am I teaching her how to vary her behavior according to circumstances?
- Am I helping her to see herself doing important work?
- Am I helping her to believe that the future holds promise for her?
- Am I training her to be a good problem-solver?
- Am I training her to manage change?
- Am I teaching her to cope effectively with doubt, fear, frustration, and disappointment?
- Am I teaching her how to make her own decisions?
- Am I teaching her how to play hard but fair?
- Am I helping her to recognize and appreciate her own unique gifts, regardless of society's opinions?
- Am I helping to create a society that will accept the contributions of my daughter, whatever they may be?

This approach takes nothing away from our daughters. On the contrary, it adds to their behavioral repertoire, putting more tools at their disposal. It opens them up to the full range of their human potential, offering them the full spectrum of behavioral choices from the uninhibited expression of compassionate, intuitive, nurturing femininity to the rugged and hardy display of persistent mastery behavior.

Finally, raising successful daughters is not about coercing them to jump through hoops of our devising. It is about giving our daughters the mastery skills to make their own choices and to be successful at whatever they choose over the course of a whole lifetime. Only in this way can we be sure they will be adequately prepared for the next century.

CHAPTER 2

The Learning Paradox

Mastery or Helplessness?

To be free is to learn, to test yourself constantly, to gamble. It is not safe.

> *Robyn Davidson, author of* Tracks, *a memoir of her 1,700-mile trek through the Australian outback with her dog and four camels*

In Chapter 1, we discussed how, early on, girls behave much like boys; they are curious, resilient, eager to explore their world and try new things. Then puberty produces a crisis of confidence that lowers girls' self-esteem, their aspirations, their resilience.[1] Despite over thirty years of second-wave feminism, too little change is occurring in our culture. We still watch helplessly as too many girls go underground with their talents.

The most important thing a mother can do to raise a successful daughter is to arm herself with as much information as possible concerning ways to develop and preserve the natural mastery and resilience her daughter exhibits early in life. In other words, mothers must learn how to *keep* daughters mastery-oriented, since it is inevitable that girls will encounter setbacks and failures in life.

It is a mistake to believe that successful people never get confused, experience doubt, miss the mark, flop, fizzle, or flounder, that they have been sheltered from or are immune to the difficulties and hardships of failure and criticism. Nothing could be further from the truth. However, they are willing to endure difficulties to reach their goals. How do they do it? Not by avoiding mistakes and set-backs but by learning a set of attitudes and responses that will sustain their confidence through difficult times and enable them to persist when plans go awry.

One might speculate that the high spirits of a young child, girl or boy, are born of naïveté. Since they have not yet encountered difficulty and failure, they haven't been damaged by it. Yet that is not borne out by the facts. For example, educators have long observed that *all* children in the process of learning encounter obstacles. They even fail initially at many tasks: the smart, not-so-smart, older, younger, males, females, everybody. In fact, learning is impossible without trials and tribulations, without some discomfort. The real question is, Why do some children persist in the face of difficulties and inconveniences in order to succeed, while others give up?

To shed light on this fascinating question, researchers designed studies on the dynamics of persistence and failure. What emerged was that there were observable differences not only between those who persisted and those who did not, but between boys and girls as well.

The boys and girls who were chosen for these studies were roughly equivalent in overall skills and intelligence. They were given problems and puzzles designed to be slightly beyond the capabilities of their age group, in order to experimentally induce confusion, obstacles, and failure. The children would have to be persistent and resilient in order to master the tasks.[2]

Because the children were matched in skill level and intelligence, one would assume that their responses to difficulty and confusion would be similar. The researchers were surprised to discover that difficulty caused some children to improve their performance, while others were so debilitated by the difficulty of the task that they couldn't solve problems they had solved previously!

Eager to probe these differences, the researchers delved still deeper into the dynamics of the two response types. They designed tests in which the children would first experience success, then failure. The results were intriguing.

As expected, some children were able to improve their performance on subsequent tests following failure. Others just quit, and their performance levels decreased following failure. What was most intriguing about the results was that the primary difference between the children whose performance level improved and those who gave up was their thinking about success and failure, or the way they *construed* their situation, the stories they told themselves while working on the problems. The following lists outline these two views of mistakes.

Those Who Improved Their Performance	Those Who Were Debilitated By Their Failure
1. While recognizing a mistake, labeled it not as a failure but as something temporary and correctable.	1. Labeled a mistake as a failure.
2. Offered no explanations for why they made mistakes.	2. Tried to explain or account for mistakes by attributing them to lack of ability: "I must not be any good at this."
3. Spent their time working on the problem and correcting their errors rather than explaining their mistakes.	3. Spent more time explaining and accounting for mistakes than trying to solve the problem or correct their errors.
4. Predicted future success.	4. Inflated present failures and predicted future failures.
5. Gave themselves encouragement through little pep talks.	5. Developed negative self-talk leading to negative feelings about the task.
6. Became more positive about the activity.	6. Expressed a desire to drop the activity.

Children who gave up said, "I failed," while persistent children said, "I'll try this!" One group saw failure (or mistakes and confusion) as a failure of *self,* while the other saw it as a failure of *strategy.* Children who gave up saw a mistake as an indication of their lack of ability, believing that failure springs from within, while those who persisted had the ability to include confusion, mistakes, and failure into a larger process of achieving their ultimate goal, which would eventually result in success. The children who gave up had acquired "learned helplessness," while the persistent children had retained their mastery.

What is particularly distressing is that study after study shows that girls tend to exhibit the responses of learned helplessness more often than boys do. By puberty, boys retain the mastery behaviors they exhibited as young children, while in girls it is lost altogether or seriously diminished. Girls consistently express greater anxiety about failing than boys do.[3] They do not recover as well from failure, and they predict future failures in new performance situations while boys predict higher performance following failure.[4] Girls reported less pride in their success than boys did and a stronger desire to hide their papers after failure.[5] Most shocking of all, one study revealed that those who are most debilitated by failure and confusion are the brightest girls.[6]

In studies involving gender differences in math, girls and boys respond differently not only to failure but to success as well. When elementary school boys are asked to explain why they did well on a difficult math test, they attribute their high scores to intelligence and effort. When girls are asked why they did well on the same math test, they attribute their high scores to the fact that the test was "easy," even though they were told ahead of time, just like the boys, that the test was difficult. Older girls, especially, tend to be less encouraged by success. They predict relatively poor future performances even when they receive the same performance feedback upon which boys predict future success.[7] When boys experience success they tend to change their opinion of themselves—that is, they internalize it. When girls, confronted with the same data, experience success, they externalize it—that is, they change their opinion of the task. Thus, we see that even when girls are presented with a positive outcome to their efforts, they do not show a mastery-oriented response to it.

Since all children make mistakes, the adults must do a form of damage control to help them retain the mastery behavior they exhibited quite naturally as young children. Unfortunately, boys and girls receive different kinds of training. When a boy's natural resilience is threatened by difficult situations, he is taught to "tough it out," "shake it off," or "fake it," and he's shown how to display confidence. These attitudes and responses are reinforced and modeled by fathers and other adult males. Unfortunately, when girls are not resilient, their behavior either goes unnoticed or is considered "feminine" and "normal for girls." What's worse, girls are often rescued from situations where boys are taught coping skills. The danger is that our daughters, in the process of learning how to be "feminine," are actually being trained into learned helplessness by a variety of forces. (Much more about this in Chapter 3.)

A music teacher who attended one of my workshops told a story that illustrates this point. "I teach private lessons to young violinists," she began. "Two of my students are brother and sister. Their parents bring them to their separate music lessons. With the boy, the parents tell me I need to be demanding and strenuous. His father says, 'Act like a coach and just tell him what to do. Expect him to do it and he will.' With the girl, they tell me I need to be understanding and sympathetic. The mother says, 'She needs to feel that you care about her. She needs to be encouraged.'"

Perhaps these recommendations stem from the parents' knowledge of different temperaments in the boy and the girl. Perhaps not. I submit that the different approaches will result in different temperaments for the boy and the girl. Either way, it is as if the parents are asking the teacher to prepare the boy and the girl for two completely different worlds. I am not willing to say which is the better approach since I do not know the children personally, but I am suggesting that one child is not being prepared for resilience in the outside world while the other child is not receiving the nurturing he may in fact need.

Thus, girls and boys are trained differently. Girls may acquire learned helplessness along with "femininity" because our society continues to reinforce old stereotypes, albeit more subtly than thirty years ago. In the process, all girls are at risk for losing the risk-taking and resilience that was natural to them before their identity became mixed up with societal beliefs about females being helpless, diffident, and decorative.

Patterns, Characteristics, and Components

The first step in helping our girls retain the mastery that came to them naturally as children is to understand the differences between mastery and helplessness.

Both mastery-oriented behavior and learned helplessness contain three basic characteristics:

1. A core belief
2. A style of explaining bad events—that is, an explanatory style
3. A set of behaviors

THE CORE BELIEF

The core belief is the foundation upon which future choices will be made. A girl's core belief concerning her capabilities, as well as her beliefs concerning the nature of learning itself, will determine her future choices and responses to life.

While a girl is developing, her core beliefs are not yet solidified, although by puberty she will already have experienced pressure to be "feminine." Even during puberty, however, the process of forming core beliefs is going on. The girl is very much in the process of creating and deciding, somewhat unconsciously, what her core beliefs about herself are going to be. Her developmental task is to try on many different personas and experiment with many different types of behavior. One style of behavior, the one considered "feminine" by our society, will become increasingly important for most girls as they mature.

Those who are mastery-oriented have the core belief that effort and time—not destiny, heredity, or luck—are the forces that produce results. Mastery-oriented people also understand that effort *over* time is critical. This belief enables them to persist over longer periods. Thus they are willing and able to expend effort even in the midst of obstacles, confusion, and setbacks.

Of course, realistic thinking must also be a part of this core belief, but only to an extent. Certain outcomes and goals do, of course, depend upon innate talent, ability, or luck. For example, the average individual, no matter how much training she receives, will never be capable of hitting the notes required of an operatic soprano. Girls with certain body types are simply not going to become gold medal Olympic high-jumpers. Others will never invent breakthrough technology. Certain levels of achievement and success require a raw talent upon which to build, and every individual must work within the confines of the genetic, historic, or cultural hand she was dealt.

But so-called realistic thinking can become a dangerous preconception, especially with children. Although a child may not possess the innate musical ability to become a soloist who performs at Carnegie Hall, she may have, with *effort expended over time,* the talent to become a violinist in her school orchestra or the organist for her church choir. She may play local gigs around town or just be good enough to play for friends at parties or at home for her own enjoyment. In the light of individual differences, then, thinking realistically may mean that the initial desired outcome requires readjustment. But insisting a girl think "realistically" during the process of forming her beliefs about her capabilities may preclude her reaching certain goals despite apparent shortcomings.

In contrast, the core belief of learned helplessness is that there is no connection between actions and the final outcome of events. Ultimately it says, "Regardless of what I do or how long I do it, I do not believe I can achieve my desired outcome." Exhibited by those who have not learned resilience in the face of difficulty, this belief leads to reluctance, timidity, and eventually to total avoidance of risk-taking, best summarized as a "no-matter-what-I-do syndrome." The adult version of this would be "No matter what I do, I just can't get out of this dead-end job" or "No matter what I do, I just can't save any money" or "No matter what I do, I just can't seem to leave this lousy relationship" or "No matter what I do, I can't lose ten pounds." An adolescent version might go something like this: "No matter what I do, I can't understand math" or "No matter what I do, I won't be as pretty (or popular or cool) as Tiffany, Heather, and Jennifer" or "No matter what I do, I just can't get a boyfriend" or "No matter what I do, I can't get a good grade in science."

In this belief system one hears a subtext, albeit subtly, of destiny at work. In other words, those who have boyfriends, understand math, get good grades, are elected to office, program computers, play the violin, or are superior athletes have been somehow preordained to accomplish these wondrous things. To those with learned helplessness, the success of others seems like divine providence rather than a result of the hard work and effort that undoubtedly have gone into these endeavors.

EXPLANATORY STYLE: HOW WE CONSTRUE REALITY

Explanatory style is the way in which an individual explains bad events to herself, the way she construes events. Since everyone experiences negative events in life, explanatory style is critical. Here is how it works.

Humans have a need to make sense out of the frequently strange, seemingly random, and often confounding events of life. In order to satisfy this need, we weave stories out of the events of life: tapping memory, making connections, seeing relationships, forming concepts, and drawing conclusions. This is simply the natural activity of the mind. This is what the mind does, although its conclusions are not always valid.

The truth is more amorphous. "Reality" is open to multiple interpretations. Many of us have had the experience of believing reality to be a certain way, yet with greater maturity or simply more information and experience, we learn that the explanation we have clung to with such tenacity is simply wrong or, at the very least, limited. With this experience, it becomes apparent that reality is more fluid and subject to interpretation than we thought.

Your daughter will try to make sense out of her life and create stories that will explain the events she encounters. As long as her life is going smoothly, there is no problem, but when difficulties arise, as they inevitably will, your daughter's explanatory style (the way she construes and explains reality) will determine whether she is likely to stay the course and remain hardy or give up. If her explanatory style is positive, it will sustain, support, and motivate her. If it is negative, it will erode, undermine, and sabotage her.

Both the core belief and the explanatory style are internal processes. They take place in your daughter's inner world, hidden from view, an endless stream-of-consciousness narrative that will accompany her actions and make her draw conclusions about her life. Unless she tells you, you cannot determine whether her core belief and explanatory style are mastery-oriented or helpless. It is at this point, however, that the process moves from an internal one to an external one.

As was stated earlier, mastery-oriented people are able to maintain their resilience and hardiness not because they avoid confusion, mistakes, and failure but because they have learned positive ways in which to construe reality, positive ways to explain difficulty to themselves, positive ways of interpreting bad events.

How your daughter explains a life event to herself can be more important than what might actually have taken place—assuming she can ever know what actually took place. When your daughter understands that reality is open to multiple interpretations, she will become more willing to interpret difficulty in different ways and more likely to change the story. When she takes this into her heart and mind at the deepest levels, it is indeed a profound realization. Some individuals find this amorphous quality of reality deeply unsettling. Others find it liberating.

Don't dismiss a positive explanatory style as a mindless Pollyanna approach to life ("Just be happy!"). Examine the specific aspects of both the positive, or mastery-oriented, explanatory style and the negative, or helpless, explanatory style as shown below:

Mastery-Oriented Explanatory Style	*Helpless Explanatory Style*
• Dynamic: All things change.	• Stable: Nothing changes.
• Specific: The problem is limited.	• Global: This will affect everything.
• External: This is not necessarily my fault.	• Internal: It's my fault.

A mastery-oriented girl will have an explanatory style that is dynamic, specific, and external. This way of thinking enables her to monitor and control negative emotional responses to events.

First, in her acknowledgment of the dynamic aspect of life, she acknowledges the great truth that nothing stays the same. When nothing seems to be changing, that seeming is simply due to human limitations and perceptions, both physical and intellectual. Observing any life event in retrospect will readily teach your daughter that it was a changing process that occurred over time.

Second, she is encouraged by reminding herself not to let a problem in one area seep into every other aspect of life. While it is true that some situations are harder to control than others, it is also true that other areas of her life remain under her control at all times, even in the most difficult circumstances. She has the ability to control her own reaction to life.

Third, and finally, she acknowledges that in any situation many different variables coexist that will determine results. This external aspect releases her from taking responsibility unduly for people and events she cannot influence. In this way, she avoids internalizing blame when something goes wrong.

In contrast, the explanatory style exhibited by a girl with learned helplessness is stable, global, and internal. This way of thinking does not sustain, nourish, or motivate her through difficulties.

First, a girl with learned helplessness will tell herself that a bad situation is never going to get better. According to her way of thinking, the passage of time and the choices made by the individual will have little or no effect. This is a stable explanatory style.

Second, she will be convinced that difficulty in one area of her life will inevitably cause difficulty in other areas of her life. She resists the notion that a problem can be contained. This is the act of globalizing her problem.

Finally, the most damaging explanation of all is that she blames herself for everything that goes wrong. She jumps to the conclusion that every mishap, misadventure, and misunderstanding is caused by her personal ineptitude. This is internalizing the problem. She overlooks the reality that many factors outside of her control are working at all times.

Let's contrast the two styles using as examples the responses of two teenage girls. We will call them Zoe and Jessica. Zoe exhibits mastery, Jessica helplessness. Both did poorly in math last year. Now they are making out their schedules for next year and deciding whether to take another math course. Each girl's style of explaining events is different. Zoe's mastery-oriented response will reveal a dynamic, specific, external style, while Jessica's helpless response will reveal a stable, global, internal style.

Keep in mind that both girls struggled in math last year. The difference, then, is not in their external, observable situations. It is internal and hidden. Let us look closely at the individual responses of Zoe and Jessica to determine the underlying assumptions that derail Jessica but keep Zoe on track.

The Dynamic Response

"It's a new semester, and I have a different teacher for algebra," Zoe might say, or "I'm more motivated now, and I won't be distracted by my friends, because they will not be in my class this year."

Zoe responds this way because she acknowledges the dynamics of change. She knows that nothing remains the same. This semester she is perhaps more mature with the greater brain capacity that growth represents in a teenager. Nor is her classroom the same. The teacher has changed, the students will have changed, and therefore the interactions and dynamics of the classroom will be different. Zoe realizes that whatever her problems were in the past—poor study habits, lack of maturity, a poor teacher, or distracting classmates—those problems no longer exist. A "that was then, this is now" mentality acknowledges new opportunities for change.

The Stable Response

Jessica, however, might say, "I can't take math. I did badly in math last year; therefore, I would do badly in math again this year."

Although there are those who would argue that Jessica's interpretation is valid, there is a lot of inaccuracy revealed in her response. First of all, it precludes any possibility of a successful change in self or change in circumstances. It fails to acknowledge that both people and circumstances can and do change. People can and often do succeed where they have failed previously. They do make and act upon new decisions, which in turn influence final outcomes.

Jessica's belief, however, prevents her from understanding or acknowledging that learning itself is a process of change, that growth is a process of change, and that changes occur within *her* without her knowledge. These changes occur developmentally, intellectually, and incrementally. Her abilities do not stagnate, nor does the world around her stagnate.

Finally, this response presumes she can see the future. It presumes that the future will be just like the past, that the outcome will be the same. It does not take into account that when present circumstances change, they create the opportunity for future outcomes to change as well.

The Specific Response

"It's only one class," Zoe might say. "I'll bring up my GPA in other classes." This response reveals Zoe's belief in her ability to offset a bad grade in math with a good grade in a different course. She is less fearful because she perceives *another* area of control that, although different, is still closely related enough to be pertinent to influencing the final outcome. Subsequently, she is able to keep one math class in perspective. She doesn't see events spiraling out of control in every area, spelling disaster and doom. She is willing to take a risk by perceiving control in another area of endeavor.

The Global Response

Jessica, however, might say, "If I get a bad grade in math this year, it will affect my whole grade point average."

This response reveals that Jessica is willing to sacrifice the opportunity to learn a new subject that could lead to greater success in learning something else in the future—computer programming, for instance—simply so that she can maintain a kind of homeostasis. It reveals a reluctance to take risks for fear of upsetting the status quo. Essentially she says to herself, "I am willing to take a risk only if the results will not negatively affect anything else in my life."

Of course, this is not a real risk. Instead, this response reveals Jessica's desire for no inconvenience, embarrassment, or difficulty to occur as a result of her decision. Furthermore, it assumes that inconvenience and difficulty are *bad* things to be avoided. This is inconsistent with life, which teaches that growth and development occur *during* difficulty. No inconvenience, no growth. To decide that difficulty must be avoided is a mistake that sounds the death knell for future achievement. To decide this in high school is a tragedy.

Jessica reveals a desire for certainty. The problem with the desire for certainty is that opportunities are missed for the sake of safety. She concludes in advance that risk will affect everything in her life in a negative way, that she has no control, and that everything else will also go wrong.

The External Response

"I'm not stupid. I was just learning something new," Zoe could say.

To some, this response may have a ring of irresponsibility to it, especially if it's coupled with typical adolescent declarations such as "The teacher didn't like me" or "The teacher was unfair." However, when an external explanation such as this is coupled with a willingness to take personal responsibility to learn and a determination to perform better regardless of the obstacles encountered, then it is not irresponsible and enables real change. The truth is that everyone makes mistakes when learning something new, and very often the individual learns even more as a result of those mistakes.

The Internal Response

"I'm just not smart enough to understand math. I get confused. I'm dumb," could be Jessica's response.

This response is perhaps the most self-sabotaging of all. It internalizes one's failure by faulting *oneself*, by taking blame. Jessica hasn't been taught to consider other equally valid reasons for her problem—for example, lack of math readiness, poor study habits or instruction, classroom distractions, or immaturity, which is different from intelligence. She is able to determine one and only one reason for her failure—her own perceived lack of intelligence.

The truth is that an individual may fail at any given task for a number of reasons. Perhaps Jessica did not receive adequate instructions or direction. Perhaps she was not developmentally ready for the task. Perhaps she didn't get enough sleep the night before her final exam. Perhaps she did not receive the emotional or financial support she needed. Maybe she was never taught how to learn— that is, how to ask questions, explain events in a self-supporting way, and develop strategies for sustaining projects even when things go wrong.

Consequently, if she believes that the failure in math class is proof of her lack of ability or intelligence, if she believes *she* is a failure because her project failed, and if she believes all future attempts will fail as well, then she is exhibiting the response style of learned helplessness. It then becomes likely that she will give up and fail again. On the other hand, if she is taught that success is a process that will *include* failure along the way, she is more likely to stay resilient as a consequence of having a more realistic picture of herself and of the nature of achievement.

A SET OF BEHAVIORS

Eventually, the internal dynamics of each style can be translated into a set of behavioral choices that are observable in the world. In this particular category, we will examine learned helplessness first in order to form a background against which to contrast the more desirable choices a mastery-oriented person would make in the same circumstances.

Mastery Behaviors	Helpless Behaviors
1. Chooses learning goals	1. Chooses performance goals
2. Makes no comparisons	2. Makes inappropriate comparisons
3. Is highly strategic and creative	3. Lacks alternative strategies
4. Copes with and uses fear	4. Avoids and resists fear

Learning Goals versus Performance Goals

Do you know people who do only what they are already good at? People who choose to do only the things they already perform well at? These individuals may be exhibiting a helpless style.

Here is how this style operates. People who have acquired learned helplessness tend to choose goals that will either win them approval or help them avoid criticism. They choose only those activities in which they have already proven themselves, those activities in which they already perform well. These are called *performance goals.*

Mastery-oriented individuals, on the other hand, choose goals in which they seek to learn a new activity, master a new task, or acquire a new skill. These are called *learning goals.* Choosing to set learning goals shows the individual is willing to endure criticism, relinquish approval, and tolerate some hardship and criticism in order to acquire a new skill or new information.

The tendency for one with learned helplessness to choose performance goals over learning goals makes perfect sense if that individual's explanatory style of learned helplessness is taken into consideration. Since learning something new almost guarantees confusion and mistake-making, particularly if the material is challenging, and because the tendency is to construe every mistake as a failure, those with learned helplessness doom themselves to feel bad every time they make an error. They personalize the impersonal process of learning and wind up feeling even more insecure. Eventually they are unable to withstand the onslaught to their self-esteem. To avoid this painful state of self-doubt—which, ironically enough, is the result of their own negative explanatory style—they choose performance goals rather than learning goals.

When mastery-oriented people encounter these same frustrating events, they do not experience emotional pain on top of the already stressful confusion. Furthermore, they feel less put upon to account for their errors or justify their mistakes, and they are able to utilize their time more efficiently in actual problem-solving.

It should be obvious that learning goals are critical, especially for young people. Since they are in an exploratory period of their lives and do not know what work they will be pursuing, they must keep their options open as long as possible. I would encourage performance goals only for a child who shows signs of being a prodigy—a concert pianist or a budding tennis champ, for example. Unfortunately, in the area of math, too many girls start avoiding learning goals as early as eighth grade, when they begin opting out of a higher-level math class, usually algebra.[8] Obviously this is much too early in their educational careers. By doing so, they limit their options and their potential.

Because studying high-level math and science almost guarantees mistakes and confusion, one must be willing to endure these frustrating states of chaos and befuddlement. One must learn to believe that it is okay to make mistakes because *everybody* does, including smart, capable, successful people. Even Einstein got confused. One of his famous quotes may help your daughter feel less inadequate in math. He said, "No matter what your difficulties in mathematics, mine are still greater, I can assure you." This notion was reinforced by a math professor who told me, "To succeed in math you must be willing to bang your head against a wall." A woman math and computer whiz kept insisting that she was not smarter than the average female in math. When I pointed out that there must be some difference, because she had advanced higher in this field than most women, she replied, "I just have a higher tolerance for confusion." While we laughed when she said this, I now appreciate her insight more fully and pass it along to you.

No Comparisons versus Inappropriate Comparisons

Perhaps the best way to illustrate this behavioral difference is to relate a story from my childhood.

When I was a girl, dancing was my life for well over a decade. As a ballet student, I had just enough talent to be dangerous, and so I reached a relatively advanced level—toe shoes and the whole bit. Around twelve or so I decided I wanted to go to New York and become a famous ballerina. My dancing instructor was pleased, of course, and wanted to encourage me in this endeavor, so she began taking me to see professional ballets. Due to her efforts and generosity, I had the glorious good fortune to see Rudolf Nureyev and Margot Fonteyn dance *Romeo and Juliet.**

As I sat in the audience, an awestruck adolescent, watching Ms. Fonteyn defy the laws of gravity and space, I remember thinking, "No matter how long I practice, no matter how hard I try, I'm never going to be that good." You can probably predict what I did. I quit dancing.

All those years of work, struggle, time, and money; all those years of my parents schlepping me back and forth to dancing lessons in snowstorms; all the sheer joy of moving my body to music; all that discipline to force my body to do whatever I bade it to do—all of it went down the tubes in one spectacular display of learned helplessness—and all because I sat there, a thirteen-year-old child, comparing myself to the world's greatest living female dancer. I compared myself to an inappropriate person and thus came to an inappropriate conclusion concerning my abilities, and ultimately, my future.

A ballet classmate of mine was not concerned that she might not be the equal of Margot Fonteyn. At eighteen she auditioned for and was selected to join a professional troupe. She toured with the company in Spain, Japan, and Australia—not as prima ballerina but in the chorus. Today she owns a dance studio, choreographs local ballets, and is an active member of the performing arts community.

I cannot judge which of us made the better decision or who is more successful. I love my life as a writer and speaker and would not change that. I don't know if I would be writing at all had I stayed with dance. I do know, however, that even a great love of dancing was not sufficient to sustain me though this debilitating aspect of learned helplessness or to prop up the sagging self-esteem it engendered. It took another seventeen years, until I was a much less limber thirty-year-old, before it finally dawned on me that in the

---

*Thank you, Shirlee Carlisle, wherever you are.

process of giving up a professional career in dance, I had also forfeited the most reliable source of pure bliss in my life. Once that realization dawned, I began dancing again, but this time for my own pleasure and delight. Now I feel successful as a dancer, even though my future will be limited to dancing in front of studio mirrors.

Mastery-oriented individuals do not compare themselves to anyone else. To be sure, they ask questions of others and love to pick the brains of successful people to learn as much as they can. They are also willing to ask for help when necessary—it's not helpless to ask for help—but they do not compare themselves or their performance to inappropriate others.

Being Creative versus Lacking Strategies

If one blames oneself for confusion and failure or fears the negative judgment of others (internalizes failure), if one believes that a specific problem will inevitably affect all other aspects of one's life (globalizes failure), and if one believes the problem will never get any better anyway (stabilizes failure), why would one be motivated to create, generate, or develop alternative strategies? In other words, once the interconnectedness of explanatory style and behavior is understood, it becomes obvious why the explanatory style of learned helplessness does not lead to persistence or, more importantly, to the creative problem-solving that helps to increase persistence.

If, on the other hand, one understands that the failure of one strategy is simply that, the failure of a *single* strategy; that timing is a critical component in any undertaking; and that success includes some failure along the way, then one is motivated to investigate many alternatives for reaching goals. Furthermore, one is able to sustain this motivation over long periods of time.

Developing a variety of alternatives—that is, being creative—entails effort and time. Since another word for exerting effort over time is "persistence," one can see how that effort is directly correlated to the creativity aspect of mastery. To learn persistence, one must be taught creative thinking skills. One must learn how to brainstorm, plan, analyze, synthesize, reorganize, make a mistake, practice, fall down, try again, synthesize some more, reorganize, analyze, make another mistake, and so on.

My years as a public school teacher taught me that creativity is a cognitive process that exists in all children to some degree and that can be enhanced. Although words like "synthesize" and "brain-storm" are too sophisticated for a child to understand, the truth is that kids can comprehend these complex concepts, as long as the language is simple. More importantly, even if they can't understand them, they can do them.

Therefore, if a girl is experiencing self-doubt about taking math, or if she is running for office or trying out for the team, she can learn to plan, strategize, and create as many alternatives as possible for reaching the goal and then to restrategize if and when those tactics fail. Whether it's getting a tutor, joining a study group, making new friends, studying with a private teacher, or practicing one full year before trying out for the team, whatever is required, she can learn the mastery skill of creative problem-solving and strategic thinking and planning, *if it is taught to her.*

Using Fear versus Resisting Fear

Stop for a moment and ask yourself this question: what is the purpose of fear? Fear must be a part of the design of nature because it exists in all mammals. Fear has an evolutionary purpose; otherwise the process of natural selection would have eliminated it long ago in some forgotten millennium.

What is the purpose of the physical reaction to fear—churning stomach, sweaty palms, rapid breathing, quaking and shaking? *Energy.* Fight or flight. Whether one chooses to defend oneself or flee the scene, one had better be quick, fast, and strong—in essence, action-oriented.

Some people describe this shot of adrenaline as terrifying and uncomfortable. Given these labels, it is to be avoided. Others who experience the same physical manifestations describe them as stimulating, exhilarating, thrilling, intoxicating, and even fun. These people are the thrill-seekers and risk-takers. If an individual can learn to avoid labeling the fear as either good or bad, and instead simply allow it to unfold, she will discover that nature itself has provided the energy she needs to do what must be done. What is needed is provided *within the fear itself.* A wise man helped me to understand the nature of fear, and I would like to pass his words along to you and your daughter.

"After all these years of standing in front of large groups," I complained, "I still get stage fright. It's the only part of my work I dislike. I wish I could make it go away."

Much to my bewilderment, he replied, "Why would you want it to go away?"

I was so dumbfounded I was unable to answer him. I had expected him to sympathize with my predicament and say something soothing like "Oh, yeah, that must be really awful." It was so perfectly obvious to me that fear was bad that I couldn't even imagine why he didn't understand. As I stood there trying to figure out what to say, he said kindly, "Don't call it stage fright."

"What do you mean? What should I call it?" I replied.

"Why must you call it anything?" He paused. "Listen," he said. "When you speak in a large room before a large audience, you must generate a great deal of energy to penetrate not only the space of the room itself but also the hearts and minds of your listeners. What you are labeling stage fright is simply your body generating the energy required to do the job, the personal power that will be necessary to do what must be done."

I still get shivers up my spine when I recall this story, for it reframed, once and for all, my conception of fear. I am not exaggerating when I say it was like a miracle to me. What had been a negative experience was promptly transformed into a positive experience, one to be welcomed.

Now I no longer resist what I used to call stage fright. When the physical sensations occur, I say to myself, "Oh, good, my mind and body are doing what is necessary so that I can do what must be done. I am confident that I will be prepared to handle this job," and then I appreciate and allow, rather than resist and resent, the sensations flowing through me.

The lesson this man gave me is the secret treasure of the mastery-oriented person: the realization that fear is a natural and integral part of bigger, more important processes such as learning, problem-solving, creativity, growth, change, risk, transformation, and resilience. Those who are mastery-oriented understand that fear contains a hidden gift—the energy to sustain them through the process.

This may be one of the most critical areas of difference in the upbringing of girls and boys. Boys are taught that fear, anxiety, and apprehension do not have the power in and of themselves to block

Mastery's Top Ten

10. Expect mistakes, confusion, ambiguity, setbacks, obstacles, and even failure.
9. Regard achievement as a process that *includes* failure.
8. Recognize that failure is a state, not a trait.★
7. Understand the difference between "response-ability," which is action- and future-oriented, and blame, which is passive and past-oriented ("Too late, nothing can be done").
6. Construe events in a way that preserves and increases self-esteem (use a positive explanatory style).
5. Spend your time problem-solving rather than explaining why you made the error.
4. Do not compare yourself to others.
3. Remember a failure is usually a failure of strategy, not self. Strategies can be changed an infinite number of times.
2. Take credit for a job well done (internalize success).

And the Number One Reason to Hang In There...

1. It's okay to fail, get confused, make mistakes. Everybody does!

★Thanks to Peter H. Johnson and Peter N. Winograd for this phrase from "Passive Failure in Reading," *Journal of Reading Behavior* 17 (1985), pp. 279–301.

them from reaching their goals. They are taught how to tolerate these emotions. Girls, on the other hand, usually are not taught that fear is just a part of life to be dealt with, that it has no greater power over them than they allow it to have. They aren't taught that it will inevitably occur and can be experienced and faced without sacrificing the goal that engendered the fear in the first place. Instead, when fear arises they are often given the message "Okay, you don't have to do that task." When they don't have to, they don't, and they sacrifice important aspects of learning.

In Chapter 3, we will see how keeping girls fearful actually serves some societal and parental agendas, and we'll examine the consequences of these agendas on our girls. We will also examine the causes of learned helplessness and contrast them with the sources of mastery.

CHAPTER 3

Causes and Effects

The enlightenment is not in the answer, but in the question.

Eugene Ionesco

Danielle is eight months old. She is learning to talk. She mispronounces words. She points to where the music comes out and says, "Radido." Everybody laughs. So does Danielle.

Melissa is one year old. She is learning to walk. She falls down. She gets up. She falls down. She gets up. She falls down. She gets up.

Amy is two. She knows exactly what she wants and doesn't want, and she makes her wishes quite clear to her parents by shouting "No!" whenever things do not suit her.

Rachel is five. Her parents must keep a watchful eye on her because she likes to wander around and talk to the next-door neighbors every chance she gets.

Michelle and Chelsea are twins with freckles. They are in second grade. They are learning to ride their bicycles. They fall down and skin their knees. They get right back on their bikes.

Joni, Hannah, Piper, and Sara are chums. They run around together in a little clique. They are in third grade. When the boys hog the jungle gym on the playground, the girls form an ad hoc committee and go to the teacher. When the teacher tells them to solve their own problem, they gather more support from other girls in their class. When they are about twenty-strong, they march en masse to the playground and demand that the boys vacate the jungle gym and share fairly. The boys, grumbling but outnumbered, do so.

Lisa is in the fourth grade. She has been trying to answer the teacher's questions in math class every day. She sits quietly with her hand in the air, but the teacher does not call on her. After class one day, Lisa goes to the teacher and politely but firmly requests that she be acknowledged. The teacher, embarrassed, apologizes and promises to call on her.

Mary is in the fifth grade. The class bully keeps knocking her books off her desk. One day she calmly stands up, walks over to him, grabs him by the collar, and yanks him halfway out of his seat. She leans down in his face and yells, "Knock it off!" The class bursts out laughing. The bully never knocks her books off her desk again.

Naomi and Shelley are in Mary's fifth grade class. They come home after school inspired by the girls-against-boys competition that Mr. Lowry instituted in math class that day. "We won!" shout the exuberant girls. Shelley adds, "I'm going to ask if we can challenge them in science class too!"

Toby and Jessica are in the sixth grade. They want to work on the computers at school, but the boys always get to them first and monopolize the work stations. The girls grumble to each other but say nothing to the boys. They stand behind the boys' chairs and watch while the boys play video games and work on the computers.

Ms. Brainard teaches seventh grade. Whenever she rewards her class with a free day, the boys rush to the game closet and grab the chess, Monopoly, and Go sets. The girls write notes to each other and draw on the board.

Ms. Reed is an eight grade counselor. She facilitates an after-school mentorship program for girls. The girls, ages thirteen to fifteen, complain that the boys got a new locker room and showers, but the girls didn't. When Ms. Reed suggests they make a formal complaint, they respond, "Yeah, but nobody will listen to us. Everybody knows that boys' sports are more important than girls' sports."

Ginny is a tenth grader. A first-rate violinist, she auditioned for and won a seat in the prestigious Young People's Philharmonic of her hometown. It required many hours of dedicated practice to keep up with the pace at rehearsals, but Ginny rose to the challenge. Shortly after achieving her goal, she began dating a boy. Within six weeks she informed her parents that she wanted to drop out of the orchestra because it was taking too much of her time. Distraught, her parents tried everything. Her father gave her a good talking-to. Her mother tried bribery. Nothing worked. Ginny dropped out of the orchestra.

Trish is in the eleventh grade. Math is her favorite subject, and she gets A's, but she has decided not to enroll in a math class as a senior. When her parents, appalled, ask her why, she replies, "Because I'm sick of the boys." When her father refuses to accept this reason, she elaborates: "They act so obnoxious, jumping out of their seats and waving their hands and shouting at each other. I don't want to have to act like *them.*" Her father continues to argue, but her mother, who empathizes with her daughter's reaction, pauses, unsure how to proceed.

Carla, a twelfth-grader, is the star forward on the girls' basketball team. She is disheartened at every game because there are hardly any spectators, while the bleachers at her boyfriend's basketball games are so crowded that there is often standing room only. When her boyfriend tries to persuade her and a few of her teammates to offer incentives to encourage more people to attend, all the girls insist it would be a waste of their time and flatly reject the idea.

The stories you have just read are all true. Only the names have been changed to protect the innocent. The younger girls faced the challenges of learning and problem-solving very much the way the boys did—by being persistent, assertive, resilient, unafraid, lively, inquisitive, full of the spirit of debate, and willing to challenge the opposite sex. Then, as their stories graphically indicate, the process that debilitates many of our girls began to occur, making them quiet, timid, and reticent. One begins to wonder if all girls are doomed.

"I don't agree that all girls will become fearful of competition or chronically depressed," said one workshop mom. Then, with a little less confidence, she added, "Will they?"

"Well, my oldest daughter didn't give up and drop out of math or fall in love with an abusive boy," responded another. "She stayed the course, was intelligent and fun, did well in college, dated nice boys, and made me proud."

"My daughter acted as a mentor to her friends and helped them to keep a high opinion of themselves," said another.

"That's right," I responded, "Not all girls will manifest serious symptoms of learned helplessness, but even among the resilient girls, there tends to be a *period* of self-doubt, and however long or short, it is a danger zone with the potential to derail them for longer periods."

Though the crisis faced by most girls will vary according to the individual, her temperament, and her circumstances, the question remains: how and why do so many girls go from lively and confident to unsure and self-deprecating? Furthermore, how do we minimize this possibility in the life of an individual girl?

The best way is for modern mothers to arm themselves with as much information as possible in order to understand (1) the differences between influences that strengthen mastery behavior and influences that instill learned helplessness, (2) why these influences exist, and (3) how these influences interact with and reinforce each other. Mothers also need to know how these influences operate in the personal, cultural, and familial contexts of daily life.

What Is Self-esteem?

Before we examine in greater depth the influences and causes of learned helplessness and mastery, we need to clarify a potentially confusing concept: self-esteem. It is often mistakenly understood to be synonomous with mastery behavior. There are differences between mastery and self-esteem, but they work together to keep girls resilient.

Over the last decade the discussion of self-esteem has become almost mantralike in the literature on children, especially female children, and in some ways this concept is so overused that it has become practically meaningless. It has come under increasing attack by scholars, teachers, mental health practitioners, and educational psychologists, even by Martin Seligman, the man responsible for the research on learned helplessness, which is presented in his book, *The Optimistic Child*.

Mastery and self-esteem enjoy a close relationship, since the components of mastery behavior lead to confidence, belief in oneself, and self-efficacy, but they are not the same, nor does one automatically lead to the other. Mastery leads to attitudes, behaviors, and responses that increase one's likelihood of staying resilient and capable of persisting through difficulty. Self-esteem, according to Dr. Nathaniel Branden in *Six Pillars of Self-Esteem,* is defined as "the feeling of being worthy, deserving, entitled to assert our needs and wants and to enjoy the fruits of our efforts" and "confidence in our ability to think and to cope with the challenges of life."[1] The difference is that mastery is based on performance and self-esteem is based on feelings. A problem arises when the definition of self-esteem, as used and understood by most people, blurs the distinction with mastery—in other words, it blurs the distinction between the way one feels about oneself and one's actual ability to perform in challenging situations.

On the one hand, we want our children to feel good about themselves in all circumstances. This will help them to stay resilient and persistent during the periods when they are not doing well and are at their most vulnerable. On the other hand, we don't want to produce a generation of children who feel good about themselves but who have no skills, can't perform according to high standards, give up easily, and are only engaging in bravado. When mastery-oriented people fail, they can feel good about themselves because they tried their best and will continue to pursue their goals. They do not persuade themselves to feel good while abandoning their goals. This is the so-called self-esteem that is being attacked by educators and others.

The truth is that self-esteem—that is, confidence in one's ability—and feeling worthy, deserving, and entitled (self-esteem) are not necessarily based on the reality of one's ability to meet high standards (mastery). Performing well (mastery) often leads to good feelings about oneself (self-esteem), but not always and not necessarily with lasting results. One may lack confidence, or self-esteem, in a certain area, but with the *willingness* to expend effort over time (created by a mastery orientation to problems), one may gain confidence. So while it is easy to see how the two are related, it is not a foregone conclusion that they always go hand in hand.

The emphasis on self-esteem as a "feeling" causes confusion in some people, who conclude that they should feel good all the time. Feeling good all the time is contrary to the experience of life. The truth is, sometimes we feel good and sometimes we don't. Feelings are unstable and capricious. This myth about feeling good all the time will become especially pertinent during puberty when your daughter's feelings will not only change with lightning speed and a mercurial whimsy, but will occasionally be quite negative. (More about this in Chapter 10.) In the final analysis expecting to feel good all the time is rather immature.

Furthermore, the illusion is often perpetuated in our society that success and self-esteem are irrevocably linked and that success produces self-esteem—in other words, good feelings. The problem with this kind of thinking is that success, like feelings, comes and goes. If one's success diminishes or undergoes a change, one's self-esteem often suffers as well. In addition, successful people don't go around feeling good all the time. They have good weeks and bad weeks just like everybody else. This is true even for the star performers. If one's self-esteem is based solely on one's success or level of performance, it is resting on shifting sands and will be subject to a wide range of ups and downs.

The real task of establishing self-esteem in a child must be based on something much more profound, substantial, and reliable. True self-esteem is the realization and appreciation of one's intrinsic self-worth, regardless of how one may be feeling or performing at any particular time. Therefore, to build true self-esteem in our daughters we must help them learn that they have worth, dignity, value, and merit regardless of their level of performance, their appearance, their grades, their intelligence, their personality, their popularity, or any other category we can come up with. True self-esteem must lie beyond the categories and measurements of a changing society. It is a deeper, perhaps even a spiritual, issue. Because true self-esteem is an inner certainty of self-worth and not subject to capricious emotion, fleeting thoughts, changing social values, or unreliable success, it is a more authentic, more substantial asset upon which to draw.

Of course, a certain amount of what passes for self-esteem among some adolescents, male and female, is neither self-esteem nor mastery. It is bravado and posturing, and the degree is often dependent on outside circumstances. For example, in rough neighborhoods and those with gangs you will find that a false show of self-esteem, a defiant and swaggering attitude, is calculated to deflect aggressive types on the lookout for vulnerability. By the same token, for some girls, dating dangerous boys may be a display of bravado.

While self-esteem must be nurtured to enable girls to feel good about themselves, astute mothers will understand that it must be developed in conjunction with mastery behavior. Together they form a substantial foundation for achieving one's goals.

The Contexts in Which Girls Learn Helplessness

1. *Personal* Personal experiences with confusion, setbacks, and failure can lead girls to draw inaccurate conclusions about themselves if they are not taught to maintain the coping attitudes and responses of mastery behavior.

2. *Cultural* Collective cultural beliefs about the "nature" of females and femininity determine how girls are raised. Also, a violent society that, to some extent, regards females as prey, contributes to fear and learned helplessness.

3. *Familial* Actions parents take or do not take will have consequences for either mastery or helplessness.

The Personal Context

The research on learned helplessness has shown that the greatest cause of learned helplessness at the personal level involves an individual's direct experience with an uncontrollable situation, one in which an individual's efforts to problem-solve do not produce meaningful feedback. This occurs when feedback is inconsistent, arbitrary, or meaningless, so that outcomes are not contingent upon the individual's actions or efforts. When an individual is unable to experience a gradual reduction of uncertainty based on what she does, she acquires helplessness.

By contrast, when an individual is in a controllable situation—one in which the feedback is meaningful and consistent, responds somewhat predictably to an individual's actions, and is congruent with the effort expended—then she is motivated to continue even if the situation is difficult and challenging. At the cognitive level, her way of thinking and her explanatory style enable her to continue problem-solving.

If her efforts at problem-solving do not produce consistent results, on the other hand, the individual then experiences what is known as cognitive exhaustion. She loses her willingness to invest more mental energy in a process that does not produce results or lessen her uncertainty. Her motivation and performance will decline and the negative explanatory style and emotions of learned helplessness will be aroused.[2]

For example, a child may not be performing well in a subject because of poor study habits. If she changes her study habits and subsequently improves her performance, she will be motivated to continue because her behavior produced the desired outcome. The outcome was consistent with her actions.

On the other hand, if a child has a learning disability and that, not poor study habits, is the cause of her difficulty, simply studying harder or longer will not produce an outcome that is consistent with her efforts. Studying harder and longer will just be a recipe for burnout, and she will start to display cognitive exhaustion.

Learned helplessness also occurs when a child does not receive parental responses consistent with her behavior. Suppose a parent is going through a crisis, is mentally ill, or is simply exhausted from working two or three jobs. The child has been struggling in a particular area and one day brings home a good grade on a quiz. The parent may ignore the child or even act or speak abusively. The child studied hard and improved her grade, but the parent's response was inappropriate and not consistent with the child's behavior.★

Finally, with regard to uncontrollable situations of a more systemic nature, I would be utterly remiss if I did not mention the social and political factors that perpetuate learned helplessness in all children. They are poverty, neglect, abuse, illiteracy, and racial or gender stereotyping. If we are to eliminate learned helplessness in any child, we must eradicate these forces to the best of our ability, especially since these uncontrollable circumstances in the life of a child perpetuate learned helplessness almost without exception.

Issues pertinent to our girls become evident here. First of all, it is imperative that the source of the problem be accurately identified, so as to prevent her from automatically internalizing the problem as a failure of self. A child with a learning disability, for instance, who

---

★It is interesting to note that many children of alcoholics do not seem to acquire learned helplessness, but instead just keep trying harder to win parental approval. This may be due to another psychological motivator known as intermittent reinforcement. Studies show that any behavior that is intermittently reinforced—say, two or three times out of every four or five attempts—will increase. If the reinforcement is random, the behavior increases even more. The behavior of the child of an alcoholic is often intermittently and randomly reinforced, since the response is based upon the parent's level of sobriety rather than the child's behavior.

tries hard without being taught how to adjust for the disability, is likely to conclude that she's just stupid. Once this attitude develops, it is difficult to undo. Better to accurately identify the source of problems as early as possible.

Second, we need to determine when appropriate actions have been taken and it is time to set a new goal. The girl with a learning disability may have to readjust her goals in light of the new information about her disability. She may have to be satisfied with going slower at first until she learns new skills. This is realistic thinking.

This notion of an uncontrollable situation has subtle repercussions with respect to math classes, where the learning styles preferred by boys have become the norm. The atmosphere is competitive, with a focus on the abstractions of math. Boys jump out of their seats and wave their hands to compete with one another. Teachers concentrate on the abstract concepts without regard to real-world application, contributing to girls' alienation in math class.[3] When coupled with attitudes, typical math classes become an uncontrollable situation for girls.[4] Even if girls try harder in this setting, they do not necessarily succeed, and teachers still do not call on them. As a result, girls still feel alienated from mathematics as a field of study. Given this bias, many people have concluded that girls are just "bad at math" rather than attributing the problem correctly to the fact that math classes often instill helplessness in girls.

Conversely, when the learning style preferred by girls is given equal time in the classroom, their understanding and performance in math improves. In "girl-friendly" classrooms, students work collaboratively in teams or groups, sit in circles, and learn about the real-world application of the math concept they are studying. Girls fare better in this setting.[5] They enroll in future math classes and feel better about math as a subject of study. Most importantly, they do not believe that they are too stupid to learn math.

Some people will assert that if we are to raise successful daughters we must teach them how to cope effectively in competitive "masculine" situations. I agree. After all, many of their future co-workers will be males who will exhibit this competitive style. Girls must learn the attitudes boys learn ("It's okay to make a mistake because everybody does") and the skills (waving their hands in the air and becoming vocal if necessary) to compete successfully.

At the same time, however, if we insist that girls learn in a way that alienates them, we will be defeating our purpose, which is to give them the education they need. To truly provide girls with equitable treatment we must establish an environment and a teaching style that will enable them to learn at maximum efficiency and stay confident of their abilities. Of course, a less competitive style will appeal to some boys as well. Eventually learning styles will be considered a matter of personal temperament rather than an issue of masculinity and femininity, and teachers will use a variety of styles in order to reach all their students effectively.

When this controversy of preparing girls for competition with boys arises in my workshops, I often compare girls to the aspen trees that are native to my home state of Colorado. Why aspens? Because there are similarities in the requirements of their upbringings.

You see, aspens are extremely hardy and resilient trees once they reach maturity. Because they are also beautiful, many Coloradans plant them in their yards, usually with limited success. This is so because most residential areas of Colorado are situated on the plains, and aspens are native to the mountains, where the conditions are different. If a homeowner is indifferent to the special needs of the aspen tree, which has been removed from the environment most conducive to its growth, the tree is unlikely to survive. If, on the other hand, the gardener recognizes that the tree is in a hostile environment and makes the effort to give the tree what it needs, the gardener will be rewarded one day with an incredibly hardy tree in full maturity.

The analogy to girls is apt. If the needs of girls go unrecognized while they are in the developmental phase of childhood; if they find themselves in the uncontrollable situation of a hostile environment (what author Mary Pipher calls a girl-toxic culture), they may not make it. If, on the other hand, an effort is made to give girls the support they need in a hostile environment, they will be hardy and resilient in adulthood.

Parents need to work on two fronts simultaneously. First, they must teach girls the most internally resilient ways of coping with the situations and environments they will encounter. At the same time, mothers must also work to change those uncontrollable situations and hostile environments where and when they can. While it is important that girls learn the attitudes and skills necessary for competition, it is also important that advocates for girls work to create a society more conducive to the growth of girls where cooperation is a valued commodity and a norm.

In later chapters we will discuss what parents can do to prevent a helpless response in a girl who finds herself in an uncontrollable situation—a girl-toxic environment. For now, however, we will continue our look at the causes of learned helplessness.

The Cultural Context

Following a period of social upheaval such as the second wave of the women's liberation movement of the sixties, sociologists estimate that it can take up to 250 years for behavioral change to percolate through the many levels of society. This is particularly true for belief systems such as sexism, racism, and ageism. Laws can be passed, of course, but the attitudes and behaviors that signal genuine change at the human and cultural level follow at an almost glacial pace.★

To make matters worse, in our society the social, cultural, and historical influences of sexism have contributed toward learned helplessness in women. One such influence involves society's collective beliefs about femininity and masculinity. Given the devaluation of feminine traits by our society, especially when they are equated with helplessness, it is not always easy for a girl to sustain either her self-esteem or her mastery

In the historically male-dominated arenas of finance, business, politics, technology, and science, for example, feminine traits are often perceived as a sign that women are too soft to cope with the harsher realities of life in these fields. In my professional work training mentors to work with women in the workplace, the women report that they are often advised to harden themselves and act more like men if they are going to succeed. A female Ph.D.

★A sociologist who studies the impact of telecommunications on society recently pointed out to me that this process may be speeded up somewhat due to the impact of the media. Nevertheless, if you doubt the truth of this statement, consider the tribulations of African-Americans who are still coping with the consequences of slavery nearly 150 years after emancipation.

candidate attending my workshop told the group that one member of her dissertation committee, a male professor in microbiology, informed her that women were too emotional to make good scientists!

Girls continue to be rewarded in school for displaying traditional feminine traits. While teachers call this behavior cooperation, it could be called submission and passivity. Here is how it works. As any teacher knows, a classroom can easily veer out of control if too many students become too enthusiastic, jumping out of their chairs, waving their hands, shouting answers, and demanding attention. Therefore, a good, dependable block of well-behaved students is a life raft for the classroom teacher who must maintain control. These dependable students are usually girls. Because the teachers need them so badly, they reward the girls for their submissive behavior.

Researchers report that girls who are cooperative are rated by teachers as more intelligent than others and are given higher grades.[6] Another study found that teachers evaluated girls by considering both performance and good behavior.[7] As a result, girls who complied with classroom rules received good grades on their report cards despite their test results.

This form of grade inflation partially explains a paradox long recognized in education: while girls get better grades, boys score higher on standardized tests. Because girls are being positively reinforced for the performance goal of good behavior rather than the learning goal of taking risks, being competitive, and mastering a difficult subject, they ultimately learn less. The end result is lower scores on the SAT and other standardized tests.

Finally, the consequences of society's devaluation of women and femininity can be observed by witnessing the behavior of adolescent boys, who can be quite hostile to girls, especially when they are in groups. A fourteen-year-old girl in one of my workshops said of her fraternal twin brother, "My parents think they have done such a great job of teaching my brother to treat girls with respect, but they don't see him at school with his friends. He acts all full of himself and like he thinks girls are stupid, just like the rest of the guys." Walk down the halls of any elementary of middle school, where boys who wish to insult or humiliate each other routinely yell such charming epithets as "You woman!" or "You wuss" (and we all know what *that* really means). In high school, this posturing can and does progress to sexual intimidation and abuse.[8] In addition, homo-phobia among males is directly related to their fear of appearing effeminate. Girls learn early on that the traits associated with their sex are not only unappreciated, they are trivialized, denigrated, and even condemned.

In addition, girls realize at puberty that boys are judging them almost solely upon their appearance, not their inner qualities. Com-petence and intelligence can actually become a hindrance to receiv-ing the boys' approval. Even a girl who has developed a high level of mastery can begin to feel weakened by these forces, especially if she does not measure up to the contemporary ideal of feminine beauty: thin, blond, pretty, and athletic.

We know from the research on learned helplessness that when groups feel devalued they tend to blame themselves instead of the real problem: cultural prejudice. They judge themselves rather than holding society responsible. If they take on the values of the culture and believe the fault lies with them, they lose both their motivation and their self-esteem. Or, if they *do* reject the values of the society, they wind up feeling alienated from the dominant culture. Thus, old people may feel burdensome and worthless, or they dislike young people; minorities may feel inferior and debased, or they may sal-vage their self-esteem by rejecting anything white; and females may feel debilitated, weakened, and reluctant, or they may engage in male-bashing.

Young Latinas in particular speak of a double standard within their families, where boys are treated better. They say their brothers have more freedom and fewer family and domestic responsibilities.[9] According to one survey, as many as 80 percent of young Latinas said that they would not enjoy being homemakers. However, more than one-third believed that they would be forced to assume that role because of cultural pressure and family expectations.[10] As you now know, their beliefs about their future will be critical in deter-mining that future.

African-American adolescent girls, on the other hand, manage to retain their self-esteem longer than either Anglo or Latina girls. At ages nine and fifteen, black girls showed higher levels of self-esteem than did the other two groups.[11] But they often do this by rejecting white values. Although this helps them retain their self-esteem, they pay a price by becoming alienated from the resources of the dominant culture, and their chances for future economic self-sufficiency and security are sabotaged.★

The other cultural cause of learned helplessness in females is the reality of our violent society, which regards women as prey, to some extent. Rock-and-roll lyrics and jacket covers, slasher movies with lovely young women as the victims, slick Madison Avenue ad campaigns, and magazine covers subtly promote the violence against women by making it look sexy and titillating. The verdicts in many high-profile legal battles involving sexual harassment or abuse send the message that it is easy to get away with victimizing women. Much of the posturing that occurs among adolescent boys implies that the domination of women is masculine and cool and that women make easy victims.

As girls mature, they become increasingly aware of these realities. Eventually, this makes girls wary of taking risks, and, quite frankly, who can blame them? Parents encourage this wariness. We do not want our daughters out there taking risks.

The traditional cultural response of overprotecting girls in order to keep them safe simply doesn't work. They still get pregnant, they still get raped, they still get involved with abusive men. Inculcating fear in girls or rescuing them *may* (no guarantee here) prevent a girl from taking risks, but it is more likely to produce an individual who will be unable to fend for herself if she encounters real danger. Even more to the point, the belief that a girl must be protected does not teach her the skills she needs to keep herself safe (more about these skills in Chapter 9).

Whether the danger results from an external source, such as an antagonist, or an internal source, such as one's own behavior, unsafe is still unsafe. The hard truth is that kids, male or female, are not always safe. Yet because most people believe that boys must be prepared for their future lives as providers and wage earners, many parents control their fears and allow their sons to test their limitations and push their boundaries despite the possibility of danger.

★Interestingly enough, there is little research, and therefore much to be done, on how Asian girls (the so-called model minority) handle the passage to womanhood. Nor are the trials and tribulations of Native American girls as they cope with Anglo value systems well researched.

While you may or may not agree with this practice, the point is that we have different standards for teaching risk-taking to boys and to girls. Parents overcome their fears about safety and teach their sons to stand up for their rights, defend themselves, and learn about their limitations by testing the boundaries. But they teach their daughters to be cautious and careful, to accommodate others in order to avoid provoking anger, and to curb risk-taking behavior. In so doing, they inculcate fear in girls. Thus, when learned helplessness ("I need help," "I'm scared," "I can't do it") rears its head in the life of a boy, adults take steps to correct this deficit ("You can handle it," "You can make it," "Try again"). When a girl shows the same behavior, parents may accept it in the hope that it will keep her safe. They may even unconsciously perpetuate what is called premature rescuing.

The Familial Context

PREMATURE RESCUING

The third cause of learned helplessness occurs at the interface between the reality of violence and the belief that females are vulnerable and in need of protection. This gives birth to a fear-based response on the part of parents, leading them to rescue girls in situations where they do not rescue boys. Sometimes, in fact, they rescue girls even before they need it!

In a fascinating study by Jean Block, fathers were videotaped helping their sons and daughters solve a difficult puzzle.[12] They helped each child separately, working one-on-one. With their sons they began with the principles of problem-solving and task mastery. When the boys, frustrated at their inability to solve the puzzle quickly, began crying and throwing puzzle pieces, the fathers just ignored this emotional behavior and continued to focus on the tasks of problem-solving. With their daughters, they began in exactly the same way, with the principles of problem-solving and task mastery. When their daughters began to cry and show emotional distress, however, the fathers comforted them with reassurances such as "That's okay, honey. It's just a game." Some of the fathers actually picked up the puzzle pieces for their daughters and placed them in their proper slots even before the girls asked for help. This parental behavior, premature rescuing, is almost guaranteed to teach learned helplessness.

Premature rescuing sends a powerful message. It says, "You cannot do this alone. You need my help." Mothers, of course, engage in this same behavior and often model for their daughters the desire to be rescued. Having been rescued themselves as young girls, as adults, they expect to be rescued when the going gets tough. These mothers have learned helplessness.

You can see the danger here when both parents have been conditioned by subtle stereotypes. Parents don't wake up one morning and say, "I think I'll rescue my daughter today and make her helpless." Rather, both parents, having been raised and conditioned in a sexist society where powerful stereotypes tell us that a man shows love for a woman by protecting and rescuing her. If the average father is inclined to rescue and the average mother is inclined to *be* rescued, a potent message, perhaps never spoken aloud, will be sent. Then, no matter how many inspired pep talks are given, the deeper message—"You need help"—has already been sent. When help is premature or inappropriate, it actually causes the helpless behaviors we wish to eradicate.

Thus, helplessness in females can be perpetuated under the innocent, even noble, guise of love. In our attempts to counteract a violent society and in our eagerness to keep our daughters safe, we inadvertently act in ways that instill or reinforce learned helplessness.

Of course, there are situations from which a child must be rescued. No one would allow a four-year-old to run out into traffic or go off with a stranger in order to test her limitations. Here is a good rule of thumb: if you would not rescue a boy, do not rescue a girl. Girls must be allowed to fall down and skin their knees, defend themselves, and learn resilience and persistence, just like boys. Neither sex must be debilitated by faulty parental belief systems. Treating your sons and daughters differently when it comes to determining whether they are in danger, and failing to build their coping skills when they are, does not serve the goal of raising mastery-oriented daughters.

This is the bottom line: to create strong, brave, and resilient girls, we must change our thinking from "How do I keep my daughter safe?" to "How do I make her strong and capable of protecting *herself?*"

An astute education professor of mine said it best in a class about introducing computers into the classroom. (This was back in the Early Pleistocene Period of education. Many of you will remember it, since you were educated during that period yourselves.) In making the point that kids are natural learners until well-meaning adults hamper their instinctive curiosity, he said, "Just get out of their way and let them learn."

Even if it seems that a fearful attitude will somehow act as a talisman to keep danger at bay, even if you feel a need to hover or be anxious, remember that this is *your* problem. Do not pass your fearfulness on to your daughter. In other words, do your sentinel duties as invisibly as possible. If you must keep watch, stay in the background and do not be obvious about it. It is crucial that your daughter does not see you hovering.

GRATUITOUS PRAISE AND CONSTANT CRITICISM

Many of us, especially teachers, have witnessed the results of confused parents who think that the way to build mastery and self-esteem is to give constant and gratuitous praise. If a parent presents self-esteem in this way, as built upon something as flimsy, changeable, and unpredictable as praise from others, several unpleasant results are likely: (1) the child may become a complete bore whom no one can stand; (2) the child may stop believing the parent; (3) the child may become a people-pleaser, constantly trying to be what other people want; or (4) the child may depend solely on outside sources to feel good about herself and may therefore lose the autonomy necessary to supervise her own inner responses.

Gratuitous approval does not result in mastery behavior or high performance and will probably not result in true self-esteem either. The child who becomes a bore may have self-esteem but may lack skills, resilience, or the ability to think strategically. The child who stops believing the parent loses whatever self-esteem she may have had and becomes impervious to parental guidance. The people-pleaser will be rendered incapable of acting in a mastery-oriented fashion if mastery behavior causes conflict with those around her. The child who is externally motivated may lose her ability to feel good about herself without outside praise. How does a parent deal with such awesome complications and instill both self-esteem and mastery? The goal is to produce girls with high self-esteem who are also mastery-oriented. Achieving this goal rests on the dual responsibility of building both from *within*.

All children, girls and boys alike, must develop self-esteem by feeling and experiencing unconditional love that is based on their intrinsic worth as human beings regardless of the level of their performance. This is achieved not by giving constant or gratuitous approval but by being a good friend to one's daughter; by helping her to understand that even if she isn't brilliant or beautiful or funny or cute or superior, she is worthy of respect and deserves to be treated with consideration. You can accomplish this by spending time with her, by not withholding affection when she isn't performing up to the standards you desire, by helping her see that failure and confusion are temporary and natural and not a part of her identity, by modeling compassion, by teaching her to stand up for herself, by not making her feel bad if she gains a few pounds, by teaching her that she herself is the only person who ultimately has the right to assess her worth, and by teaching her that she has dignity as a human being, no further qualifications needed. In other words, treat her as you would treat a dear and cherished friend.

For example, you would never say to a cherished friend, "Gee, Mildred, I think you're a great person and I love spending time with you and all, but I might like you a little better if you were promoted." And you wouldn't say, "Annabelle, I have a lot of respect for you and what you have accomplished and you're great fun, but I would be closer to you if you'd lose ten pounds." We love our friends unconditionally for who they are, not for what they have achieved, how they look, how they serve us, or what they can accomplish at some point in the future. We do not withhold our affection until they meet some standard we have set for them.

It is strange how most people would never even think of judging a friend, but they feel free to judge their own children, although perhaps more subtly, when they fail to meet parental agendas or gratify parental egos. Attacks on a child's basic feeling of self-worth as a human being will do devastating and long-lasting damage.

Standards are important, however. Therefore, while you remain conscious and vigilant in establishing in your daughter a sense of intrinsic self-worth that does not come and go with every difficulty and reward, you must also endeavor to instill true and long-lasting mastery skills. These skills are of the kind that can be applied in all situations and in all circumstances. Like self-esteem, mastery skills must be built from within if they are to be real and long-lasting.

Thus, in all the activities of girls, whatever their age, they must be encouraged, rewarded, inspired, and acknowledged for all behaviors that reflect mastery or the refusal to accept a passive role. Some of those behaviors may not be consistent with society's notion of "feminine behavior," but your daughter's sense of mastery and her overall self-esteem will nevertheless be enhanced. You can guide your daughter to think and act masterfully by teaching her how to identify correctly the source of a problem, especially if it is an external one; by teaching her the difference between blame and responsibility; by teaching her how to strategize her way past any obstacle; by instilling a strong work ethic; by telling her the truth about what will be expected of her; by teaching her that the life of an individual and the achievements of an individual are processes, not products; by not rescuing her prematurely or otherwise, when she makes a mistake, experiences discomfort, or makes a bad decision; and by teaching her life's greatest truth—that everything changes and that mastery behavior and success require a lifelong effort and commitment.

Finally, in dealing with girls, you must not fail to consider the events and trials of puberty, when the traits of femininity, however they are perceived by your daughter's generation, will become increasingly important to her. In our society the pressure is on girls to be attractive in order to have high self-esteem. We must have compassion for the stress this creates in them, and we must understand and respect their desire to attract male attention.

In summary, the job of establishing in girls both high self-esteem and a mastery orientation to life is a big task, particularly given some of the social and cultural messages girls receive. Without mastery and self-esteem, they may flounder. If they feel good about themselves only in a superficial way, dependent upon circumstances of life that may change, but tend to give up easily and are unable to meet high standards, they will be ill-equipped to deal with life and attain economic self-sufficiency. On the other hand, if they are capable, competent, and skilled but dislike themselves, they may lead productive lives, but they will not necessarily be happy lives. Only when they have access to profound and reliable feelings of intrinsic self-worth and a highly developed set of skills will they have the right stuff to be both successful and happy individuals.

PART II

What Mothers Can Do

CHAPTER 4

Mothers as Role Models

Show me a woman who runs for school board and I'll show you
a daughter who runs for governor.

> *Laura Liswood, author of*
> Women Leading at the Top

The Clan

Once or twice a week around my mother's kitchen table, amid
steaming cups of coffee, warm bagels, and sweet rolls, there would
congregate a coterie of lively women. They would affectionately
call the gathering a kaffeeklatsch. I remember the women always sat
in the same chairs: Pat, the neighbor from across the street, exotic,
raven-haired, barely twenty-one years old and already the mother of
three; Laura, the neighbor to our left, overweight, redhaired, acerbic,
and hilarious; Ethel, the neighbor on the right, a gravel-voiced
hawk with perpetual nicotine stains on her fingers; Zoe, big-busted
and big-eyed, a cute Gidget type who could cuss like a truck driver; and my mother, who presided as the reigning matriarch.

With the sun streaming in the window illuminating their faces
and hands as they gestured, threw their heads back laughing, and
poured themselves more coffee, I would hover around the warm
kitchen sneaking doughnuts and eavesdropping. As I listened to
their tales of their families, their husbands, and even the intimate
details of their sex lives, I absorbed clues to what it meant to be a
woman—how to act, what to think, how to make my way in the
world. Sometimes, and with greater frequency as I grew older, I
would even be allowed to join them, as long as I abided by the seen-

and-not-heard rule these tolerant, loving women silently enforced. They knew, even if I didn't, that a learning process was taking place.

Unfortunately, during the last several decades, such kaffeeklatsches have suffered bad press. The group that functioned for me as an authentic Council of Elders would now be dismissed as a bunch of housewives with nothing better to do than sit around and gossip. In truth, it was (forgive my overwrought prose here, but I really believe this) a convocation of collective female consciousness, a congress of way showers. It was the clan. At the very least it was a cluster of adult women bestowing their wisdom on a youngster.

Looking back, I think the most powerful aspect of that kaffeeklatsch—other than the transmission of a feminine sense of community—was that it offered me the opinions and perspectives of adult women rather than other teenagers, a perspective that was often in strong counterpoint to the media messages of that period. The stories and personal insights I remember hearing were presented with a good deal more chutzpah and with mastery-oriented attitudes as well. Just listen:

- "Men have to be trained to be husbands. They don't come out of the box that way."
- "Women have to be twice as good as men to get noticed on the job."
- "I told Steven, 'If you think you can bully me without consequences, you're wrong. If I have to wait until the middle of the night and hit you over the head with a cast-iron frying pan, I will. If you doubt it, just try raising your hand to me one more time.'"
- "During our separation it hit me that I was totally dependent on Ed's income. Without his salary I was penniless. That's when I went back to school and got my CPA."
- "I would tell my daughter to wait a long time to have sex because, by waiting, I know I learned a lot more about my body and what I respond to. You know how men are. They are always in such a rush to do it. If Fred and I had done it too soon, I don't think I would have learned so much about my body."
- "Even if I gained fifty pounds, John would still love me. He's hooked."
- "I wish someone had told me to get an education instead of rushing into marriage. I lost a good deal of my youth because I

got scared no one would ask me and I married the first guy who did."

These were powerful messages from adult mentors and members of the clan, even if they were in disguise as 1950s homemakers. Even though I had no way of knowing it at the time, their words, spoken from direct experience, were teaching me the ropes. Their lessons stayed with me over many years as I matured.

Growing up in the fifties, when the model mother was Donna Reed vacuuming in her pearls, my own mother was an unusual role model. She was a jazz pianist who played gigs and came home at four o'clock in the morning. She had musicians over on the weekends to jam. She negotiated contracts, hired and fired musicians. Maintaining her self-esteem in the often cutthroat world of the music business, where a three-month gig was equivalent to a gold watch, made my mother strong and resilient—a savvy lady, a tough cookie, a force to be reckoned with. Having observed her firsthand, I know that she did not really like the business end of music, but she did it. She was the risk-taker in the family. My dad, on the other hand, was Mr. Security. Employed at the same company for over twenty-five years, he would argue with my mother over whether or not to go into the nightclub business. My father's philosophy was "If you've got a penny, save it." My mother's philosophy was "If you've got a penny, try to make two out of it."

Having lost her father at the tender age of sixteen months (he was poisoned by cattle buyers in 1911), my mother was reared by her grandmother, Sarah; her mother, Rebecca; and her aunt Blanche in an all-female household. While Rebecca and Blanche worked every day in a garment factory making overalls, Grandma Sarah did the work of raising my mother. Thus, as a child, my mother saw nothing but women taking care of business, and by that I mean *all* business—earning money, doing household repairs, nurturing a family, and raising a child.★

I refer to my mother's unique upbringing because she is and continues to be, even in her eighties, an unsurpassable role model for female mastery behavior. Not only can mothers teach mastery and risk-taking, just like fathers, they can do it in spite of stultifying

★This situation mirrors the current circumstances of many African-American women in families where no males are present.

societal and cultural norms that may work against them. As pervasive as it was, the circumscribed model of the 1950s mom did not alter the impact of my own mother on me; nor did the Victorian ideal of womanhood that was still prevalent during my mother's childhood, with its images of women as decorative, helpless creatures too frail to be expected to cope with the harshness of life, alter the effect of my mother's many "mothers" on her.

Today's mothers come in a variety of styles. They may be entrepreneurs, athletes, secretaries, politicians, nurses, doctors, teachers, sole proprietors, accountants, social workers, programmers, waitresses, day-care providers, or engineers, or they may choose to stay home and make raising their children their full-time occupation. Daughters can identify with their mothers and be taught the important life skills of mastery that used to be the male domain. In this chapter you will have an opportunity to evaluate your own mastery level and your potential for modeling it for your daughter, but first I would like to address two issues that often surface in my workshops.

Once they understand the subtlety of learned helplessness, some mothers experience discomfort. They realize that they must confront their own patterns of learned helplessness in order to be effective role models for their daughters. Some wonder if they are successful enough in their own lives. Mothers who work inside the home rather than outside the home are particularly vulnerable. The following conversation from a workshop illustrates this point.

It began when Peg, a systems analyst at the National Center for Atmospheric Research and the mother of Caitlin, who wanted to be a veterinarian, began discussing her daughter's struggle with organic chemistry.

"My daughter is overwhelmed," said Peg. "Recently she evoked the old girls-are-not-as-good-in-math-as-boys-are routine, and I quickly reminded her that *I* am good in math. I also reminded her that math is confusing for everyone, not just girls. I told her about the confusion I face almost daily in my particular field."

"I know what you mean," said another. "I'm in business for myself, and I face financial problems and decisions of hiring and firing that require me to take risks and cope with criticism. I share these with my daughter so she can see what I am up against."

A third woman chimed in: "I'm an attorney and a partner in a big law firm. I am constantly exposed to sexist attitudes from my partners. Some doubt my capacity to get in there and mix it up with the big boys. Either way I—"

"Wait a minute," interrupted an apprehensive mother in the back of the room. "This is making me feel defensive. What about those of us who *aren't* scientists or entrepreneurs or attorneys? I'm from that dying breed of women who used to be called housewives. What about *our* daughters? Does this mean they are doomed?"

Doomed? Certainly not. From a mastery point of view, what is important is that you set an example of willingness to take positive risks, try new things, and remain persistent, hardy, and resilient through difficulty and criticism. That is the measure of your success as a role model, *not* whether you make partner at the firm, make a fortune in investments, or make the bed at home.

The woman who called herself a member of a dying breed—the housewife—then brought up an interesting point. What is a housewife these days anyway? Just for the fun of it, I looked up the word "housewife" in two dictionaries. One was my old college dictionary from twenty-five years ago; the other was brand new. Guess what? There was a slight but telling difference. The older dictionary defined a housewife as "a woman who manages her own household." The newer one defined it the same way, but with an added twist: "a woman who manages her own household as her main occupation." In addition, the new dictionary had an entry for "house husband," while the older one did not.

More to the point, however, there is the feeling some women have that being "just a housewife" is some sort of cop-out. (Although I do not believe early feminists intended for this negative connotation to arise, it did. I believe that this negative connotation arose not from feminism but from the old patriarchal habit of devaluing "women's work.") I know from my own childhood that even the so-called conventional housewives of the fifties were anything but cop-outs. I was blessed to be exposed to women of the 1950s who were creative, intelligent, and adventurous. My own mother was a musician, my aunt owned and operated a movie theater and drive-in with her husband, and my best friend's mother was a potter, radio collector, and map enthusiast.

Likewise, the mothers and homemakers who attend my workshops and who appear to be "just housewives" are involved in so many activities, community responsibilities, and personal projects that they defy the label "housewife." One mother is an equal partner with her husband in buying fixer-uppers in Victorian neighborhoods, refurbishing them, and then selling them. She tears down walls, installs hardwood floors, does electrical wiring, replaces the grout in shower stalls, and handles bankers and real estate brokers. A mother of three is a marathon runner who trains year-round. She regularly finishes in the top five of her age category in the amateur division of the races she runs. Still another is the volunteer arts director for a major nonprofit outfit. She oversees a marketing staff, a group of volunteers, and a six-figure budget for three yearly fundraisers.

All mothers—career mothers, stay-at-home mothers, and those who work part-time—can model the responses and attitudes of mastery behavior to keep their daughters' aspirations alive and their confidence high when the going gets tough, just as good fathers do with their sons. It is natural for girls to want to model these behaviors. Why should they believe, much less act on, our pep talks glorifying mastery behavior if we don't act on them ourselves? And, more importantly, without direct experience on our part, how can we be sure our advice is valid?

After leading workshops designed to help mothers model the behaviors of mastery and positive risk-taking, training teachers in classroom interventions to build mastery in female students, and conducting research on adolescent girls, I know that the first step is to help you determine the effects that *your* attitudes and behaviors have on your daughter. Here is a quiz designed to get you thinking in that direction.

Taking Stock: Your Mastery Inventory

Part I: You as an Individual

In this first set of questions, select the answer that best describes you. Do not make your selection based on what you think the right answer should be. Choose the one that is the most honest and accurate description of you.

1. When I experience a failure or setback I tend to
   a. Be completely unconcerned with whose fault it is and keep working.

b. Be mildly concerned but not blame myself for or lose sleep over it.

c. Be upset with myself and lose a lot of time fretting about it before finally getting back to work.

d. Blame myself, lose significant amounts of precious time, hate myself, procrastinate, and undermine my motivation.

e. Give up altogether.

2. When something breaks, I usually
   a. Fix it.
   b. Ask someone or hire someone to fix it.
   c. Hint around for somebody to fix it.
   d. Put it aside for later.
   e. Live with it.

3. When something is challenging, I tend to
   a. Get more excited and energized.
   b. Get more determined to master it.
   c. Get nervous and feel like procrastinating.
   d. Indulge in avoidance behavior such as sleeping, eating, "getting organized," or any activity other than the one posing the challenge.
   e. Quit and never go back to it.

4. When faced with a new technology, I feel
   a. Excited and eager to learn something new.
   b. Curious and willing to tackle it.
   c. Hesitant and reluctant to touch it.
   d. Completely uninterested or bored.
   e. Nauseated and anxious.

5. My reaction to unplanned changes in my schedule is usually
   a. Endless wonder at the spontaneity of life.
   b. Openness and curiosity.
   c. Controlled anxiety.
   d. Resistance.
   e. Outright opposition.

6. The idea of playing team sports makes me want to
   a. Join.
   b. Coach.
   c. Watch.
   d. Sleep.
   e. Wretch.

7. My typical decision-making mode is
   a. Relatively swift and decisive.
   b. Well thought out and thorough.
   c. Hesitant and unsure.
   d. Anxious.
   e. Totally passive—I rely on others to make decisions.

8. When it comes to financial matters, I am
   a. Confident and willing to take an occasional risk.
   b. Competent but unwilling to take a risk.
   c. Careful and cautious.
   d. Nervous and anxious.
   e. I don't make financial decisions other than balancing the checkbook.

9. If I had to enroll in a math class tomorrow in order to keep my job or get a job, I would
   a. Have no problem; I'd just do it.
   b. Not be thrilled, necessarily, but I'd do it anyway.
   c. Be nervous but I would get a tutor or find another way to get help.
   d. Procrastinate, miss registration, or get sidetracked with other concerns.
   e. Refuse to do it.

10. My reaction to criticism is generally
    a. Calm or indifferent.
    b. Relaxed and willing to listen.
    c. Concerned and mildly fearful.
    d. Anxious, hurt, and tearful.
    e. Complete debilitation.

Part II: You as a Mother

In this set of questions, select the answer that best describes how you interact with your daughter. Again, do not make your selection based on what you think is the right answer. Choose the one that is the most honest and accurate description of you.

11. For moms with daughters under age eight: When my daughter feels intimidated or demeaned by another,
    a. I deal with the situation immediately and speak with the person who is causing her problems.
    b. I wait until I have thought it through and then speak to the person.
    c. I think about it, postpone acting, maybe say something, maybe not.
    d. I encourage her to try harder to fit in.
    e. I comfort my daughter but say nothing to others.

    For mothers with daughters age eight or older: When my daughter feels intimidated or demeaned by another,
    a. I teach her to be assertive and act quickly. I help her figure out what she wants to say, and then we do some role-playing so that she can practice her response and be prepared for a variety of responses.
    b. I encourage her to stand up for herself.
    c. I comfort her, encourage her to think it over before acting, maybe say something, maybe not.
    d. I comfort her and encourage her to try harder to fit in.
    e. I comfort her and teach her that making waves brings future trouble.

12. My level of concern with whether others approve of my daughter is
    a. Nonexistent.
    b. Mildly interested.
    c. Moderately concerned.
    d. Very concerned.
    e. Eager for others to approve of her.

13. If my daughter began talking about attending an all-girl college, and if money was no object, I would
    a. Be very pleased and encourage her to do so.
    b. Be pleased and let her make up her own mind.
    c. Be open to the idea but concerned for her social life.
    d. Suggest she consider a school where she would have an opportunity to meet and date college boys.
    e. Discourage it and encourage her to attend a coed college.

14. If my daughter suggested we enroll in a self-defense class together I would
    a. Tell her to sign us up! I want to learn how to take swift, decisive, and effective action to save my life, and I want my daughter to learn the same.
    b. Have no qualms. I believe in self-defense classes and learning to be aggressive, if need be, to save one's life.
    c. Like to think I would sign up, but I'm not sure how I would react.
    d. Probably resist and come up with an excuse.
    e. Encourage her to do so, but I would not participate.

15. If my husband suggested enrolling our daughter in a gun safety class and wanted to take her to the shooting range to practice, I would say,
    a. "Good idea!"
    b. "Okay."
    c. "Well, I don't know...."
    d. "I don't think this is a good idea."
    e. "Absolutely not. No way!"

(I realize this is a tricky question that may not measure mastery attitudes so much as religious and spiritual values and attitudes surrounding violence. Nevertheless, I invite you to reflect upon it. Try to keep in mind that the ability to handle a gun is simply a skill. I am not suggesting that you keep a gun in your home or that you imply to your daughter that gun-handling skills will enhance her safety.)

16. If my daughter reacts to criticism by becoming depressed and anxious, I will
    a. Counsel her to "Consider the source of the criticism. If you respect, admire, or care about the person who criticized you; if that person seems to have good intentions and be knowledgeable, intelligent, and kind, then perhaps you can learn something from the criticism. Try to determine what you can learn. The person may have reasons that have nothing to do with you and may be jealous, uninformed, or just petty. Don't take it personally."
    b. Sympathize and explain that criticism is part of life. Ask her what reasons the person might have had for making those remarks. Are they based on something that actually occurred or something inside of the critic? I would share with her what I do when I am criticized. I'd tell her what works for me and what doesn't.
    c. Sympathize and indicate I know how she feels. Criticism hurts.
    d. Ask her to explore what she might have done to provoke such a comment. Then we would discuss ways of changing her behavior to avoid future criticism.
    e. Criticize her for becoming depressed or anxious, and tell her to buck up.

17. If my daughter suggested we take a basic computer programming class together, I would say,
    a. "Cool! Let me mark the dates on my calendar."
    b. "Fine. I'm willing to try it. Sounds like a good idea."
    c. "Sounds good, but I'm too busy. Maybe another time."
    d. "Oh, I don't know. I'm not sure I want to try that. Computers make me crazy."
    e. "No way. I hate computers."

18. In terms of popularity, I tell my daughter
    a. That it feels good to be liked, but being a good person who earns the respect of others is equally important to her happiness.
    b. That having people like you is better than not having them like you, but it's not the be-all and end-all. There are other sources of happiness in life.

c. That I do care if people like her.

d. That she should make an effort to please others so they will like and approve of her and make her feel good about herself.

e. That being popular is important.

19. The idea camping in the wilderness for four days alone with my daughter, just the two of us, sounds

a. Like an exciting adventure.

b. Like a great opportunity to get away from it all and enjoy some privacy and quality time together.

c. Interesting, but I want to know a lot of details before trying it.

d. Like an opportunity to encounter dirt and wild animals that I would just as soon avoid.

e. Like a stupid and dangerous idea.

20. If my fourth grade daughter goes on a diet, I will

a. Talk with her and explain that, while I understand that her appearance is important to her, it is only one aspect of life and that many other aspects are equally important to her happiness, well-being, and development. I will then encourage her to get involved in sports, dance, and other physical activities.

b. Tell her that people of all weights, shapes, and sizes are valuable, beautiful, intelligent, and fully capable of achieving all their goals. I will encourage her not to make her appearance the center of her life, and I'll encourage discussion of why good looks alone will not bring happiness.

c. Tell her she is lovely and also get her father involved in giving male approval to her.

d. Probably say, "You're too young for that. I won't allow it."

e. Suggest that we diet together and give each other moral support.

Scoring and Commentary

To determine your score, go back over the test, give yourself the following points, and add up the numbers. I recommend taking this test on two or three different days. Since it is self-rated, your answers can be influenced by your mood or by external events that may make you feel better or worse. My experience upon taking it several different times was that my score varied by about five points. If you are on the cusp of a score, retaking the test may be enough to move you into another category, up or down. If you are in the middle, retaking it won't affect you that much.

A responses = 5 pts.
B responses = 4 pts.
C responses = 3 pts.
D responses = 2 pts.
E responses = 1 pt.

80–100 points—Amazon Warrior

If this is your score, it means that most (or all!) of your answers were in the two mastery-oriented categories—the A and B responses. This is an extremely high score and a very unusual one. In the event that an armed insurrection of the matriarchal forces should ever erupt, we want you as our generals and field marshals. I say this only partially tongue-in-cheek, because truly, if you scored this high you are a strong and resilient woman willing to take a risk to reach your goals or even just for the thrill of it. You don't blame yourself when something goes wrong or assume that bad events can't be changed for the better. Undoubtedly you are already modeling self-reliance and positive risk-taking for your daughter. Bravo and congratulations!

60–79 points

If you chose mostly A and B answers, with a few C, D, and E responses, you are a little harder to predict. Sometimes you take the bull by the horns when necessary, but sometimes you don't. You can be quite mastery-oriented in some areas, but you exhibit (or model) learned helplessness in others.

The best thing for you to do is to review your answers and try to identify your areas of weakness, lack of confidence in yourself or in your daughter, and fear of risk-taking. Then look at these weak areas to see if there is a pattern. Perhaps you will find an area of fear around physical risk-taking. Perhaps financial. Perhaps emotional. If you do detect a pattern, that is an area where you need to apply the techniques offered in this book in order to begin making the changes that will set a mastery-oriented example for your daughter.

40–59 points

If you scored in this range, you may still have enough mastery to get the job done, but you are reluctant, hesitant, and inclined to doubt yourself. You may not take the initiative, or perhaps you take action only when you're forced to do so. Another possibility is that you are highly mastery-oriented in a particular area, but you suffer from a lack of belief in yourself in all the others.

This score may also indicate an individual who is hiding learned helplessness behind subtle and covert disguises such as boredom, irritation, procrastination, and lack of interest, time, or money. Are you truly not interested in that new activity, or are you avoiding taking a risk and possibly looking foolish? Do you really not have the time to learn that new subject, or are you avoiding the discomfort of the learning curve? Can you really not afford to spend the money on that new business idea, or are you just unsure of your own creativity? Nobody but you can take a thorough and searching second look to determine what's really going on in these responses. As your daughter matures, she will see through your excuses. Eventually, from watching you, she will learn how to make them herself.

Finally, even though you may take action when you have to, you put yourself through a lot of hand-wringing and gnashing of teeth before finally tackling the problem. This causes you unnecessary grief since, most of the time, you have to go ahead and do the thing you have been avoiding anyway. I do understand that many risks are painful and hard to undertake. Still, we should give ourselves a break and minimize the time we spend suffering.

20–39 points

The E responses indicate serious learned helplessness. These responses show a near total lack of belief in your ability to learn something new, change bad habits, bounce back in the face of difficulty, or create new and better situations for yourself. This lack of belief in yourself can manifest itself as passivity, reluctance, or even inertia. This is particularly distressing when you consider that certain kinds of passivity are considered feminine, especially during conflict or in situations where physical intimidation and hostility are required, such as fending off an attacker in a dark parking lot in the middle of the night.

In place of the subtle social, cultural, and personal enhancers of learned helplessness, you must substitute activities, techniques, attitudes, and behaviors that will make your daughter a mastery-oriented and positive risk-taker. Unfortunately, the easiest way—simply telling her—is the least effective. I wish I could report that pep talks alone would suffice, but the truth is that girls must see us act in the ways we recommend for them. They must see us get confused and make mistakes, yet remain persistent and resilient. They can see us cry, become frustrated, and feel like giving up and witness that these behaviors do not permanently stop us in our tracks. We must do for our daughters what fathers typically do for their sons: model mastery behavior over time and coach them through it in an experiential way. Like boys, girls must learn from their adult role models.

You need to get involved, together with your daughter, in positive risk-taking experiences such as learning something new (the experiential aspect) and then setting the example of mastery behavior for her to imitate (the modeling and coaching aspect). Mother-daughter mastery projects are great vehicles for this valuable teaching and learning experience. Think of the suggestions in the rest of this chapter as a sort of teacher's guide, a reference to which you will return again and again as you make your way through some of the suggested projects.

Based on my own research showing that girls benefit from these activities, I guarantee it will be a worthwhile investment of your time. Based on testimonials from the mothers who have participated in my groups, I guarantee it will be a challenge for you to determine who learns more—you or your daughter.

Mother-Daughter Mastery Projects

CHOOSING A LEARNING GOAL

Your first task in modeling mastery is to choose learning goals over performance goals. The possibilities are endless. Have fun!

Physical Learning Goals

1. Take a ropes course or wilderness survival course together.
2. Learn to Rollerblade.
3. Learn to dance.
4. Join a team sport you have never played before such as volleyball, soccer, touch football, or basketball.
5. Start a competitive mother-daughter racquetball team.
6. Learn a martial art.
7. Take a self-defense course.
8. Go on an extended backpacking trip.
9. Learn to ski.
10. Learn to water-ski.
11. Learn to snowboard.
12. Take yoga or Tai Chi classes
13. Get certified in scuba-diving.
14. Go snowmobiling.
15. Go sailing, wind-surfing, or sky-diving.

Intellectual and Financial Learning Goals

16. Take a computer class together.
17. Play the stock market.
18. Start a mother-daughter poker night.
19. Do some household repairs.
20. Change the oil in the car.
21. Learn to play an instrument.
22. Learn a foreign language or visit a foreign country together.
23. Join an animal rights group or some other controversial group together.
24. Build something out of wood.
25. Learn a game of strategy such as chess, Go, or backgammon.
26. Start a reading group.
27. Take a course at a university or museum.
28. Create a Web site.
29. Make a financial plan for a small business.
30. Do a science experiment, using one of the kits available at museums or through environmental organizations.

AVOID INAPPROPRIATE COMPARISONS

The second mastery behavior to model is to avoid making inappropriate comparisons. In fact, avoid comparisons altogether. They do not promote a mastery attitude, and they can damage self-esteem.

Comparisons often inadvertently model a negative aspect of femininity. Trivializing one's own accomplishments by comparing them to someone else's can masquerade as humility—a culturally sanctioned feminine behavior. In fact this kind of humility borders on self-deprecation. Avoid it. Model femininity for your daughter in other ways.

Comparing yourself to others sets up the dangerous dynamic of judging your worth based on accomplishments and success only. As we saw earlier, success can ebb and flow. Judging your worth based on these inconstant factors will not sustain self-esteem during the rough periods of life. Therefore, to properly model mastery for your daughter, you must not undermine your own self-esteem by engaging in comparisons.

As the two of you learn a new game, sport, instrument, or subject, do not compare yourselves to gold medal Olympians, Pulitzer and Nobel Prize winners, supermodels, millionaires, elected officials, or celebrities. In fact, do not compare yourselves to anyone, even each other. The only valid comparison might be to your own progress. For example, it's okay to make the observation that two weeks ago you could barely manage to stand up on your new in-line skates, but now you are able to teeter along for a few yards, wildly flailing your arms and screaming. Acknowledge this breakthrough! Be playful. Don't be heavy-handed about success. Be happy for your own and your daughter's progress, especially the first small steps. Take yourself lightly and have fun.

BE STRATEGIC AND CREATIVE

Modeling strategic and creative thinking for your daughter means allowing her to see you make, change, and execute plans, change them again, and then execute your new plan. Involve her whenever possible. Let her observe you and work with you as your assistant or apprentice as you make out a budget, organize a committee, plan a fund-raiser, mobilize a political campaign or local legislative reform, acquire a sponsor, develop a church seminar, figure out how to afford the new addition to your home, argue a case with your boss, write a grant, or present your point of view before a board or even your own husband. Witnessing you in the process of strategizing, and even participating where and when she can, will be invaluable lessons for her future, regardless of whether that future entails painting water-colors in the garage or running for public office. The ability to strate-gize is a key component of persistence in reaching any goal.

Remember to be creative in developing alternative strategies. For example, be creative about money, since it is easy to use lack of money as an excuse for not trying something new. Suppose you can't afford to take tennis lessons from a pro, for example. Barter for the lessons with something you know how to do. Sup-pose you can't afford a computer. Rent or trade a bicycle, guitar, lawn mower, or something else you have lying around the house unused for a computer.

Sometimes being creative in developing alternative strategies involves an apparent change of direction. Although persistence is a mastery-oriented behavior, there are no formulas. Take an honest look at the situation to determine if you and your daughter have been persistent. If so, then perhaps taking an alternative tack is the more mastery-oriented approach. My mother, the musician and music teacher, taught me that some people will take naturally to one instrument but not to another. Therefore, sometimes the most cre-ative alternative strategy is simply to pick a different instrument, metaphorically speaking. If the violin is not your daughter's style, have her try the piano, flute, cello, or guitar or something nontradi-tional for girls like the trumpet, drums, or saxophone. (Next to President Clinton, Lisa Simpson is the most famous amateur saxo-phone player in the country.) If she doesn't like soccer, try volley-ball. If she doesn't like chess, try backgammon or Go.

Because there are many exciting ways to break through problems and develop a variety of routes toward a goal, let your daughter experience the thrill of strategizing and problem-solving. That's how she will learn. Besides, it will be fun for both of you.

DON'T RESIST FEAR—USE IT!

Using fear may be the most critical behavior of all to model and perhaps the hardest one to master. It is all right to *experience* fear, even to admit it. Just don't let your daughter see it permanently stop you. Demonstrate for her that fear does not have to block progress toward a goal, that it is a natural part of embarking on any new adventure or undertaking and that she can experience fear while she continues to push through her comfort zones.

The way to keep on track is to remember that life never lets anyone off the hook. Life never says, "Okay, you don't have to," just because we are scared or anxious. Since life is what we are preparing our daughters for, coaching them through fear is a requirement for training any resilient individual.

In Part III you'll learn how to use fear to your advantage rather than resist it as an obstacle. For now, suffice it to say that, to the extent you can, you must model for your daughter that fear and anxiety are not necessarily in and of themselves bad things to be avoided. Use some of the Mother-Daughter Mastery Projects on pages 79–80 to model for her that the energy existing within fear can be accessed and utilized to move an individual forward. You do not have to be a fearless individual to do this. You need only be willing to try. If fear is accepted as a natural part of life, as an energy source, it has the potential to transform both lives and individuals.

Teach by example that fear is as natural a state in the flow of experience as joy or relaxation or excitement. In fact, all states, including fear and anxiety, are part of life's tapestry of emotion and give life the texture and richness we crave. Without the full range of emotion, a certain blandness and complacency, the most insidious and covert saboteurs of goals, can take over one's life.

Take advantage of your young daughter's natural taste for thrills. Ride roller coasters together. See scary movies. Ask her what she would like to do. One workshop mom and her daughter even got tattoos together! Be open and see what happens.

As you set the standards of mastery behavior for your daughter by your own actions, attitudes, and choices, remember the explanatory style of the mastery-oriented. Keep in mind that the actual process you are modeling for your daughter will be fluid, involving a mastery-oriented explanatory style that accompanies, permeates, and weaves throughout the behaviors as they take place in real time. In practice, explanatory style and behavioral choices are interlocking and inseparable and make up a whole cloth. Therefore, throughout your daughter's childhood and the mastery projects you undertake together, remember the overarching concept of construing reality in a mastery-oriented fashion, as exemplified by the mother in the story that follows.

"You Mean It's Not Necessarily My Fault?"

"All my life I have felt like everything bad that happened was my fault," said a mother at a seminar. "When I got pregnant as a teenager, it was my fault for not using birth control. When I had trouble losing the weight after Annette was born, it was my fault for not working out enough. When my husband left me for another woman, it was my fault for not being attractive and charming enough to keep him. When I was passed up for a promotion at work, it was my fault for not being talented and hard-working enough. When I started my own business and the bank wouldn't loan me money, it was my fault for not being credible and savvy enough to know how to handle lenders. It just never ended."

She paused, tapping her pencil. "Then one day, for no reason I can determine, I became incredibly angry. It dawned on me that *everything* could not be my fault. I was willing to take responsibility when necessary, but this was getting ridiculous. My anger grew until I could barely contain it. I went around with a chip on my shoulder for quite a while. But I didn't like being angry all the time. Finally I began to see that anger wasn't necessary if I learned to see things differently. I could use this anger as a tool to increase my self-esteem rather than as a weapon to beat myself up."

This inspiring story illustrates one of the most debilitating aspects of learned helplessness: the tendency to internalize failure.

If success and failure were both viewed as processes, it would be less threatening to discuss setbacks, confusion, and mistakes. The tendency of adults to discuss openly only our successes while cloaking in mystery any failures along the way gives our children the false impression that successful people never make mistakes. As adults we know that people become successful because they have learned to tolerate confusion, setbacks, and even failures. Unfortunately, when kids—especially girls—fail, they believe it is because they are stupid. Well, it's time for a change.

The mother continued, "I began teaching Annette that things could go wrong for many reasons. The funny thing was that, in teaching her, I learned it myself.

"I started paying more attention to the things I said in front of her. Whenever I caught myself putting myself down or blaming myself or feeling that a temporary setback was the end of the world, I paused, thought it over, and either decided to say nothing at all or changed the content and tone of what I was about to say.

"I knew I had succeeded when my daughter lost the election as class president in her sophomore year." (The other workshop participants emitted a cross between a shocked gasp and a compassionate sigh when they heard this.) "I know," she continued, "it sounds crazy to consider my daughter's loss a success, but wait until you hear the rest of the story.

"When Annette told me she had lost the election, she said, 'You know, Mom, I could've won if I'd acted cute and stupid.'

"I asked her what she meant, and she replied, 'Well, the girl who won turned the election into a popularity contest, like an election for homecoming queen instead of class president. My campaign was about trying to make changes and do something worthwhile, not just getting voted most popular girl.'

"I told her that I was very proud of the way she had handled herself. She said, 'Well, I feel sad, but I'd rather feel sad than phony.'"

This is testimony to the power of teaching girls that every setback is not a failure and that the reasons for failures are varied and change over time. Teach your daughter that

Mistakes will be made.

Confusion will arise.

Failure is okay, even to be expected.

All people, including the successful ones, experience doubt and dismay.

When failure loses its power to harm her and make her self-esteem plummet, the willingness to learn—an intrinsic trait of a secure, confident human being—will be liberated and will unfold quite naturally.

So don't forget to model mastery self-talk. It reveals your internal dialogue. Is your talk style helpless: stable (this will never change), global (this will affect everything else), and internal (it's probably my fault) type of explanation? Or are you able to construe events in a healthy, hardy, and resilient style: dynamic (all things change), specific (the problem is limited), and external (this is not necessarily my fault)?

Monitor yourself carefully in order to avoid statements such as the following:

Stable

I've never been very good at...
My mother was never any good at...
Women are not very good at...
I always have trouble with...
I'm so clumsy.
I'm so uncoordinated.
I just don't understand math.
No matter how hard I try, I just can't...
I'll never be able to get this.
Some people are just naturally better at...

Global

I've tried everything. Nothing works.
Everything else depends on getting this part right.
Nothing ever works out the way I planned.
Everything is all screwed up.

Internal

What's the matter with me?
Why can't I get this?
How could I be so stupid?
I just haven't got what it takes.
I always screw up this part.
I don't know what made me think I could do this.

You need to model a mastery-oriented way of interpreting events to teach your daughter. Invariably at workshops with mothers, someone brings up the concern that by teaching girls to externalize failure and confusion, we will be training them to be irresponsible or to violate others by blaming them for problems. Although I understand these concerns, I do not agree. First, women tend to constantly blame themselves; therefore, I find it necessary to encourage and coach in the opposite direction, if just for the sake of balance.

Second, girls need to learn the difference between responsibility and blame. You've heard this before, but it bears repeating: Response-ability is action-oriented and therefore mastery-oriented; blame, on the other hand, is passive. Attributing problems to internal inadequacy teeters perilously close to blame; therefore, any method of circumventing this destructive trajectory—in this case, attributing failure to external causes—is both useful and beneficial to girls.

At the same time as you monitor your own speech style, listen carefully to your daughter's. Counter negative comments with examples that give her a new way to think about negative events. You will have the greatest impact if you counter with a mastery response the moment you recognize the helpless one. Teachers call this a teachable moment. Seize it! Some examples are on the following page.

In each case, the counterstatement involves discerning which aspect of the learned helplessness your daughter has internalized and then countering with a mastery-oriented response. For example, number one and number four both involve not only internalized blame but also a stable worldview—in other words, a feeling that the situation is never going to change. The counterstatement in number one points out that the daughter's strategy may need to be changed, and in number four that is also a factor. Neither one blames the individual.

Let's take a closer look at response number five, which presents a philosophical issue. First, it highlights the global reponse, the one that says, "This is going to affect everything else." Because of the way GPAs are computed, your daughter is right: a bad grade on her report card will lower her GPA. And because this is true, you as a parent must make a decision. Do you want to reinforce performance goals, telling your daughter to do only what she is already good at, ensuring a good grade by avoiding subjects that might pose more of a challenge? Or do you want her to learn how to tackle

Negative Internalized Response	Your Counterstatement
1. No matter how hard I work on this, I just don't get it.	1. Perhaps you haven't hit on the right approach yet. Let's work together on a plan.
2. When I get lost, I feel stupid. or I get so confused I can't even figure out what to ask. or I'm too stupid to learn math.	2. I know what you mean. It's easy to feel that way when you get confused. Remember, though, that everyone gets lost and confused, even the smart and successful people. It's part of learning. It's okay, even though it feels a little uncomfortable. You can learn to tolerate it, especially if you know it's not bad.
3. I get confused because in fourth grade I was absent a lot (or what have you). or I always have problems with... because...	3. You don't have to explain why you're confused. You're learning something new, that's all. Problems are to be expected. Just spend your time solving the problem rather than explaining why it is difficult. It's okay to be confused.
4. I'm so uncoordinated.	4. Only for *now*. As you practice the moves, they will become more natural. You'll get used to moving your body that way. Right now, it's all new. Give yourself a chance to learn. Don't beat yourself up for being inexperienced.
5. I can't take science; it's too risky. If I get a bad grade in science, it's going to spoil my GPA.	5. Let's find out if there are alternatives. Perhaps you can audit the class, or can be tutored. Anyway, the most important thing is not just to get a good grade but to try.

Negative Internalized Response	*Your Counterstatement*
6. Some kids are better at this than I am.	6. That's not necessarily true. Perhaps they have had advantages you have not. Maybe someone at home helps them or they have learned better study habits.

new goals and challenging subject matter, the learning goals that will require mastery-oriented skills?

This can become a complicated issue, especially if a parent or child has pinned her hopes on a special college and feels compelled to maintain a high GPA as a requirement of admission. I understand this dilemma, and there are no easy answers to it. Personally, I am in favor of choosing the learning goal over the grade (performance goal), but that is a philosophical decision you and your daughter must make on your own. On the one hand, ensuring that your daughter's GPA remains high enough to gain acceptance to an Ivy League school or some other lofty institution may be the best choice to ensure her future job marketability, economic self-sufficiency, or some other personal goal. On the other hand, choosing learning goals may be better preparation for the shocks and surprises of life. Think it over carefully. As long as both choices demand that she meet standards and face challenges, she will be learning important mastery skills for life.

Taking Action versus Wishing and Hoping

Taking action encompasses most mastery behaviors. Take every opportunity to teach your daughter how to take action. Action is mastery-oriented; wishing, hoping, and complaining are not.

One mother related how her fourth grade daughter and friends decided they wanted to form their own volleyball team. Since the school was unable to supply the funds, the mother suggested the girls solicit members of the business community as sponsors. With parental guidance, the girls organized themselves, created a business plan, gave presentations through the local Chamber of Commerce, and acquired the funding they needed. One girl said, "I thought they would just give us the money. I didn't know we would have to persuade them!" Even when activities like this are not entirely successful, they are priceless for giving your daughter the experience of how one goes about influencing outcomes. A different girl, for example, whose attempt to circulate a petition at school failed, said, "Well, I know more now about democratic stuff than I did before." And another girl who did not qualify in her chosen event on the girls' track team said, "At least I got in shape!"

The difference between response-ability and blame is the difference between taking action and being passive, between looking forward and looking back, between lighting a candle and cursing the darkness.

An example of lighting a candle rather than cursing the darkness, of being action-oriented to effect change, is offered by several nonprofit organizations in my community that collaborate with one another to teach girls and boys awareness and prevention of dating and relationship violence, sexual abuse, and harassment. They take programs into the schools and teach girls not only to mentor each other in these areas but also to mentor their teachers regarding sexual harassment in the hallways and at school-sponsored activities. By teaching girls how to do this, they teach them response-ability and empower them to change the very fabric of the institution.

To truly encourage the mastery behavior of taking action, allow your daughter to take calculated risks, to fail, to try a new strategy, and then to try again. Allow her to make her own decisions, even when they are in conflict with yours, and either reap the rewards or suffer the consequences. Do not rescue her when she makes a mistake, experiences discomfort, or makes a bad decision. Allow her to be self-sufficient and find out for herself what she can and can't do. Teach her how to present an argument and argue a case. Teach her the skills of assertive behavior. Encourage her to stand up for herself, verbally and physically. (If you are the parent of a teenage girl, you may think she already has enough skill at being assertive and standing up for herself verbally. As we will see in the chapters on adolescence, however, just because she stands her ground with you

Encourage your daughter to take action by teaching her the principles of a democratic society:

• Organizing	• Making speeches
• Building community	• Arguing a case
• Circulating petitions	• Networking
• Acquiring funding	• Gaining support of peers
• Strategizing and problem-solving	• Being elected to office

Encourage her willingness to show leadership qualities:

• Pioneering and trailblazing	• Speaking out in behalf of others
• Taking a public stand	• Questioning authority
• Taking charge of a situation	• Questioning authority
• Taking charge of others by organizing, giving guidance, or instructing	• Being willing to make decisions
• Being highly visible or involved	• Being willing to solve problems

Support her efforts to defend herself in all situations:

• Asking questions or arguing her point	• Showing an interest in martial arts classes
• Refusing to accept blame for something that is not her fault	• Showing an interest in any form of self-defense, which may even include a class in gun safety, if she so desires★
• Learning to set boundaries and enforce them	• Learning how to say no

★While I am personally against guns, the stories and life experiences I have heard in my workshop prompt me to make a point of noting that some mothers choose to make their daughters aware of how to handle a gun safely should the need arise. *Please be advised that I am not advocating keeping guns in the home or the use of guns as a necessary mastery skill your daughter must learn.* Use your judgment based on your life experience and value system.

does not mean she does so in other situations with other people, or to her best advantage.) Allow her to participate in activities with adults so that she will learn by watching them. Finally, empower her to change the institutions that affect her life by familiarizing her with the tools of a democratic society that appear on page 91.

CHAPTER 5

Mothers as Mentors

Mothers are there to tell you how to make it in the world. My mother did it for me, I did it for my daughter, and she is doing it for her daughter.

Lena, seventy-six-year-old grandmother
and workshop participant

"You know, all this mastery stuff makes a lot of sense," said one mother, a thirty something woman in leggings, Ray-Bans and Reeboks, "but I'm not sure I can really model all of it. Some of it I already do pretty well, like not taking the blame for everything. But I have some of my own fears to overcome around risk-taking. Am I setting a bad example for my daughter?"

This is a recurrent theme in my workshops. Some mothers feel uncertain about their ability to model mastery behavior and positive risk-taking. I understand their misgivings. Having been raised as girls in this culture, they were not prepared as well as they could have been. I tell them to model where and when and as often as they are able. It is good for girls to see adult women act in ways we advocate for them. Girls want to observe us as we work through the challenges of positive risk-taking.

On the other hand, I let the mothers know that while modeling is good, it is not the only way. Even when you are not able to model a certain behavior to the extent you would like, you still have a potent role—as a mentor. Your more comprehensive life experience and world knowledge qualify and enable you to act as a wise counselor to your daughter.

Undoubtedly there will be times, particularly during puberty, when your daughter seems impervious to your wisdom, your advice, and even your simplest declarations. The truth, however, is that she is not as impervious as she appears. Resistant, yes; impervious, no. She just wants you to think she is impervious. The trick is learning how to advise and counsel her so that she is able to hear you. (More about this in Chapter 10.)

In the meantime, as her mentor, you can comfort yourself with the knowledge that a long period exists prior to the resistance phase of puberty, during which your mentoring will be laying the foundation for the future. Also, though puberty and the resistance that accompanies it are nerve-racking to you, they are, after all, temporary.

Knowing how your daughter forms her beliefs and opinions about herself, particularly as they relate to mastery and helplessness, will be valuable knowledge for you, as her mentor, to have. You will be empowered to say and do the right things in a variety of circumstances. To that end I have provided an overview of principles and psychology of self-concept to aid you in your role as guide and facilitator of resilience, mastery behavior, and achievement.

How Your Daughter Comes to Know Who She Is

Every individual has certain ideas about who she is; she will describe herself in certain ways; and she will see herself as this, not that—as either helpless or mastery-oriented or some combination of the two. This is what the mind does. It pieces together experiences and events, accesses bits of memory, categorizes them, and weaves together a "story of me." This story of me may be positive, uplifting, and mastery-oriented or it may be replete with helplessness.

For all individuals this process of self-concept is in a constant state of flux, forming and re-forming throughout life. Beliefs about the self are not set in stone or written in the womb. Our beliefs about who we are evolve, devolve, transform, and remold themselves throughout the journey of our lives. Many contingencies influence these changes: the work we are doing, or not doing; the rewards and recognition we are receiving or not receiving; our own changing values and interests over time; our health; external circumstances; and significant others or the lack thereof, to name just a few.[1] While the self-concept is in a state of flux, however, our earliest beliefs, ideas, and conclusions about who we are form the critical background against which all future beliefs will be sketched. Therefore, if you can establish in your daughter a base self-concept that is hardy, resilient, and mastery-oriented, it will serve her all her adult life through the myriad challenges she will face.

To be a truly effective mentor to your daughter, then, in addition to your own life experience you need substantive information regarding how self-concept (as differentiated from self-esteem) is formed. Think of it this way: Everyone has a self-concept, but not everyone has self-esteem. Self-concept may incorporate either a positive and mastery-oriented perspective or a negative and helpless one; it may embody resilience and persistence or frailty and fragility; and it may or may not embrace high self-esteem.

While the process of forming one's self-confidence is ongoing, most experts agree that four identifiable factors act upon an individual to form her beliefs about herself.[2]

1. People come to see themselves as they believe others see them.
2. People compare themselves to others.
3. People observe their actions and experience their outcomes and consequences.
4. People prioritize their personal traits so that some are more important than others for their overall self-esteem.

In your mentoring, you will ensure that your daughter gains a positive self-concept. We will go through each of the four factors so that you can learn how to mitigate negative cultural messages and misconceptions before they become a part of your daughter's self-concept.

PEOPLE SEE THEMSELVES AS THEY BELIEVE OTHERS SEE THEM

People come to conclusions about who they are based on other people's reactions to them. In the psychological and educational literature these reactions are called reflected appraisals. The people you encounter in the daily business of life act as mirrors, constantly reflecting back to you their opinions and judgments, both subtle and direct. The direct ones, like labeling another person's behavior, are the easiest to recognize. The more subtle ones, like expectations based on gender or behavior such as premature rescuing, are trickier to expose and can be more dangerous for that reason. Either way, reflected appraisals are extremely potent stuff, for good or ill.

Reflected appraisals are really messages sent to us by others concerning our identity, our worth, our self. They come in a variety of poses, challenges, disguises, opportunities, and personalities. Let's examine some common types of reflected appraisals that our children experience on a daily basis, as well as the messengers who send them. A discussion of the consequences of these on a girl's concept of who she is will follow. The most common types of reflected appraisals are labels and expectations, challenges and opportunities, discipline and anger, feminine and masculine stereotypes, and society's messengers—media, schools, and peers.

Labels and Expectations

Labeling is a direct reflected appraisal, as when a teacher describes a child as "slow" or "the class clown" or "a behavior problem." I once saw an adorable three-year-old boy at an amusement park. Across the front of his baseball cap was written "Here comes trouble." While I'll admit it was kind of cute, the cap elicited comments from adults that were textbook examples of negative reflected appraisals such as "Uh-oh, here comes Mr. Problem Child" or "So you're trouble, huh?" or "I got my eye on you, big guy." The parents of this child were setting him up for comments that could reinforce a potential problem by displaying this perhaps temporary personality trait for others, even total strangers, to comment on.

While the people doing the labeling are almost always eager to justify it, the label should never be considered the ultimate truth. For example, all "problem students" do not cause difficulties for all their teachers. A child who is a hellion in one classroom might be an angel in another. When I was a teacher I had a female student who was the bane of my existence. We just didn't like each other. I caught her in the act of writing obscenities on my classroom door. When I brought up my problem with others in the faculty lounge to get advice, I learned that I was the only teacher for whom she misbehaved! It was a great and humbling lesson for me.

Some reflected appraisals are indirect and subtle. As was mentioned earlier, prematurely rescuing a girl sends the message that you don't believe she is capable of doing a task on her own, that you believe she needs help. On the other hand, giving her a chance to work it out, waiting for her to ask, and allowing her to experience a little discomfort or test out a variety of alternatives will send the message you believe she is capable of handling adversity and figuring out solutions for herself.

Reflected appraisals are potent because they tend to become self-fulfilling prophecies. Studies of teachers' and parents' expectations have shown that children perform at the level expected of them and that they take on the roles assigned to them by the adults in their lives.[3] Expecting your daughter to go to college is a reflected appraisal that tells her you have confidence in her intelligence. It is more likely to result in college attendance than not sending that message. As mentors, then, it is important to reflect to girls in ways both subtle and direct that you see them as capable, competent, and resilient.

Challenges and Opportunities

You can show your daughter you believe she is capable, competent, and resilient by giving her tasks that appropriately challenge her. I will give you some ideas for presenting challenges to your daughter, but first I want to take a moment to draw attention to the word "appropriate."

It will be empowering for your daughter to feel challenged, but if the challenges become too intense, too difficult, or too frequent, you may wear her out or, worse, create the very self-doubt you are trying to avoid. Some parents become so obsessed with challenging their children to develop their skills that they simply exhaust them. Always forcing a girl to run faster, throw harder, climb higher, or get a better grade sends the subtle message that what she has accomplished thus far is not enough. She must always strive to outdo herself. This can lead to exhaustion and feelings of inadequacy. Granted, this is a judgment call and a delicate one at that. My advice is to avoid a tyrannical approach, one that shows you are never satisfied with her current performance.

Notwithstanding this caveat, there are ways to present challenges to your daughter so as to develop her mastery skills, strengthen a healthy self-concept, and establish self-esteem.

One potential stumbling block can be a mother's own limited and unexamined beliefs. Mothers in my workshops often express doubts about the capabilities of women or about the limited opportunities for women to overcome the restrictions of a sexist society. (They call it being realistic.)

One group of workshop mothers seemed so inspired, so revolutionary, that I let my Joan of Arc alter ego out of the closet just long enough to wax poetic about raising daughters as saviors of the planet. I felt I was really inspiring these women to go forth and challenge the dominant paradigm when suddenly a bewildered look came over the face of one mother who had been a live wire earlier in the workshop. I kept an eye on her, expecting her to raise her hand any minute. She didn't let me down.

"Wow," she began when I called on her. "I just realized something. I can't even *imagine* my daughter as one of the saviors of the planet. Isn't that terrible? Is even my *imagination* under the control of cultural expectations?" Then she said pensively, "I'm not sure."

"Well, what do you think?" I encouraged her. "Try to say something more about that. What do you mean, exactly?"

"Well, when I try to think of the greatest future I can imagine for my daughter, it turns out that my ideas are limited by something I can't quite name."

"Give us an example," I said.

"Okay. My first thought was that Heather would make a great investigative reporter. Then I thought, Wait! Why just a reporter? Why not managing editor or publisher of the whole damn newspaper? That's when it hit me that even my imagination, which should be free and unlimited, is held back."

Would mastery-oriented female leadership result in a kinder, gentler nation, peacefully prospering and facilitating the developmental potential of all its citizens? Would technology become a tool for feeding the starving masses rather than a tool of destruction? Would television promote communication, compassion, and consensus rather than violence and death? Would Congress focus more on the responsibilities of individuals and society and less on the endless preoccupation with their rights?

Imagine, if you will, a truly egalitarian society where new inventions spring from a population of female scientists, inventors, and engineers; where women participate in the creation, development, and control of technology; a society in which women play a decision-making role in the use of the media, and explain the world on the nightly news, giving us their interpretation of international events; a society where the equal representation of women in high-status, high-paying jobs is common. Imagine a society in which women and girls are free to walk alone on a warm, summer evening if they so desire; a society in which your daughter can legitimately dream of and plan to become the leader of her country; in short, a society where the aspirations and inspirations of the female population enjoy the recognition of a full and public forum.

Who knows? But unless we can imagine it first, it is guaranteed not to happen.

So use your imagination. Let your daughter become the one for whom you dream the big dreams. Maybe you already do. Think about it. What did you want to be when you were nine? Did your dream change by the time you were sixteen? For example, I wanted to be a surgeon when I was in the fourth grade. By the time I was in college, I wanted to be an English teacher. Nothing wrong with being an English teacher, but the educational requirements for a surgeon are vastly more rigorous and the status and earning potential vastly more remunerative. Something must have happened along the way.

Have you ever imagined your daughter doing the following jobs or recommended them to her?

- accountant or auditor
- aerospace engineer
- agricultural scientist
- air traffic controller
- alarm system installer
- architect
- biomedical engineer
- broadcast technician
- chemical engineer
- chiropractor
- civil engineer
- composer
- computer programmer
- computer repair technician
- conservation scientist
- dentist
- drafter
- fish and game warden
- forester
- geophysicist
- industrial designer
- judge

- mechanical engineer
- metallurgist
- molecular biologist
- physicist
- podiatrist
- power plant operator
- sound technician
- surveyor
- systems analyst
- tool and die maker
- urban planner

Granted, not all of these jobs will enable your daughter to achieve the status of savior of the planet, but you get my drift. Until we learn to see our daughters succeeding in these traditionally male-dominated careers—which, not coincidentally, are much higher paid than nearly all traditionally female-dominated careers, our daughters will never learn to see themselves in these roles, much less as leaders of the free world.

Findings of a new study by Dr. Ann B. Miser show that girls still see themselves doing traditionally female work.[4] Boys and girls were asked to list the top five jobs they could see themselves doing, then to list the top five jobs they could see a classmate of the opposite sex doing. Dawn gave typical responses. She envisioned herself in the same professions as her parents—teacher and veterinarian. After that, however, it was hairdresser, day-care worker, and waitress. Then she listed the jobs her friend Jason could do—engineer, doctor, and scientist.

The day after Take Our Daughters to Work Day I read an account of the event in our local newspaper. The five girls interviewed, whose ages ranged from seven to twelve, went to work with their parents in computer labs, banks, and family-owned business. When asked what they wanted to be when they grew up, the girls answered, "Movie star," "Dress designer," "Ice skater," "Model," and "Famous dancer."

These reports underscore the urgent need to broaden our daughters' vision of themselves and their capabilities, to challenge them in new directions—a perfect job for a mentor. To correct this vision deficit in our girls, mentoring mothers must keep chipping away at sex-specific work roles. Mothers can make their daughters' dreams bigger, more encompassing, and more intellectually challenging by helping their girls realize just how high they can allow their aspirations to go.

As mentors, mothers must remain alert to the conclusions of

researchers who imply that monumental change has already taken place. Take, for example, the commentary that erupted following a 1995 survey by *Working Woman* magazine, which suggested that women had finally arrived as financial equals to men. This was based on survey findings that reported the wage gap between the sexes is closing and that women now earn between 85 and 95 percent as much as men earn.[5]

Encouraged? Well, not so fast there, little lady. These cheery statistics will certainly apply if your daughter becomes the dean of arts and sciences at a state university or the CEO of a multimillion-dollar corporation. While I am exaggerating to make my point, the statistics apply only to professional women in 38 industries, as opposed to the 367 industries listed in the Labor Department's *Occupational Outlook Handbook* for that year. Moreover, the media failed to report that females in banking, accounting, financial management, and health care management are still earning less then men. They also failed to report that being white is a big advantage, since white women's incomes are 75 percent of their white male counterparts' earnings. Black women, however, earn only 63 percent as much as do their male counterparts. Finally, the most important statistic of all got left out: the fact that the gap in salaries is closing and therefore women *appear* to be making financial progress only because men's salaries are decreasing (11 percent since 1974).[6]

So if your daughter chooses a nontraditional job, she will earn *approximately* the same salary as a man in a similar job. Should she, however, choose a more traditional female-dominated career, her wages will be curtailed by as much as 20 to 30 percent, according to the U.S. Department of Labor Women's Bureau.[7]

While her earning potential and status may be foremost in *your* mind, other aspects of a job may be more motivating to your daughter. Since girls are generally not encouraged to be adventurous, this might be an interesting way to capture her attention. When she says, "I want to be in medicine," you can say, "Paramedics see a lot of action and adventure. If you can tolerate the gore, you'll have a real opportunity to save lives." If she says, "I want to be a musician," you could say, as my mother said to me, "Do you realize that a musician plays a single instrument, but the conductor plays the whole orchestra?" And so forth. If your daughter already has extremely high aspirations, just say, "Go Girl!"

Finally, remind your daughter of the progress she is making right now. Say things like "Remember when you couldn't read? Now look at you. Your nose is always in a book," or "Remember when you couldn't ride a bike? That took some effort!" or "Remember when you couldn't play that song? Now it sounds great. How long did it take you to learn it anyway?" These comments are great reminders. In this way you help her keep in mind that the challenges of life and learning are processes, not static goals that exist independent of time and circumstance. Eventually, as you show her the way, she will learn to do this on her own as she proceeds through difficult subject matter and challenging life situations.

Discipline and Anger

Inept disciplining and anger can also broadcast some very debilitating messages. How many times have you heard frustrated parents utter statements like the following:

- What's the matter with you?
- What is your problem?
- Can't you do anything right?
- Why can't you get it together?
- What part of "no" don't you understand?
- Are you deaf?

I am aware that these comments are made to children when parents are at their wits' end, but when understood in the context of a reflected appraisal, they can lead a child to certain negative conclusions. One realizes that, based on the above comments, a child is likely to reach the following conclusions:

- There is something wrong with me.
- I have a problem.
- I can't do anything right.
- I can't get myself together.
- I am stupid.

As a mother striving to keep your daughter resilient, you cannot afford to have her reach such conclusions, particularly since she is likely to carry them into her adult life. Therefore, even in anger and frustration, avoid making comments that contain negative judgments. Instead, just be straightforward about your requests:

- I want you to…
- You are not doing as I requested, so I am going to…
- Let me make this clear. I expect you to…
- I am angry with your behavior, especially since we agreed you would not do this.
- Do you need clarification as to what I expect?

While these rejoinders clearly establish your superiority in the power relationship as the parent—the one in charge—they actively engage the child without commenting on her worth, her inferiority, or her dignity as a human being. Therefore, the best course of action is to avoid words and phrases that contain judgments based on whether or not your daughter is doing what you request. At puberty, this can really backfire.

Regarding the use of sarcasm: avoid it. If you have ever been the recipient of sarcasm you know how condescending it is. It is a subtle type of reflected appraisal that devalues the recipient. Sarcasm eschews any need to support an argument with evidence or strengthen a point of view with logic, since the recipient is too limited or dense to "get it" anyway. If you use it to make a point, you are setting a precedent for your daughter, who will ultimately use it on you and others.

Unfortunately, sarcasm enjoys a certain degree of popularity among the young and has come into vogue in their conversational style. Your daughter may learn it from others and use it as a weapon, either in presenting an argument or in defending her actions. If so, you may want to discuss with her its power to devalue another, for it is possible that she just thinks it is funny and misses altogether its destructive quality. In that case, make her aware that sarcasm must be used only sparingly and with great judiciousness, just as one would wield a dangerous weapon.

Finally, when disciplining, refrain from asking clarification questions—in other words, don't ask her why she broke that window, left without permission, or told that lie unless you actually want to engage in a dialogue. Asking a question will invariably elicit reasons that generally sound like excuses to parents. Simply stating what you expect, rather than asking for reasons—which, in most cases, you really don't want to hear anyway—is a more effective technique.

Feminine and Masculine Stereotypes

When the reflected appraisals of routine daily life reinforce feminine and masculine stereotypes, they can undermine a girl's mastery. These stereotypes can be particularly virulent if and when the feminine stereotype includes helplessness or the need for protection while the male stereotype is one of self-sufficiency and resilience.

A mother in a workshop told the following story: "My husband and I were at the park with our kids, a boy and a girl. He's seven. She's nine. All of us were learning how to skate on those new in-line skates. Jeremy and Alison were holding hands and skating downhill—too fast, really—and they collided with a parked car.

"My husband and I rushed over to see if they were hurt. Since they were wearing helmets and other protective gear, they were more shook up than anything else. My husband was encouraging them both to get up and try again. I, on the other hand, kept asking my daughter if she was okay and comforting her. My son, who was just as shook up as my daughter, was not getting that kind of attention from me. I just kind of let my husband do the male thing with our son.

"Finally my husband turned to me and said, 'Quit making such a big deal. Let her get up and skate, for God's sake.' It didn't hit me until he said that that I was treating them differently. The embarrassing part is that I consider myself an aware mom!"

The reflected appraisal both children received from their mother in this case was that the girl was more fragile and in need of protection and comfort than was the boy.

If these kinds of interactions happened only rarely, they would probably have little effect. But reflected appraisals based on sex are constantly reinforced in a million different ways, and they have long-lasting consequences in the formation of every child's self-concept. It is rather like placing braces on teeth. By applying subtle but unrelenting pressure to the teeth to grow in a particular direction, eventually the teeth become "set." This is precisely the effect of society's reflected appraisals based on sex. Over the years, through subtle and unrelenting pressure, individuals learn to act in these rigid and codified ways.

The fact is that the sexes are more psychologically similar than they are different.[8] Even in areas assumed by most to indicate differences between the sexes, when closely examined, these so-called differences lie more in interpretation or research methodology than in reality. Take empathy or compassion, for example. In test studies where people are asked to rate themselves, women typically rate themselves as more empathetic than men do. However, in studies that actually measure physiological responses to the suffering of others, or those that measure behavioral indicators of empathy, such as taking action to relieve another's suffering or distress, there is, in fact, little difference. The results are the same in studies with both adults and children.[9]

Even aggression, that supposed bastion of male dominance, is subject to scrutiny. While it is true that males are more physically aggressive, females display aggression as well. One need only spend a little time on the playground of an elementary school to see the truth of this statement. You will observe the fourth grade boys having fistfights and playing King of the Mountain on the jungle gym. And what about the girls? They are busily ostracizing a member of their clique for some real or concocted infraction of the group's ever-changing rules. As a mother you already know that this form of childhood blacklisting can become quite vicious.

Now, if aggression is defined only physically, then yes, boys appear to be more aggressive than girls. If, however, we expand the definition to "behavior with intent to dominate another," we can see that the girls are every bit as aggressive as the boys. The difference lies less in degree than in style. Girls are simply behaving in an aggressive manner that is socially sanctioned for them.

Interpretation of aggressive behavior becomes even more complex when girls and boys relate to each other. In studies of young children, girls behave more assertively among themselves than they do when boys are present, when they become more passive. (This is echoed in studies of college students as well.[10]) So, even aggression becomes a matter of interpretation and subject to change vis-à-vis the circumstances.

Therefore exercise caution in the reflected appraisals you communicate and in your assumptions about your children's identity based on their sex. Be as sex-neutral as possible in your comments and your behavior as well as in mundane activities—the division of labor around your house, for example. Refrain from reinforcing stereotypes that certain behaviors are specific to one sex but not the other. Treat boys and girls as similarly as possible.

Being a good mentor to your daughter in this critical area of self-concept means being vigilant about the messages you send regarding femininity such as:

- Girls are not good in math and science.
- Girls are not as assertive as boys.
- Girls are more sensitive and empathetic than boys.
- Girls should be small and dainty.
- Girls should be soft-spoken.
- Girls should be more polite than boys.
- Girls are not good at repairing things.
- Girls do inside work. Boys do outside work.
- Girls shouldn't brag. (Neither should boys!)
- Girls should be spared hardship and discomfort.
- Girls are in greater danger than boys are and need more protection.

Society's Messengers: Media, Schools, and Peers

Society, via its messengers—the media (primarily television and advertising), schools, and peers—also reflects to your daughter its evaluations of who she is based on a notion of femininity. This means that in a number of situations, areas of the country, specific cultures, and social milieus she will be expected to be nice, friendly, sweet, and perky—the All-American Girl.[11] Some communities, families, and schools now add smart, educated, athletic, and accomplished to the list. I get tired just thinking about trying to be all these things to all people.

Let's begin with advertising. (We will be discussing television in greater detail in Chapter 7.) Even though the expectations for girls are now broader in scope than they were not so long ago, the one area that has not changed is that women should be—indeed, must be—attractive to men. The media, particularly advertisers, are the archenemy when it comes to the establishment of a healthy self-concept in a girl. For it is here that the most damaging reflected appraisals come into play.

I use the word "archenemy" quite purposefully, without any sense of hyperbole or melodrama, for I regard the premeditated and calculated attempts by advertisers to promote products by *lowering* female self-esteem as despicable and misogynistic. Creating the illusion in both sexes that an acceptable woman is a statuesque, ultra-beautiful, emaciated, long-legged waif is diabolical, particularly given the fact that the models used to create this illusion are, in fact, anomalies. Not only are they deviations from the norm, but even they are not considered beautiful enough. They have to starve themselves to reach a state of "true desirability."

The damage done to women and girls is irrelevant to scheming advertisers, however, because, as every first-year marketing student knows, perception is reality. By creating the perception that an average female is unacceptable, life mimics art (these ads are often extraordinarily artful productions) and average women and girls begin to feel unacceptable. In order to be desirable to men, who are also inundated with these images, the average woman must improve herself. Otherwise, she would have no reason to buy the advertisers' products. Clean hair would be sufficient. Silky, soft, smooth, fluffy, shiny, thick, bouncy, tousled, voluminous, wavy, and radiant hair would be gratuitous. I gathered these adjectives simply by thumbing through hair care ads in a popular fashion magazine. A strong and healthy body in and of itself would be a prized possession. The outlay of time and money to become lean—or downright skinny, as preferred by many teenage girls—muscular, sleek, sculptured, well defined, big-bosomed, and flat-stomached would be recognized "as a national mood weighing women down," in the words of Naomi Wolf.[12]

If your daughter is lucky enough to grow into a young woman whose face and form are consistent with whatever cultural ideal of feminine beauty is currently in vogue, her self-concept will include beauty. If she grows into a young woman who does not match the cultural ideal du jour, her self-concept may include a whole range of extremely negative and even vicious self-descriptions. In my workshops for teenagers, I have heard healthy, beautiful young girls call themselves fat, ugly, dumb, gross, thunder thighs, and Miss Piggy.

As mentors to our daughters and in service to their developing self-concepts, we must teach them how to deflect the assault of advertising. Although it will be an uphill battle against a powerful and well-financed foe, our only chance is to buttress them against these attacks through awareness. Without developing out daughters' awareness, we leave them utterly vulnerable, for like sponges, they will mindlessly absorb the subtle but potent negative images to which they are being exposed. Teaching girls resistance in this area also entails mentoring them in how to interpret the messages and images of beauty in the world around them. There will be more details about this later, but for now, suffice it to say that we must make our daughters aware that *advertisers seek to lower their self-esteem as a way to get their money.* You also must mentor your sons, by making them aware of these realities, since they are the ones to whom girls will be trying to appeal.

Finally, as a mentor, you must also be aware of the media messages that assault us on a daily basis, not on television, not in magazine ads, but in the most unlikely of places. Ten years ago, in *How to Father a Successful Daughter,* I wrote about an "innocent" little poster I had seen in the post office that portrayed extremely stereotypical roles for males and females. Today, a decade later, as I stood in the post office I realized how little had changed. The poster, like the previous one, still features males over females, four to one. This time, in the first two frames we see two men—one white, one black—in business attire, opening what is obviously an important piece of mail. The third frame shows two boys as stamp collectors. The only female on the poster is holding up stamps for us to look at, smiling down upon them, much like the models on quiz shows who wave their arms about while displaying new cars. Once again—at the post office, anyway—females are stereotypically passive and decorative.

I cite this to emphasize that even if your daughter is not receiving stereotypical gender messages (reflected appraisals) at home, she is getting them everywhere else in our society. As her mother and her mentor, and so that you can take appropriate action in her behalf, you must be aware of these forces, particularly subtle ones like that poster. Sometimes, particularly when she is young, appropriate action will mean going directly to the source of the problem: writing the postmaster general, talking to a teacher or another parent, or simply turning off the television. Later, when she is older, appropriate action will mean teaching her the attitudes and responses of resistance. You might say to your daughter, "Look at that poster. Imagine if the roles were reversed. Imagine if there were four females. Imagine two girls as stamp collectors. Imagine a man smiling down at some stamps and passively displaying them to the viewer."

Teachers form yet another group of society's messengers who send subtle appraisals to girls about their intelligence and capabilities. Numerous studies have shown that teachers underestimate the intelligence of girls and have lower expectations of their achievements.[13] Furthermore, when boys perform badly, teachers attribute the problem to lack of effort or laziness and suggest they try again. When girls do poorly, teachers attribute the problem to lack of ability in the subject area and do not encourage them to try again, or they "help" them by providing the answer.[14] In addition, teachers perceive well-behaved girls as more intelligent and reinforce good, cooperative behavior by bestowing higher report card grades.[15] According to one team of experts, teachers may be responsible for the performance deficits of girls on standardized tests through this form of grade inflation by creating the illusion of a higher level of skill than the girls actually exhibit.[16]

Schools, at all levels of education, send a more generalized reflected appraisal based on sex. Basically the message is that boys have greater value than girls. The hard evidence shows up in school programs that routinely encourage boys to excel while permitting girls to lag behind.[17] In most cases, a lack of awareness on the part of administrators, teachers, parents, and in fact the entire school community, unintentional though it may be, must be corrected. (Turn to Chapter 8 for recommendations on how to foster female achievement within schools.)

The last, but certainly not the least, of society's messengers is her peer group. We will examine girls' influence on each other in more detail in Chapter 10, on puberty. But reflected appraisals that girls get from the other important group of peers—boys—is best understood by presenting it in the next principle of self-concept.

PEOPLE COMPARE THEMSELVES TO OTHERS

"Others" can refer to both individuals and groups. One of the "others" to whom girls most emphatically compare themselves to is *boys*. Unfortunately, in almost every category, the message seems to be "It's better to be male."

In *Failing at Fairness: How America's Schools Cheat Girls,* the authors, Drs. Myra and David Sadker, say it with great candor:

> To all the world boys appear to be the favored gender, heirs apparent to society's rewards. They are the recipients of the lion's share of teacher time and attention and the featured figures in most textbooks. Sitting atop high standardized test scores, they haul in the majority of scholarship dollars, claim more than half of the openings in the most prestigious colleges, and are destined for high salaries and honored professions.[18]

Indeed, girls can't win either way. When boys succeed, they get more attention, and when they fail, they get more attention. A mother in one of my workshops, a fifth grade teacher, said, "The boys in my school are either learning how to take their place in society or rebelling against the idea. Either way, they do it competitively and aggressively and wind up with all the teacher attention. Girls sit quietly, cooperate with the teacher for the most part, and get ignored." Again, from the Sadkers: "Girls suffer silent losses, but boys' problems are loud enough to be heard throughout the school."[19]

When girls compare themselves to boys, they themselves come to the conclusion that it is better to be male. What is most distressing is the lack of change. To illustrate this same point back in the mid-1980s, when I was writing *How to Father a Successful Daughter,* I cited a fascinating study from 1982, which has since been replicated with very nearly the same chilling results. These results show us that both girls and boys value males more highly and see advantages to being male.

Boys and girls of different ages are asked to answer this open-ended question: "If you woke up tomorrow and discovered you were the opposite sex, how would your life be different?" The answers showed that the boys had a startlingly low opinion of girls. Here are some of the comments of the researcher:

> Perhaps the most disturbing theme which consistently appeared in the responses...was the implication that males are inherently of greater value than females....By far the greater number of comments which denigrated the opposite sex were written by

boys…who often selected titles for their responses using phrases such as "The Disaster," or "The Fatal Dream," or Doomsday.[20]

In 1994, after more than a decade of posing this same question to 1,100 students in Michigan, Myra and David Sadker continue to get the same results: girls, for the most part, are intrigued at the thought of changing genders and see opportunity, security, respect, and freedom; boys, on the other hand, are appalled, disgusted, and humiliated at the thought and see restriction, loss, and devastation. For example, 42 percent of the girls see many positive outcomes in becoming a male, while 95 percent of the boys saw no advantage whatsoever in the change.[21] Furthermore, just as in the study more than a decade ago, boys were extreme in their expressions of horror:

My friends would treat me like dirt.
I would scream, duck around corners.
I would hide.
No cat liked me. No dog liked me. No animal in the world. I did not like myself.

To 16 percent of the boys, becoming a girl is so unacceptable that they fantasize committing suicide. Listen to their comments:

I would stab myself in the heart fifty times with a dull butter knife.
I would kill myself right away by setting myself on fire.
I'd wet the bed, then I'd throw up. I probably go crazy and kill myself.
I would be heading over to the cemetery right now and start digging.

Finally, the words of the researchers eerily reiterate the comments of that other researcher a decade earlier: "Although we have read hundreds of boys' stories about waking up a girl, we remain shocked at the degree of contempt expressed by so many…by such jolting themes of revulsion."[22]

This study has several disturbing aspects. The first is the lack of significant change over the years. The second is the revelation that *both* sexes devalue girls. Girls do so by eagerly anticipating becoming boys. (One can hardly blame them.) Boys do so by reviling the thought of becoming a girl, to the point of having suicide fantasies. Third, and most important from the standpoint of resilience and self-esteem, is that both sexes paint a picture in which being a boy is a vastly more desirable state than being a girl. Out of the mouths of babes comes the truth about how females are viewed in our society.

Here we have a double whammy. First, in comparing themselves to boys, girls notice that boys are granted greater freedom, are offered more opportunities, and reap greater rewards. Thus, in comparison, girls feel devalued, trivialized, and ignored. Second, since boys indulge in such derogatory rhetoric and express such contempt for girls concerning their worth, the girls' self-concept suffers further. Girls don't get no respect!

If you are also the mother of a son, being a mentor to your daughter means seeing to it that your home is as hospitable to her as it is to your son and as conducive to her development as it is to your son's. Here are some ways to do that:

- Be sure that all household duties are equitable in degree of difficulty, time commitment, and desirability—in other words, make sure your son also has to clean the toilet. Your daughter should also see her father doing housework, particularly if you both work outside the home.
- See to it that a son is not granted greater access to the computer or video games.
- Hold the males in the household responsible for putting a meal on the table and for cleaning it up.
- Be sure that the boys in your household are not granted greater freedom than the girls. If you restrict your girls, restrict your sons as well.
- Be sure any baby-sitting responsibilities are equally divided among older brothers and sisters.
- Remind your husband to spend as much time with his girls as he does with his boys.
- Ensure that family members attend the sporting events of sons and daughters equally.
- Do not emphasize different things for boys than for girls—success and meeting challenges for boys, appearance and being sweet for girls.

• Compliment both daughters and sons for achievements, overcoming adversity, and self-reliance as well as kindness to others.

Of course, some of the "others" to whom your daughter will compare herself are the models and actresses she sees on television and in magazines. Again, you should employ a policy of awareness-building for your daughter at an early age, using explanatory style (detailed techniques are given in Chapter 7). This policy will be the main weapon in the arsenal of resistance.

It is especially incumbent upon mothers to raise their sons' level of awareness of the conspiracy to make boys dissatisfied with average females. Boys need to understand as well as girls do that they are being manipulated for the sake of profit. By making your son aware of these realities you are lessening the impact of advertising and mentoring both boys and girls.

Although dads will be discussed later in this chapter, it should be mentioned here that a father may have to be reminded of his own attitude toward females and how it will be reflected in his own behavior and that of his son, who will learn these attitudes from him. Whatever differences in treatment a father exhibits toward his girls and his boys will not go unnoticed by his daughters when they compare themselves to their brothers. Dads should therefore be made as aware as everyone else in the family of the necessity for equitable treatment of females within your household. (If you possess little influence over the males in your family, mentor your daughter from an early age. Make her aware of the consequences of choosing a life partner who refuses to listen to and respect females.)

PEOPLE OBSERVE THEIR ACTIONS AND THEIR OUTCOMES

In this third principle of self-concept involving actions and outcomes there emerges a clear link between one's explanatory style, which can be either helpless or mastery-oriented, and the formation of one's self-concept. Here is a recap of how this link works.

Since the explanatory style—the way of construing events—of learned helplessness does not even recognize the individual's ability to influence outcomes, it sabotages both mastery behavior and one's self-concept. This is true because establishing a positive self-concept rests upon observing the connection between one's actions and the final outcome. A negative self-concept results when the individual does not recognize, or cannot perceive, the link between actions and outcomes. In the formation of one's self-concept, it becomes an "If ...then" equation:

If self-concept is formed by observing one's actions and their outcomes,	
then the explanatory style of learned helplessness in which **Effort ≠ Outcome** produces a **negative** self-concept.	then the explanatory style of mastery in which **Effort over time = Outcome** produces a **positive** self-concept.

Being a good mentor to your daughter in this arena means teaching your daughter to accept credit for her successes and to own them. Teach her how to accept accolades and praise without belittling herself. The mastery-oriented, yet gracious, response is to say a simple thank-you or "Yes, I did do a lot of hard work. Thank you for noticing." (It wouldn't hurt to teach boys the same confident yet courteous reply.)

Furthermore, should you hear your daughter refusing to acknowledge a success (such as detracting from a high score on a math exam by saying "It was an easy test"), respond immediately with "Nonsense! I saw you studying late last night. Take some credit for all that effort. It paid off." Or say, "Nonsense! You're a smart and capable girl. That's why you aced that test. It had nothing to do with it being easy." Or "Nonsense! Do you think your brother or your father would react that way? Of course not. They would take credit for a job well done. So should you!"

In this way, by coaching girls to exhibit confidence with humility, accept kudos without arrogance, and take credit without negating their accomplishments, we create in them a self-concept that includes mastery, femininity, and genuine self-esteem. That self-concept will serve them all the days of their lives.

PEOPLE PRIORITIZE THEIR PERSONAL TRAITS FOR THEIR OVERALL SELF-ESTEEM

During your daughter's puberty, the traits associated with femininity assume a position of maximum visibility and importance. The traits that her society, family, and peer group have labeled "feminine," and that your daughter has internalized, will move to the top of her priority scale for her overall self-esteem. As has been emphasized throughout this book, if your daughter's perception of femininity is tainted by helplessness or passivity, she could have problems with regard to her aspirations, ambitions, and level of achievement.

As we will examine fully in the chapters on puberty, it is to be expected, though not necessarily welcomed, that all of the principles of self-concept become subordinate to this one during puberty, when girls officially take their place within the patriarchy—that is, when they become potential sexual partners to males. Two forces are at work here. The first is natural: it is the biologically inspired, hormonally enhanced desire to appeal to the opposite sex. The second is cultural: it results in forcing girls into the unhappy and potentially servile position of trying to appeal to the very group that has denigrated them in childhood. (Remember the waking-up-as-the-opposite-sex study?) Many teenage boys do not alter their opinion of females even when they become sexually interested in them as they mature.[23]

These forces are powerful in their collusion. We must honor the physical change as a force of nature that is hardwired into the species and that will endure despite human wishes and human tinkering. (The call of DNA and the urge to propagate the species resist tinkering, unless it's done in a lab.) By the same token, we must resist the cultural force as a phenomenon that can, and indeed should, be subject to human wishes and human tinkering.

In Part III, we will look at techniques and strategies to help our daughters resist the debilitating aspects of the cultural force. For now, however, suffice it to say that mentoring your daughter in this arena means emphasizing adaptability and guiding her through the nuances of varying her behavior appropriately according to the circumstance in which she finds herself. Mastery behavior in this arena entails learning how to vary her behavior in a conscious way. She needs to be aware that there are times for femininity and times to turn it off; times when it is appropriate to be sweet, sensitive, flirtatious, and sexy, and times when it is appropriate to be competitive, ambitious, assertive, and serious; times to be nurturing and compassionate and times even to be hostile and aggressive. If you reinforce this throughout her childhood, she will be better able to call forth this adaptability as she needs it. This is particularly critical during puberty when she enters, as a potential equal, and for the first time in a serious way, the environment of a patriarchy, working shoulder to shoulder with males as companions, friends, and life partners.

Mentoring Your Daughter's Father Through Her Girlhood

Your daughter's father is the single most important male in her life. He provides her initial encounters with maleness and sets in motion certain impressions about men and beliefs about herself in relation to them. She will carry these impressions and beliefs into adult life. Some of you, as mothers, will be called upon to counsel, encourage, and guide her father as well. Since he has grown up a male in this society, there are issues about raising a girl with which he will be unfamiliar and perhaps even uncomfortable.

A daddy is an individual, so he may be fun and playful or stern and serious. He may be attentive and loving, always fussing over his little girl, or he may be indifferent, emotionally distant, or cold. Whatever kind of daddy he is, his involvement, or lack thereof, will be one of the paramount influences in the formation of his daughter's self-concept.

"When I was a little girl the highlight of my week was going to the dump with my father on Saturday morning," said the woman in a blue silk suit across the table from me, a corporate executive. "It was always just the two of us. First, we would stop at the doughnut shop. I'd get a doughnut and milk. He would have coffee. During that time we talked like friends, not like father and daughter."

"What did you talk about?" I prompted her.

"Oh, we would talk about our lives. I would talk about school. He would talk about work."

"Your father would talk to you about work?" I asked incredulously.

"Yeah, isn't that something?" When I got a little older, he would even ask me my opinion about things. I think it was his way of teaching me to think things through and to hear how I solved problems. But I also believe he was genuinely interested in my point of view."

The woman speaking is the vice-president of a major eyewear and pharmaceutical company. She is the very embodiment of what we admire as successful in our society. Poised, savvy, a major player, she exudes the qualities of mastery, confidence, resilience, and risk-taking.

"It was our time to be together," she continues, "just two people who liked being together and who cared about each other. It wasn't like a parent-and-child thing, with all the baggage that goes with that.

"Now I'm forty years old, but when I go home to visit my parents, my dad and I still go to the dump together on Saturday morning," she says, her eyes shining. "It has become our ritual. That is when I get to be who I am with my father. I can discuss with him life as an adult, whatever that means at the moment. Not just as his daughter or some kind of an extension of him. I am my own self, and he respects that."

As I write this, I feel a deep longing for my own father, who passed away when I was thirty. The man I call my father was not actually my biological father, who died when I was eight months old, but my stepfather, whom my mother married when I was two and a half. Since he was the only father I knew, it feels false to call him my stepfather. As far as I am concerned, by being the man who was willing to put up with all the hassles, problems, pain, and struggle of daily parenting, he earned the title of father. I loved him, and I miss him.

I mention this to emphasize that biology is one thing and parenting another. In today's complicated parenting relationships, with divorced families, stepfamilies, and blended families, deciding who is your daughter's father becomes complicated for some mothers and poses a challenge to me as a writer. I will leave it to you to decide who qualifies as a father to your daughter. To my way of thinking, any man who interacts regularly with your daughter, whether he is her real father, a stepfather, a grandfather, an uncle, or even a male teacher or a neighbor functions as a father figure, and the information herein is pertinent to him.

All this is to introduce the importance of a father to a daughter. You know it because you are a daughter and you know how you feel about your father. I know it because I am a daughter too. But does your daughter's father know it? That is the key question. If he does know it, he is probably already actively involved. Bravo and kudos to him! What's more, your work as a mentor will go more smoothly. If he is not actively engaged with his daughter, you must do some remedial work and team-building.

First, make him aware of his importance in her life. It will be a motivating factor. Don't hesitate to use it. Communicate to him that if he wants his daughter to speak of him with the respect and admiration shining in the eyes of the corporate executive quoted earlier, he must get actively involved with her today.

I choose the words "actively involved" quite purposefully, because some fathers, handicapped by the old, outdated models that rigidly confines the father's role to that of provider and protector, do not become actively engaged with their daughters. Some of them are quite involved with their sons, going camping, hiking, biking, fishing, hunting, putzing around in the workshop, tinkering in the garage, attending sporting events, and doing house repair. Many of these same fathers—who dearly love their little girls, by the way— do not spend as much time with them as they do with their sons.

The reasons for this are numerous, and I have heard them all, over the years, from the fathers in my workshops. Most of their reluctance seems to be based on a feeling of ignorance. Although the variations are plentiful, the theme is the same: because they grew up male, they don't seem to know what to do with their daughters. They know what to do with their sons because they were sons themselves. With daughters, however, many feel they are in strange, even alien, territory. One poor father who stands out in my memory actually said, "I thought all I could do with her was take her shopping at the mall."

For some dads, of course, there lingers a preference for boys. One father told me (confessed to me?) the following story.

"When my second child was born, another girl, my first thought was I have to try again for a boy. Then I thought, Wait a minute. What's wrong with my girls? They're not defective just because they are not male. The next week I went to the doctor and had a vasectomy."

In response to my raised eyebrows, he reinforced his statement: "Really, I did!"

Helping a father relate to his daughter is where you enter the picture as his mentor. This is an important role. Not only does it help the father, but it helps your daughter, too. You can be instrumental in bringing the two of them together.

GIVE HIM A DAUGHTER'S PERSPECTIVE: YOURS!

The most effective way to make your point about his importance in your daughter's life is to discuss with him your relationship with your own father. Good or bad, it will make an impression on him. You have instant credibility and authority as a daughter—something he will never have. In this way, you are a valuable mentor to him, a source of information and inspiration.

Like the woman who told of going to the dump with her dad on Saturday mornings, you will be speaking from direct experience. Your stories of what Dad did right and what you wish he had done differently will be compelling. If you want to sprinkle your stories with research here and there or stiffen them with expert opinions, go ahead, but even these will not carry the weight of your personal experiences, growing up in this society as a daughter of a father.

"My wife told me a wonderful story about her dad." one father began, all misty-eyed. "When she was a little girl of about four or five, every Sunday evening in the summer, right before Walt Disney came on, she and her father would walk up their street to a dairy and buy chocolate ice cream bonbons. They would bring them home, all melty and soft. They would sit at the picnic table outside, under a weeping willow tree, and eat their bonbons together.

"Sometimes he would let her feed them to him, and she remembered that he would get chocolate all over his face, just as she did. Then they would go inside and wash up and turn on the TV. She would sit on his lap and together they would watch Walt Disney. It became their bonbon ritual.

"As she told me the story, her eyes filled up with tears of love for her father," he continued. "It was such a simple little thing, and yet my wife remembers it all these years later with such fondness that it makes her cry with the power of missing him. As she talked, I realized I want my little girl to remember me like that someday.

"If I don't make the effort to spend more time with her, she won't have these stories to tell. I now realized how precious and short are these years of my daughter's girlhood. I realize if I don't get on the stick, it will be too late to build good memories."

If life with Father was a negative experience for you, you will have a wealth of information to offer concerning what *not* to do. You will make obvious the consequences of certain negative fathering styles. Your attitudes and judgments of your father's shortcomings and his parenting style will be a lesson. Your daughter's father will not want to be regarded in a negative light by his daughter when she is an adult, and you are the constant reminder that little girls grow up. Many adult women have harsh judgments of rigidly controlling, authoritarian, or emotionally absent fathers. At the very worst, many daughters have absolutely no relationship at all with fathers who were abusive, including those who were verbally and emotionally abusive.

By the same token, if life with Father was a positive experience for you, it can act as a lovely parable of the relationship that is possible between a daughter and a father who understands his role as a nurturing adult male and a deeply caring mentor. You will be able to illuminate, often quite eloquently, what your dad's love did for you. You will reinforce the importance of the time your daughter's father spends with her and the loving gestures he makes toward her by reminding him not only of what he is accomplishing in the present but of what he is building for the future. Of course, his little girl's love will be the main attraction for him and the most motivating factor, but your input as mentor and adult daughter will help him to understand the consequences of his actions—or his inaction, as the case may be—and to stay the course.

So don't hesitate to share your memories, good and bad. You can provide the wise counsel he needs with stories told from your heart—stories that can also nurture the bond between husband and wife. As one woman said, "After I told my husband a few times how much my father's criticism hurt my feelings as a little girl, I noticed that he not only quit criticizing our daughter, he also quit criticizing me! It was an added benefit I wasn't expecting."

If your daughter's father is unaware, emotionally distant, or overly busy, one way to get his attention is to have him talk to other fathers. If he could hear the stories I hear in workshops, most of which are told by middle-aged, divorced-and-remarried men working on second families, he might change his attitude.

"I'm here to do it right this time," said one father in his late forties, expressing what has become a common theme. "With my first family," he continued, "I was so busy being a corporate whiz kid that I missed entirely my kids growing up. Now they barely speak to me."

Later he said to me privately, "It's not that my kids are mean. It's just that, since I wasn't a part of their lives, they don't miss me. They don't think about me. That hurts. This time I want to do a better job. I want to be missed someday."

Another technique is to enlist the help of *his* father, your father-in-law. One young father in a workshop hesitantly raised his hand and spoke quietly: "My own father pulled me aside one day and said, 'Look, you're not spending enough time with Tiffany. Someday you're going to regret it. I know you have to provide for your family and all, but take it from one who knows—childhood is brief. Don't be stupid. You can't recover these years.'"

If your father-in-law is not a potential ally, for whatever reason, look around. Perhaps your own father, a next-door neighbor, or any good male friend of your daughter's father who is also a father and one whom he respects is a possible ally. Sometimes a man can hear advice from another man with less defensiveness than from the woman he loves, from whom he may interpret the comments as criticism.

THE FATHER'S DUAL ROLE

A dad's influence on his daughter comes from a dual role. First, dads tend to teach positive risk-taking and mastery. Research shows that dads focus their teaching skills on (1) how to compete hard but fairly, (2) how to deal with losing and frustration, and (3) how to handle power and aggression.[24] Part of the father's role, then, is to teach his daughter the same things he would teach his son—the mastery skills of positive risk-taking and resilience. In addition, he must teach specific skills like how to change the oil in the car, put a new circuit board in the computer, read a compass, throw a softball, fix the kitchen sink, climb a rope, surf the Internet, download software. (Of course, moms can teach these skills as well.)

The father's second role, however, is less obvious but equally important. Furthermore, it is a role that's impossible for a mom—even a willing mom—to take on. A father's second role is to offer, indeed freely give, male approval—both of his daughter's femininity and of her as a person. This requires a certain amount of awareness and sophistication on his part, since offering his approval means more than just giving praise.

For example, there is the issue of time. He must be spend time with her because children sense quite early that this is a parent's most precious commodity. A father who's willing to spend time with his daughter sends the clear message that he values her, likes her, enjoys being with her, and appreciates her company. This in itself is an expression of unconditional love, a reflected appraisal that she is worth it.

During the time he spends with his daughter, the father has the opportunity to demonstrate what a nurturing adult male is like. His daughter can witness this type of male behavior, bask in his attention, and absorb its benefits. She then will realize that the choice of a nurturing male as a life partner is possible for her, and she'll be likely to seek out those qualities in a future mate. You can see, and so will her father, that this is serious business. He will be setting the standard for what men should be like and, by extension, what husbands, in particular, can be like. If she spends time with a caring and nurturing father, she is less likely to get enmeshed in personal relationships with abusive or emotionally distant men.

One of the most frequently asked questions I hear from moms in workshops is "How can I get my husband to spend more time with my daughter?" I advise them to teach their daughters how to ask for what they need, how to ask for Dad's attention. Instead of allowing your daughter to mope around, waiting for her father to pay attention to her, teach her the mastery skill of identifying what she needs and asking for it. It will be much more effective coming from her than from you anyway. There is something irresistible to a father when his little girl says, "Dad, can I go fishing with you?" or "Dad, let's go for a bike ride" or a walk in the park or a baseball game, or "Dad, teach me how to work with wood" or tie a fly, find a Web site, read a compass, or play chess. Most importantly, teach her to say, "I just want to be with you. I love you."

What father could resist such a statement? He would have to be pretty hard-hearted indeed. In fact, I can't imagine any father flatly refusing. He might, however, try to put her off with statements like "Maybe later" or "I want to be with you too, honey, but not right now. I'm busy." Perhaps, at the moment she asks, he is otherwise occupied and either doesn't realize how important it is to her or is too busy to act on her request.

No problem. At that point, being a mentor means teaching her the mastery skill of persistence. Advise her to say, "Okay, when? Let's set a date." As mentors to girls on how to relate to males, we must teach them early that to sit around waiting for men to notice that you are sad and lonely is often a recipe for frustration. Learning to ask for what she wants emotionally now will save her a lot of grief and frustration in the future.

Of course, it is possible that your daughter is too young to handle a request of her father. Actually, little girls under age five are so charming and flirtatious with their fathers they usually have them wrapped around their little fingers. It is usually later that he doesn't know what to do with her. If this is the case, then, of course, it is time for you to step in and make him aware.

There will be more about fathers and their influence on daughters throughout this book, but for now, your job as his mentor is to make him aware of his unique and profound position in her life. Share with him that even though his dual role is critical, he can still relax and simply enjoy her as a child. He need not always be teaching, protecting, guiding, directing, and controlling. He need not be Mr. Answer Man. In truth, the most potent interaction of all is simply hanging out together like friends, having fun, being silly, goofing off, getting chocolate on your face, and passing time. And of course the same goes for your interactions with her. No more need be said. Going to the dump on Saturday morning and eating chocolate ice cream bonbons together says it all.

A FINAL NOTE ON FATHERS

My experience with dads over the years has taught me that the great majority dearly love their little girls and want to be remembered as wonderful fathers. If the daddy in your household doesn't seem to know how to connect with his daughter, take advantage of your unique position as his mentor to help him understand his importance in his little girl's life. He and your daughter will both thank you all of their days.

PART III

Age-Appropriate Strategies for Building Mastery and Self-Esteem

CHAPTER 6

But I Acted Like Such a *Girl*

Seven Strategies for Combating Stereotypes

I want to be a nurse, but if I were a boy I'd want to be an architect.

Fourth grade girl, quoted in a
research study

In infancy and early childhood, human beings begin absorbing the sex roles of the society into which they are born. By the time children are three years old they know whether they are male or female, and they can identify types of behavior that are considered appropriate to each sex.[1] Ensuring that children become socialized to their role in society is a long, protracted process. As we have seen, the easiest way to understand it is to draw an analogy to how braces straighten teeth. One would never attempt to straighten a child's teeth by hammering them into place. Instead, gentle but relentless pressure is placed on the teeth to encourage them in a particular direction until they are set. Such is the force of culture and its messages on all members of a society.

Take a moment to review the lists of masculine and feminine traits in Chapter 1. What you notice is that many of the so-called feminine traits are either already tinged with helplessness or are not conducive to the building of mastery behavior. Care must be taken, therefore, that the negative effects of identification as a female don't become a vehicle for perpetuating learned helplessness in your daughter.

Fortunately, we live in a time of change concerning sex roles. An opportunity exists to breathe fresh air into stale models that do not serve girls in becoming positive risk-takers. As a mother desiring to foster resilient attitudes and behaviors in your daughter, you will need to be aware of the many overt and covert sex messages that your daughter receives in the world. You also must be aware that the messages you received as a girl will ultimately influence both the way you mother your daughter and the unspoken messages you send.

Infancy

Let us begin at the beginning by obliterating once and for all the old-fashioned notion that girl babies are more fragile than boy babies. The truth is that female newborns are stronger, healthier, and more fully developed that their male counterparts. Despite a shorter gestation period, at birth girls:

- Have a more mature skeleton and central nervous system
- Have a lower mortality rate
- Are less likely than males to show birth defects
- Are less likely to be miscarried or stillborn
- Thrive better in preemie intensive care units and go home sooner
- Are less likely to show sex-linked disorders such as hemophilia and color-blindness

Many experts agree that females actually have the genetic advantage (dare I say superiority?) because they receive two X-chromosomes at conception, in contrast to the male's X and Y. This is advantageous because the X chromosome is longer than the Y and carries more genes. Also, sex-linked disorders are carried on the X chromosome. Should faulty material be found on one X string, the female has a second, backup X string that may correct or offset a problem. Males have less genetic material to work with and thus fewer options when genetic material is flawed.

Despite the facts, many parents continue to treat girls as if they were more fragile and in need of more protection than boys. From the cradle, the messages begin. For example, there is more lifting and tossing of boy babies—not a good idea for either sex, since brain damage can occur if the play is too exuberant—while girl babies are cuddled and rocked.[2] As boys mature, their fathers wrestle with them, run with them, and play hard on playground equipment, but many of them only cuddle their daughters. Mothers, on the other hand, while not changing their behavior as much for sons and daughters, tend to be more tolerant of fathers being active and playing rough with their sons than with their daughters. The attitudes that these behaviors reflect are bogus.

Keeping in mind the very important warning against lifting and tossing (*never* shake a baby in anger; many infant injuries and even deaths are caused in this manner), there is no need to be less physical with a girl baby than a boy baby. By the same token, boys love to be cuddled and held, just like girls.

Furthermore, from the moment your baby girl begins to crawl, her motivation is to see, experience, and know the world around her. The fact that, from infancy, both sexes display an insatiable curiosity and desire to explore their environment stirs up a lot of parental fears. Unfortunately, with the best intentions of keeping a baby safe, parents can say all manner of truly horrific things: "Be careful or you will get run over"—or get lost, fall down the stairs, poke your eye out, cut yourself, break your leg, get burned, drown, get electrocuted, get kidnapped. And of course it is true—all these terrible things do happen in the world.

But imagine if we did this to an adult. Suppose that as you kiss your spouse good-bye in the morning, you imagine every possible disaster that could befall him and then you warn him in an effort to keep him safe: "Bye, honey. Be careful or you'll get in a car wreck"—or lose your job, get mugged, be held hostage, have a heart attack, or become the victim of a terrorist plot. "Have a nice day!"

STRATEGY #1: ALLOW EXPLORATION

As your daughter begins to crawl, walk, explore her environment, and take the risks necessary to experience her world, allow her freedom of movement—while keeping an eye on her—so as to create the illusion of independence and autonomy. Of course you must keep her out of harm's way, since her fearlessness is born of ignorance, just remember to do so unobtrusively. For now, suffice it to say that in attempting to keep a daughter safe you may send a message that ultimately debilitates her.

Don't hover or make her feel like you are overly concerned for her welfare. Don't constantly tell her, "Be careful or you'll get hurt," and don't list all the dangers the world holds. Simply watch her closely and remove her from any precarious situation without sending her the message that the world is unsafe and therefore so is she.

STRATEGY #2: GET DAD INVOLVED

Your daughter's father should be involved in her care from birth. Studies show that children whose fathers participate in caregiving during the first six months of the child's life perform better in all three categories of development: intellectual development, motor skills, and social responsiveness. Furthermore, dads who are involved are more committed and attached and say so verbally. Finally, dads typically allow more exploration.[3]

However, there is potential for one problem that I should draw your attention to, particularly since it can be a source of tension in the wife–husband relationship. Some mothers feel jealous if their husbands are highly involved with infants, and some moms experience an erosion of self-esteem. If this is true for you, I recommend two things. First, remind yourself that both parents are critical to a child's development and you would not want to deprive your daughter of the love of her father. Second, take a look at your own self-concept to determine if it is entirely based on your role as a mother. If so, get involved in activities outside the home that have absolutely nothing to do with being a mother. Try attending an ongoing activity without telling anyone you are a mother. Eventually, as your self-concept rounds out to include facets of your nature other than mothering, you will feel safer letting the father get attention from his daughter.

Early Childhood

As your daughter matures beyond infancy into early childhood, the sex-role education that began at birth will become increasingly complex, subtle, and intense. Some aspects of identification will become increasingly powerful and will continue as part of her cultural education—whether or not we approve of them. This change is accomplished in a variety of ways through toys, games, books, sports, the media, grandparents, aunts, uncles, siblings, teachers, peers, and most importantly, parental sanction of some behaviors and disapproval of others.

This is the time to become vigilant about sending messages that ameliorate, as much as possible, those aspects associated with femininity that are tainted with learned helplessness: powerlessness, submissiveness, fragility, passivity, excessive sensitivity, excessive self-sacrifice, and the need to be rescued, protected, or defended. Mothers can offset these messages in a number of ways.

First, as a parent you must be aware of the messages you send in everyday interactions. I am reminded of a wonderful story told by a mother in one of my workshops. Her five-year-old daughter, Courtney, and her little friend, a boy, came into the kitchen one morning wearing cowboy boots, cowboy hats, holsters, and guns and pushing Courtney's miniature shopping cart. Intrigued, the father asked what they were doing. "We're cowboys and we're going shopping!" was their innocent and happy reply.

An aware parent would respond either neutrally or positively, as in "Well, have a good time!" or "Pick me up some spurs while you're at it!" An unenlightened parent would respond disapprovingly, as in "What do you mean? Cowboys don't go shopping. Cowboys ride horses. Cowboys are tough!" or "Women go shopping, not cowboys!" or any of a hundred other variations you can imagine that would discourage the two children from continuing their androgynous behavior.

What Do You Sanction? What Do You Discourage?

Be aware of the kinds of behavior you encourage by sanctioning them with approval and those you discourage through your disapproval. Like the mother who comforted her daughter on the in-line skates after a collision but allowed her son to be encouraged to get up and try again, be vigilant that you do not inadvertently perpetuate or reinforce notions of female fragility. Act and speak with awareness so that you do not send messages to your daughter that narrow her choices, place her in a subservient role, or undermine her mastery behavior.

Here's another example: "I just realized something," said a mother who looked no more than eighteen. "When my son gets into a conflict I encourage him to stand up for himself and be assertive. When my daughter gets into conflicts, I tell her to learn to get along with others, to look for ways she might be provoking the conflict. I encourage her to get along." She paused. "It just seems so unfeminine to encourage her to fight."

This is a judgment call. First, while it certainly seems unfeminine to encourage a girl to fight, it is also possible that someday she may actually be called upon to defend herself. At the risk of sounding a tad militant, I am in favor of encouraging your daughter to be aggressive if need be, even to fight if that is required, but you need not encourage fighting to encourage assertiveness and standing up for one's rights. Finally, don't forget to teach your son how to get along with others.

Toys and Dolls

Toys are another way children learn sex roles. At the very early ages, from birth to two, toys for girls and boys are quite similar: cuddly, warm, soft, and nurturing. Even in the first two years of life, however, adults tend to pick stereotyped toys for boys and for girls as well as the traditional blue for boys and pink for girls.[4]

Many (not all) girls will show a preference for dolls. Many (not all) boys will show a preference for guns and trucks. Unfortunately, some parents are tempted to use these individual preferences as proof of innate sex differences. However, parents in my workshops tell stories that come closer to the truth of individual temperament.

"I have two girls," began one mother. "One is competitive and athletic. When she was little, she liked her Tinkertoys best and loved to roughhouse like a boy. Her sister, on the other hand, is little Miss Priss. She hates to get dirty and wants to wear dresses all the time. I have to admit, her prissiness offends me."

There is nothing wrong with a girl showing a preference for dolls and stuffed animals. Girls enjoy cuddling dolls and dressing them up, and the dolls can also be a source of comfort. As an adult cleaning out my mother's garage, I happened upon a box filled with my old dolls and stuffed animals. To my great surprise I found tears in my eyes upon the discovery of a little spotted stuffed dog I had used as a pillow to cry on whenever I was upset. I must have been about three or four. It was the way I comforted myself when my parents were mad at me or when they were fighting. It still had tearstains on it. I was overwhelmed by the feelings that welled up when I met my old friend again. So if your daughter loves dolls, there is nothing to be corrected. Experiencing the nurturing qualities associated with dolls and stuffed animals is important—to boys as well as to girls.

However, since all toys teach something, it is important that she be exposed to and encouraged to play with many other types of toys as well. The most important thing to remember for this age group is not to limit your choices to dolls or kitchen utensils or dress-up clothes—the adult preferences for gifts for girls according to one study. A number of toy options are available that will help to promote her mastery behavior. I favor problem-solving toys that develop cognitive ability and skills over toys like guns and trucks, which don't build mastery behavior. My recommendation is to emphasize puzzles, mazes, books, building blocks, and Tinkertoys. Also, give her a toy microscope, telescope, computer, tool kit, and science lab until she is ready for the real thing.

What to Do About Barbie

As our culture's icon of modern femininity, a totem of the male fantasy gone berserk, and a saboteur of many a young girl's self-esteem, Barbie is more than just a doll; she requires a complete discussion to herself. Mothers need all the assistance they can get in helping their daughters block, or at least overcome, the effects of identification with Barbie as the ultimate in femininity.

Over the years in my workshops I have learned that Barbie is a source of great frustration to many modern mothers, be they baby boomers or Generation Xers. I am not exaggerating when I say that some mothers even experience a kind of grief when their daughters express desire for a Barbie, believing that it signals the beginning of a lifelong assault on their daughter's self-esteem. They fret about the preoccupation with beauty and the impossible task of achieving this warped and anomalous ideal beginning so early in their daughters' lives. This ideal is of no consequence whatsoever to a little girl with no experience or political agenda who just wants her first beautiful Barbie doll.

My heart goes out to these moms, but we have to face the facts. Being the mega-earner that she is, Barbie is here to stay—at least until after the feminist revolution. In the meantime, we must cope as effectively as possible with her influence on our daughters and her power as a symbol of feminine beauty.

This will not necessarily be easy. Part of the problem is our own conflicted attitude toward beauty. Most of us, given the opportunity, would choose to look like Claudia Schiffer or Cindy Crawford. So it's not that we would hate looking like Barbie; we just hate the pressure to try to be that pretty.

It is a useful strategy, therefore, to examine your own issues around appearance in order to foresee the unspoken messages you might be sending to your daughter. Although many adult women say they deplore what Barbie stands for, *somebody* is out there purchasing expensive hair and skin care products, joining pricey health clubs, submitting to plastic surgery, working out, and dieting. After all, these megabuck industries exist to aid in the quest to come as close as is humanly possible to resembling—you got it—Barbie.

I can almost hear the pained expressions of indignation in response to this statement:

- I don't work out because I want to look like Barbie. I do it for health reasons.
- How dare you accuse me of wanting to be a Barbie doll? I'm a professional woman.
- I hate Barbie dolls and all the vanity for which she stands.

While I am willing to concede that modern females hate the pressure to be beautiful, that pressure is so great that they succumb. In many cases, they pursue the ideal, if not for themselves, then for their daughters. (More in Chapters 10 and 11 about the messages we send our daughters regarding appearance.) Women are encouraged by the media to look thin, fit, and young and to have big breasts and long legs to be attractive to men. To some degree, this preoccupation with beauty will be communicated to our daughters, who will see us dieting, putting on control-top panty hose (a new label for an old product—the girdle—a marketing gimmick if there ever was one), buying a Wonderbra, getting breast implants (despite the health warnings), and undergoing cosmetic surgery to reduce the effects of aging.

A good beginning strategy is to examine your own beliefs and behavior in regard to femininity, appearance, weight, and beauty. Do these areas represent struggle for you? Does your self-esteem come and go based upon fluctuations in your weight and appearance? Does your self-esteem rise and fall based upon the degree of male attention you receive? Do you starve yourself?

Be aware that early in the game, probably before you expect it and unbeknownst to you, your little girl will be aware of Barbie and know who she is.

"I was in the store with my daughter when she was barely two and a half," said one mother, the executive director of a national nonprofit agency. "There was a display of Barbie dolls in different outfits. My daughter pointed and said, 'Barbie! Barbie!' I didn't even know she knew who Barbie was!"

She continued, "Now my daughter is five and of course she still wants a Barbie, and of course I still refuse to buy her one. I know it's inevitable, but somebody else is going to have to buy it for her. I refuse."

On the other hand, you may wind up buying her her first Barbie doll. That's okay. Often it's just a matter of time before she wears you down anyway. Besides, she will go to her friends' houses and play with their Barbies. When most of the other little girls have Barbie dolls, your ideals, no matter how politically well founded or based on concern for her self-esteem, will mean nothing if your daughter feels she is being deprived. And by making Barbie a forbidden item, you may enhance her appeal. If you have Barbie right there in your home, you can create more opportunities to make your political point and do the subtle remedial work on your daughter's self-esteem.

STRATEGY #3: PLAY BARBIE WITH YOUR DAUGHTER

Begin at early childhood to ameliorate the future effects of Barbie on your daughter. Poke fun at the ridiculous aspects of Barbie's femininity. Make a game of brainstorming a list of all the things one can't do in high heels. For example, point to Barbie's feet and say,

Barbie the Action Hero

Turn Barbie into an action hero by creating new activities for her. Imagine her in new roles that suggest heroic and adventurous ways for her to handle adversity with assertiveness, strength, and confidence. Make her take risks. Show her rescuing men in distress. In this way, you can influence how your daughter sees females and their role in society.

For example, instead of having Barbie live in a mansion with a pool and drive a BMW, place her in action-oriented and decision-making roles that require hard work and persistence. Be sure these occupations are nontraditional and uncommon— president of a record company, for instance, or TV network CEO, high-tech genius like Bill Gates or Steve Jobs, inventor, scientist, or astronaut. She can still wear beautiful clothes when she goes out at night with successful and caring men or when she is out with her female friends who, like her, are successful and influential.

Even better, place Barbie in daring, adventurous, perhaps even dangerous situations that have nothing to do with her looks, situations that require her to be courageous and to take bold, decisive action. Discover Barbie in the Amazon Basin where she must lead a rescue team to save a group of injured and stranded anthropologists. Have her lead an all-woman expedition to climb Mount Everest, or make her the captain of the all-woman America's Cup team as they prepare for and win the world-famous race. Have her organize a vanguard group of revolutionary women seeking to overthrow a repressive government. Have her land a plane with only the directions of the air traffic controller to guide her, or show her making her inaugural speech to the nation upon becoming president. The possibilities are unlimited, so have fun and let your imagination go wild.

"Oh, look! Poor Barbie! Her feet are deformed! Wouldn't it be awful to have feet that could wear only high heels? There are so many things you couldn't do. You couldn't go skiing or snowboarding or biking or surfing or scuba-diving. You couldn't ride a horse or go to the beach. You couldn't wear sandals or hiking boots or toe shoes or in-line skates." Point out that Barbie's wardrobe seems to be evidence of vast wealth, yet she has no discernible source of income! Brainstorm all the jobs Barbie might do to earn such a lavish lifestyle.

The main thing to remember is that dolls designed for boys are always action heroes, so they have that persona with which to identify. Girls need this persona as well, in addition to cuddly baby dolls they can nurture. As it currently stands, when girls play with dolls they are either playing Mommy or identifying themselves as sex objects. Therefore, be sure to place Barbie in situations that require her to take action and make decisions that have consequences, not in passive or decorative roles where she is required to do little other than look pretty. Lucrative but passive occupations like modeling, being a movie star, or sitting behind a desk (they now have "power suits" for Barbie to show she can be an executive) are not action-oriented enough to overcome Barbie's persona as a beautiful object.

STRATEGY #4: BARBIE'S BEEPER GAME

One attempt on the part of Mattel to give Barbie a professional image was to provide her with a beeper. Unfortunately, if you listen, most of the messages on Barbie's beeper are either from Ken or about Ken. One game to play with your daughter and her friends is to think up new messages for Barbie's beeper—messages that challenge the traditional sex roles of women. Here are some to get you started.

1. Hi, Barb. Melissa here. I have some questions about that white-water raft trip you'll be guiding through the canyon this summer. What kind of equipment will I need? Will I need my own helmet and life jacket and other stuff like that?
2. Yeah, hi, Barb, this is Ken. What time did you say I need to get dinner on tonight? What time is that client of yours arriving? Don't leave me hanging. I need to get to the grocery store. Oh, and by the way, do you want me to iron your silk dress for tonight? Talk to you soon.

3. Hello, Barbie, you don't know me. I'm Dr. Carol McIntyre, professor of environmental studies at Stanford. Recently a colleague of mine informed me that you have invented a new type of solar panel. Real breakthrough-technology stuff. My committee is interested in reviewing your prototype to learn more about your methods. Give me a call.

4. Yes, Barb, hi. My name is Bill Gates. The rumor mill has it that you have developed revolutionary new software. I am interested in opening a discussion with you about a possible partnership. I'm talking about some big bucks here, Barb, so give me a call at your earliest convenience.

STRATEGY #5: BEDTIME STORIES FOR MASTERY

At bedtime provide your daughter with powerful images of herself: great things are in store for her, and she influences outcomes. Use the bedtime story as a means to teach your daughter how to visualize herself in a wide variety of roles. Visualizing comes naturally to many children, especially the generations raised with television.

Visualizations work. Many athletes use them as a way to achieve peak performance.[5] Over the years, scores of studies in the field of educational research have shown that students learn better when both hemispheres of the brain are utilized.[6] The right side is the visual side and plays a critical role in all aspects of learning—changing our belief systems, imagining possibilities, and problem-solving. Create exciting adventures in which your daughter is an active, competent participant as a replacement for the more traditional bedtime story.

This is fun, especially if you have a flair for the dramatic or like to conjure up stories. Even if you don't, it is surprisingly easy. I have provided some stories here for you, but you can make up your own as well. Simply imagine some high adventure you have always fantasized about and then place your daughter in that role. Just be careful that you do not limit or censor these activities. Do not restrict the adventures to typically female activities, since the whole point is to broaden your daughter's horizons and beliefs about what is possible for her.

Begin by having your daughter get comfy, warm, and relaxed. Tell her to use her eyelids like a TV or movie screen. Tell her that as she hears the story, she will be able to see the pictures on her closed eyelids.[7]

Visualization 1*
Ages Four to Six
Targeted Behavior: Competition and Self-Esteem

Tonight we are going to have fun! Close your eyes and pretend you are looking at a big movie screen. On that screen is *you!* You look so happy. See that big smile on your face? You are running and playing with all your friends. (Pause.) See? There are _____ and _____ (use names of daughter's playmates). Everyone decides to have a race. You can hardly wait. You like to run as fast as you can. You feel good. You are ready. (Pause.) You *know* you can win. (Pause.) See yourself line up with your friends at the starting line. Someone yells, "On your mark." You feel happy and excited. Then you hear, "Get set." Your whole body can hardly wait to spring off the starting line and run as fast as the wind. Finally you hear "Go!" and you are off! You are running right beside all your friends. Everyone is smiling and having a great time. So are you. (Pause.) The sun is warm, and the sky is blue. (Pause.) Now you really pour on the steam. Your body does what you tell it to do and is fast and light. (Pause.) Before you know it, you are across the finish line! You are first! You won! You are so happy. It feels so good to run fast. You are laughing and smiling. (Pause.) Your friends come up and shake your hand and tell you what a great race you ran. You thank them. (Pause.) You feel happy and proud. Running fast is fun. You like your body. (Pause.) You love to win races too.

Visualization 2*
Ages Four to Six
Targeted Behavior: Safety

Tonight you are going to learn what to do if someone you don't know talks to you. Someone you don't know is called a stranger. You are not scared, though, because you are smart and know what to do.

See yourself playing with your friends or walking to school.

*Visualizations 1, 2, and 4 are reprinted from *How to Father a Successful Daughter* by Nicky Marone.

(Name some kids your child spends time with.) You are having fun. You are all laughing and talking. A car drives up. There is a stranger in it—a stranger is a person you do not know, a person you have not seen before. (Pause. Repeat.) The stranger asks you to get in the car. You do *not* get in the car. It doesn't matter if the stranger is a man or a woman. (Pause. Repeat.) Tell your friends that you should all leave. (Pause.) The stranger tells you something bad has happened to Mommy or Daddy. The stranger says we are hurt and that we said it was okay for you to get into the car. You still do not go. (Pause. Repeat.) You know that no matter what, we would never send a stranger to come and get you. (Pause.) See yourself quickly walking away. You know the stranger is not telling the truth. You are too smart to be fooled. You keep on walking or running to the nearest safe place. Tell your playmates to come with you. If they do not come, you go anyway. See yourself walking away. No matter what the stranger says, you do not listen. (Pause.)

If Mommy or Daddy is not home, go to _____'s house (give the name of a trusted neighbor). Tell us or _____ exactly what the stranger looked like and what he or she said. You do not feel afraid because you are safe. (Pause.) You are safe because you were smart and brave. (Pause.) Smart and brave. (Pause.) You feel happy to be safe. You are glad you are smart. Being brave feels good too.★

Visualization 3
Ages Seven to Nine
Targeted Behavior: Competence and Self-Esteem

You are inside a huge arena with a swimming pool. In addition to the humidity, it is unusually bright because spotlights for TV cameras have been strategically placed all around the pool area. You are wearing a regulation competitive swimsuit and a swim cap. You are climbing a ladder to the diving board. When you reach the platform at the top of the ladder, you pause for a moment to gather your courage and confidence. (Pause.) The huge audience below is hushed. They respect your need to concentrate.

★For an older child, it is wise to suggest during the visualization that she remember to get a license plate number, car color, and a physical description of the stranger.

You feel strong, capable, and completely confident in your ability as a trained athlete. (Pause.) You are ready. (Pause). This is the day you have been waiting for, training for, working toward for years.

You walk to the end of the board. You gaze down at the water rocking and swaying beneath you. You bend your knees and then press down to thrust yourself upward. Your feet tighten as you rise to your toes, swing your arms in an arc from your sides to above your head, and leap, straight and supple, high into the air above the board. (Pause.)

This is your favorite moment—the time between when you leave the board and when you enter the water. (Pause.) Every muscle knows precisely what to do. Every muscle has its own memory, trained in hundreds, perhaps thousands, of sessions. You can rely on this muscle memory, this training, to propel you to a medal. (Pause.)

You tuck your body into a tight ball, spin twice, then arch your back, thrust your legs outward, and point your toes as you stretch out into your full length. Spinning, turning, jackknifing with perfect precision and grace, your whole being is exhilarated. This is the closest you will ever get to flying. (Pause.) The air on your skin, the spinning room, and the spectators all contribute to the joy you feel at this moment. (Pause.)

You enter the water straight as an arrow. First your fingertips, then your hands, arms, shoulders, neck, torso, thighs, calves, and finally the tips of your delicately pointed toes experience the cool welcome of the sheath of water. You hear the muffled sound of applause as you propel yourself up through the water.

When you break the surface, the audience has already burst into wild applause and cheering. You smile and experience the satisfaction (pause), the power (pause), the grace (pause), and the glory of a fine-tuned athletic body perfectly executing a dive.

Visualization 4*
Ages Seven to Nine
Targeted Behavior: Risk-Taking and Self-Esteem

You are in a dense jungle. It is steaming hot. You are wearing shorts with lots of pockets; a short-sleeve shirt, also with lots of pockets;

---

*Visualizations 1, 2, and 4 are reprinted from *How to Father a Successful Daughter* by Nicky Marone.

socks; hiking boots; and a hat with netting to keep the insects off your face. You have a pack on your back and are carrying a knife to clear away jungle growth in your path. Your clothes are all stuck to your skin because the jungle air is so hot and sticky.

You are leading a group of archaeologists to an ancient Indian civilization site in Peru. You are their guide. Men and women are relying on you to get them there safely.

You are on a narrow ledge on the side of a steep hill. The jungle is so thick here that you have to clear it off the ledge as you go. There once was a path here, but it is now so overgrown that it cannot be seen. To avoid getting lost, you stop the group while you consult your map and compass.

You realize that the group has veered slightly off course, so you get your bearings by hiking closer to the little ledge where you can look more carefully at the terrain around you. Suddenly you hear a scream.

You run back to the group and learn that a man lost his footing and fell off the ledge. You yell down to him and discover that he has broken his leg. He is unable to walk on it.

Everyone turns to you for help and instructions. You tie a technical knot, using climbing rope, set your anchor points, and rappel down to him. Once there, you quickly examine his injury. At least there are no compound fractures, you think with relief. You put a splint on his leg and tie him to a rope, which the group will use to pull him up. Your main goal is to get him up to the group, where there is a doctor who can set the leg and you can radio for a rescue team.

Everything goes pretty smoothly except that he is in a lot of pain. You talk to him quietly and gently, soothing his nerves and relaxing him. You climb up after him.

Once the mission is accomplished, the doctor takes over. Everyone is grateful to you for having rescued him and brought him to safety. You say thank you, but think to yourself, It's all in a day's work!

Visualization 5
Ages Seven to Nine
Targeted Behavior: Self-Efficacy and Self-Esteem
It is a blustery winter's day. Although there are a couple of inches of fresh powder snow on the ground, the sun is shining brightly and

creating an intense glare. The biting wind cuts through even your many layers of insulating clothing and wool. Holding your open palm over your eyes like a visor to cut the glare, you gaze out into the open countryside. You see no buildings, no highways, no houses. Just bright blue sky, pristine open land, and rolling fields covered with glistening snow. The sun's intense light pounds down upon you and your dogs.

Yes, you own eight sled dogs, all barking excitedly in anticipation of your commands. This will be the first of many such days, for you are embarking on the Iditarod, a 1,200-mile trek across the tundra of Alaska, the best-known, most challenging, and greatest of all sled-dog races.

You make a final check of your gear: food, water, supplies, safety and emergency equipment. Finally—the most important check— the last inspection of your dogs. You check their paws carefully for any cuts, abrasions, or rawness. They lick you and wag their tails. Satisfied that they are all healthy, you harness up the team, soothing them with your voice, stroking their coats, laughing and joking to ease their tension.

Everything is in place, and you are ready. The dogs, well-trained athletes themselves, know exactly what they are supposed to do and they await your commands eagerly. You jump on the back of the sled, push off with your feet, yell, "Mush!" and you are off, flying across the frozen snow like Santa getting an early start.

Visualization 6
Ages Nine to Eleven
Targeted Behavior: Risk-Taking, Courage, and Strategic Thinking

It is an autumn night late in November. The trees are shorn of their leaves and appear gaunt in the darkness. The wind blows a little flurry of leaves down the deserted suburban street.

You are sitting alone in a car on a lonely suburban street with your doors locked. You are cold and lonesome. You know you shouldn't be out here by yourself, but your partner is sick with the flu and you had an intuition that tonight would be the night. Turning on the ignition and cranking up the heater, you warm your hands on a hot mug and pour some more coffee out of a thermos to help you stay awake. Being a detective on stakeout is not all it's cracked up to be, you think to yourself. As a matter of fact, it's downright boring sometimes. You feel deeply grateful to your sweet husband at home who made you this delicious thermos of coffee.

Yet this is part of the job. This sleazeball for whom you are waiting has got to come home sometime, and you are going to be here to nail him when he does. You know that he finances his upscale lifestyle in this elegant neighborhood by cheating elderly people out of their money. You can't wait to nab him. Double-checking the warrant lying on the seat beside you, you take another sip of coffee.

Just then an expensive car rounds the corner and pulls into the driveway. You snap to attention, ram your car into first gear, and quickly move in behind him, blocking his vehicle from the back so he cannot exit. His vehicle is trapped. As he exits the car, you realize he has someone with him. Instantly you call for backup. You know, however, that until help arrives, you must handle the situation single-handedly. You decide confronting him immediately with the warrant would not be a good strategy, since, if he resists arrest, you alone will be required to detain him and his friends. Therefore you decide to stall.

Thank goodness you are in an unmarked vehicle. They do not realize you are a police detective, so they are not yet suspicious, although the driver, your quarry, looks a little startled, perhaps curious.

"Hello," you begin brightly.

"Hello," he says hesitantly. "May I help you?"

"Yes. I think I may be lost." There is a pause while you think of a question, wishing you had planned this ahead of time instead of daydreaming about your husband. Then you ask, "What are the cross streets up ahead?" You think this is kind of lame, but, hey, you are thinking on your feet here.

"Why don't you just drive up there and look?" retorts his partner, who by now is looking wary and decidedly unfriendly.

"I've been driving up and down these streets. You know how twisty they are, and I'm all turned around. I could read the street signs but I don't know which direction I'm pointing." There, that should do it, you think to yourself.

His partner replies again. "I'm sorry. We can't help you. Come on, Bill, let's go inside."

You show him your badge, "All right. You got me. I hope you won't mind answering a few questions, Mr. Anderson."

"You guys again?" he says angrily, "Look, I've already answered your stupid questions on three different occasions. If you don't leave me alone, I'll call my attorney and press charges for police harassment."

"So you are refusing to cooperate with a police investigation?" At this point, you glance up the street, hoping to see your backup. Nothing.

"No, I *told* you, I *have* cooperated, but this is getting ridiculous." He starts to unlock his front door. It's now or never.

"Mr. Anderson, I have a warrant here for your arrest."

Just as you suspected he would, he tries to bolt. You deliver a kick to his groin, throw yourself on him, unaware of what his partner is up to, and deliver a solid blow that you learned as a black belt student of judo. You immobilize him just long enough to draw your weapon. "I don't want to shoot you, Mr. Anderson. I suggest you hold very still." *

Visualization 7
Ages Nine to Eleven
Targeted Behavior: Discipline, Persistence, and Internalizing Success

It is a warm, moonless night in July. It is 10:30 P.M. The summer night sky is totally black. You are sitting alone on the deck of your house. You have your telescope focused on a portion of the sky you have been watching for several nights and with which you wish to become more familiar. Although this activity certainly can be boring on occasion, you have become accustomed to it. As an amateur astronomer, you understand and even enjoy this solitary aspect of the work—gazing at the night sky through your

---

*I would not recommend this visualization as one to be done before bedtime, since it is not peaceful. It could cause a nightmare. You may wish to use it as a daytime fantasy for your daughter. I experienced some discomfort as I wrote it, especially around the physical violence and the use of weapons, but I realized that if I were writing this for boys, I would not have felt the discomfort. In the long run, I think it is good for developing her self-concept as an efficacious and mastery-oriented person. I leave it up to you to decide if you wish to expose your daughter to this visualization.

telescope, checking sky maps and making notes. Besides, you realize you might as well get used to it, since astronomy is the career you will be pursuing.

Suddenly, in the corner of your lens, you notice something that wasn't there the night before. Probably a satellite or some old space junk, you think. You focus the telescope to get a better look and to determine the location of this speck of light. As you bring the telescope into focus you realize that, based on the most recent maps of the sky, this speck is not supposed to be there. Quickly, you draw a circle on a piece of paper and put a point in the exact spot on the paper that corresponds to what you are seeing through your telescope.

You know this speck cannot be a star, because all of the stars visible through your relatively unsophisticated telescope have been charted already. But maybe, you think to yourself, just maybe, it's a new comet. You feel great excitement building from within, but you maintain your composure because you know you must be patient and verify that this object is actually moving in order to know if it is a comet.

Every night for the next three nights you eagerly await the darkness. As soon as it is dark enough to see clearly, you return to your telescope in order to chart the course of this speck of light. Sure enough, it is moving.

Early in the morning of the fourth day, you call the astrophysics department of your state university. You know you dare not waste time, because other amateur astronomers are also watching the heavens, just as you do, and may have already reported the comet.

When you report your findings to an astrophysics professor, she is very encouraging. You give her the ascension and declination of the speck of light you have been watching. Based on your detailed and organized record-keeping, which the professor praises, she believes you have something worth following up on. She advises you to call with any new information.

Your mother lets you take the day off from school to pursue this opportunity and report your findings. After several days, the professor calls back to inform you that it is official. You have discovered a new comet. You are proud and thrilled. You will enjoy a type of immortality and recognition that very few people ever have the chance to experience—for the new comet will be named after you!

Visualization 8
Ages Nine to Eleven
Targeted Behavior: Persistence, Discipline, and
Internalizing Success

You are in the dark, dank basement of the National Museum of Egypt. It smells of old books, musty manuscripts, and decrepit scrolls. World-renowned as a cryptographer, anthropologist, and linguist, you speak or read nine languages fluently, including Sanskrit and Aramaic. Even though this aspect of your career is often lonely and you would much prefer to be at the dig site itself, you are accustomed to researching ancient manuscripts in the bowels of a library, museum, or university laboratory.

You have been eager, indeed anxious, to arrive here since last night. You have a hunch that today is going to be special. All night you could not stop thinking about that scroll you uncovered locked in an old closet just before the security guard insisted you leave for the night so she could lock up.

Using the special key that admits you to the room housing ancient manuscripts and rare books, you let yourself in, put down your laptop, spread out your notes and materials on the table, and quickly make your way to that closet to pick up where you left off yesterday. Based on your earlier research, you have a hunch that this may be the one of the Dead Sea Scrolls that were lost several decades ago.

Carefully removing the cloth in which it is bound, you almost faint with excitement as you realize practically at first glance that this is indeed one of the lost scrolls. It is believed that this particular scroll contains enough information to revolutionize anthropological understanding of life in the Middle East during the time prior to Christ, and it could shed light on religious controversies throughout the world.

Slowly, carefully, and with great delicacy, you unroll the treasure before you, sit down, and prepare to begin the work that will span the coming decade and make you famous.

Visualization 9
Ages Nine to Eleven
Targeted Behavior: Being in Charge

Picture a director's chair perched precariously on a rock overlooking a deep canyon. Your name is written across the back of the chair and, under it, "Director." You are walking around with a megaphone in your hand, observing the scene carefully. You are wearing jeans, sunglasses, and a visor to keep the sun out of your eyes, and you are carrying a walkie-talkie. Hundreds of extras are positioned far below you in the canyon. Cameramen and crew members are standing around, watching alertly, waiting for you to tell them what to do.

When everything is in place, you hold the walkie-talkie up to your mouth. "Is everything ready?" you ask your assistant, who is down in the canyon.

"Everything's ready," he replies.

"People, extras, equipment, safety crew, demolition crew, everything?" you ask.

"Everything," he replies again.

You raise the megaphone and shout, "Okay, everybody, listen up. We only have one chance to do this right. As you know, this scene is both dangerous and expensive. It cost us hundreds of thousands of dollars, and anybody who screws up will answer to me. Got that?"

Everyone looks back. Some silently nod their heads. Someone shouts, "Right on, boss!"

"All right, having said that, I also want to say you are the most stupendous crew of stuntmen and women, riders and actors, ever assembled in one place. I have every faith in you and your professionalism. You all are the best in this business, the pros. You have all rehearsed and know your positions and what you are to do. Now go out there and do what you do better than you've ever done it before. Feel the fear of these people and the urgency of the confrontation in which they find themselves. Feel their dedication and determination. Feel the danger, the exhilaration. Okay, here we go."

You raise your arm. "Now, when I lower my arm, the scene will begin. The train will begin moving forward. When it hits that mark, everybody swing into action."

"Is the train ready?" you double-check one last time.

A voice shouts, "Ready!"

You lower your arm, shout "Action!" and the huge assembly begins its beautifully choreographed drama before your eyes.

Obviously, the variety of visualizations that can be generated is limited only by your creativity. Here are some suggestions for more to get you going:

Sky diver	Private detective
Mountain climber	Dragon slayer
Rescue team member	Jockey
Astronaut	Orchestra conductor
Pilot or test pilot	Judge
Astronomer	Bank president
Rock or jazz musician	Sportscaster
Soundstage technician	Archaeologist
Race car driver	Scuba diver
College professor	Geologist
Explorer	Architect
Doctor, dentist, surgeon	Chemist
Sheriff	Trial attorney
Chef	President
Circus performer	Rabbi, minister, priest
Admiral, general	Network news director
Network news anchor	White-water river guide
Talk-show host	

Late Childhood

Toys and Games

As your daughter matures, provide as many nontraditional toys, gadgets, and pieces of equipment as you can afford. By this I mean microscopes, telescopes, chemistry sets, anatomy kits, sporting equipment, walkie-talkies, tool kits, take-apart toy engines, and the like. Some girls will enjoy the variety, others will not. The important thing is not to assume that because she is a girl she will not like scientific equipment or sporting goods or tool kits.

Take Judith Resnick, for example, the astronaut who was killed in the shuttle explosion in 1986. When I interviewed her father, he told me that when Judy was a little girl she loved to watch him fix things and wanted to learn how to do it herself. " 'Daddy, show me how,' she would say. So I taught her how to fix base plugs, do electrical wiring, and replace chain pulls when she was just a little girl," he said. "Later, when she was old enough to drive, she was interested in cars and automobile repair," he continued, "so I helped her there as well."

Finally, don't forget to play board games with your daughter that require strategic problem-solving such as chess, backgammon and Go, as well as some of the more sophisticated computer games. In addition, play card games with her that involve strategic planning or the ability to bluff. Try poker, gin, bridge, and pinochle.

Take her to a family fun center and teach her how to play pool. Pool and billiards not only teach strategic planning, but develop eye-hand coordination and, most important, teach principles of geometry.

STRATEGY #6: PROMOTE YOUR DAUGHTER'S PARTICIPATION IN TEAM SPORTS

While individual sports, such as gymnastics, ice-skating, tennis, swimming, and ballet—an art form that requires athletic ability— are excellent vehicles to teach girls physical discipline as well as what their bodies are capable of, it is too easy to drop out when the going gets rough. If one drops out of these sports, the only person to suffer the consequences of that action is the individual herself.

In team sports, however, there is pressure to persist. Each individual occupies a position on the team and has specific skills, so that bailing out causes the entire team to suffer the consequences. The team has a group identity, so that dropping out affects the emotional bond among all the other individuals. Team dynamics exert pressure to persist, even when the going gets tough, when you are unsure of yourself, when you feel that the situation will never change, when you just want to throw in the towel!

This kind of persistence in the face of difficulty, where one must push through one's customary comfort zones to attain a goal, is the very heart of mastery behavior. For years, boys have learned these skills from each other in team sports. Now girls can learn them as well.

In addition, participation in field sports can teach scientific and mathematical principles—spatial relationships, trajectory, speed, and impact—in an experiential way.

STRATEGY #7: PROMOTE GIRLS' TEAM SPORTS IN YOUR COMMUNITY

Encouraging girls in team sports will require some commitment on your part to promote the events themselves. Although this may seem tangential to you, it is an important aspect of motivating your daughter. Why? Because girls' team sports do not receive the community support that boys' sports do. Go to any middle school, junior high, or high school sporting event. You will see bleachers full of cheering fans at the boys' games but empty, cavernous gymnasiums for the girls' teams.

Obviously, from a player's point of view, it is more motivating, not to mention fun, to score points, spike balls, and sink baskets with a whole gymnasium of cheering fans supporting your efforts. Increasing attendance at girls' sporting events will directly help your daughter to stay interested. Think like a promoter. Below are ten ways to do that:

1. Get other parents involved in your promotional efforts.
2. Hold contests and give things away to promote ticket sales.
3. Hold a raffle.
4. Issue two-for-one coupons to girls' games.
5. Get sponsorship from a local business or organization that is willing to help you promote it.
6. Find a local sports celebrity willing to lend his or her name for publicity purposes.
7. Invite the sports celebrity to appear at a game and sign T-shirts.
8. Encourage your daughter's boyfriend to come to her games. Saying something like "Of course you are coming to Megan's soccer match on Saturday, aren't you? I'll pick you up if you need a ride," will have a subtle but powerful effect. Parental pressure can be very effective.
9. Bribe her brothers to attend her games and get them to bring their friends along. Promise them a trip to a local pizza hangout or something equally attractive.
10. Make your husband go to your daughter's games. Many dads also enjoy coaching.

CHAPTER 7

Mastering the Media

Ten Strategies for Media Resistance

I know it's silly and superficial to want to look like a model, but it would make life so much easier.

*Brie, fourteen-year-old workshop
participant*

The ongoing blitz of media images has a profound psychological influence on children, and these images are related to gender identification and self-esteem issues. Bear in mind that the term "media" includes television programming and advertising; magazines and newspapers and their ads, covers, and stories; books and book jackets; CD lyrics and jackets; and movies. Despite the wide range of forms, however, there are commonalities. All media

- Attempt to communicate something.
- Are likely to employ the art and science of persuasion.
- Are mostly visual.
- Are designed for mass appeal and consumption.
- Serve the needs of their sponsors and advertisers.

This last aim causes the most concern. The first four can be rather neutral in nature. Communication that uses visual persuasion and is designed to reach the maximum number of people is not necessarily harmful in and of itself. However, when communication is driven by the profit motive—funneled through the particular needs of a sponsor hungry to move the product at an ever-increasing pace—the techniques used to persuade us must come under serious question. Sponsors do not exist to educate or enlighten. Sponsors exist to create customers.

You may remember from an earlier discussion that sponsors have discovered that the most effective technique for turning females into consumers, particularly with regard to beauty products, is to lower their self-esteem, a technique they do not hesitate to employ. Naomi Wolf, in *The Beauty Myth,* postulates that the images of beauty created by the media are actually devices of social control. In other words, when women feel and act too powerful, too firmly in control of their lives, something has to be done to undermine their strength. According to Wolf, the images of beauty have served this function well, causing women to strive for physical perfection. This diverts them from more meaningful goals and causes them to spend their time, money, and energy in the foolhardy pursuit of a superficial and unattainable ideal.

At the same time, the media also reflect our cultural values concerning femininity and masculinity. In other words, the media send reflected appraisals back to all of us, adults and children alike. In the past, when television was young, the images it broadcast unconsciously perpetuated old stereotypes. Today television has matured, and the powers that be do nothing unconsciously or without premeditation. They are well aware of the psychology of their images and programming. Through incredibly expensive advertising campaigns utilizing focus groups and research studies, they measure each and every physiological response in viewers, including galvanic skin response, movement and dilation of the pupils, and areas of brain stimulation in order to gauge viewer reactions to the images they create. These masters of manipulation monitor and map our every twitch in response to their creations.

I say this as both a warning and a prelude. As a parent, do not be naive. Know what you are up against. Be aware of the following:

1. Enormous amounts of research, creativity, time, money, and motives go into sophisticated media productions.
2. The people who pay for media do not expend these vast amounts of money for nothing. They have agendas.
3. Children have no mechanisms through which to filter the messages of television's powerful images, so they are doubly vulnerable. They absorb them unknowingly, like sponges.

Our most potent weapon against the negative impact of sex-role stereotypes associated with the media is *awareness.* In a way, the very last thing sponsors want is for viewers to be sophisticated and capable of filtering out subtle messages! But of course that is the best reason to turn your daughter into a discriminating viewer at an early age, especially since one of the goals of mastery is to learn to use one's intelligence in the face of obstacles. What better place to utilize mastery skills and responses than in coping with media? Therefore, most of the strategies offered in this chapter provide ways to raise a child's awareness of the tactics media sponsors are using to turn every human on the planet into a consumer.

The Early Years: Media Resistance for Ages Four to Ten

STRATEGY #1: SLAY THE ELECTRONIC BEAST

My first recommendation is the most radical: remove the television from the house. Most households aren't prepared to do this, however, so I offer a second recommendation that may be nearly as difficult to accomplish: Postpone, as long as possible, your daughter's exposure to television, and limit the duration of the exposure. I know this will be difficult, and I don't want to make you feel guilty if your efforts fail. There are times when the television is the only available baby-sitter and you need the time, but until your children are old enough to learn to be critical viewers, which can begin surprisingly early, around age seven, it is best to keep them away from TV as much as possible. One strategy many modern mothers use is to allow their small children to watch only carefully screened videos. Look for enjoyable but educational videos that do not have tie-in merchandise or other commercial sponsors.

Pay particular attention to children's programming on Saturday morning. Its target audience is boys. Television executives know, as do their sponsors, that girls will watch shows aimed at boys, but boys will not watch shows aimed at girls. Boys consider girls' shows "stupid" and "wimpy." Remember, unless it appears on a public broadcasting channel, the purpose of a children's show is identical to the purpose of an adult show—to serve the needs of the sponsor and manipulate viewers to consume their product—not, as we might wish, to educate the young.

The Saturday morning shows targeted at boys are full of negative messages about females and femininity. The majority of characters are male, and worse, these male characters are adventurous, resourceful, enterprising, daring, and heroic, while the few female characters are usually watchful, cautious, and waiting to be rescued, not to mention shapely and beautiful. The women and girls are passive and decorative, not active and decisive. No wonder the boys begin to see girls as stupid and wimpy! As of this writing, there are few action-adventure series or weekly cartoons for young girls, with female leads in the role of rescuers, risk-takers, dare-devils, and heroines.

On Saturday mornings, when most kids watch cartoons, my advice to you is to find another activity. Make a family activity of concocting large and elaborate breakfasts that take a long time to prepare. Then sit down and eat them together as a family, with conversation, not in front of the television. Clean up together as a family as well. Make cleanup time fun by turning on music and dancing around the kitchen. When the weather is nice, go to the park or the zoo, or go hiking or cycling. Invite other kids over to play on Saturday mornings *with only one rule: no TV.* Challenge (or bribe?) older siblings to go one, two, or three weeks without television. Encourage them to play board games, card games, and charades instead of watching TV. Do whatever is required to keep young children otherwise occupied and away from the television.

You can shield your daughter for only so long, however. Even if you don't have a television in the house, she will watch it when she starts going to friends' houses. At that point, you must teach her to use her mind to buffer the negative messages, and you must create in her an awareness of the messages, both subtle and overt, that are being perpetrated.

"I have a son and a daughter," one mother said at one of my workshops. "We didn't have a TV for the first five years of my kids' lives. It was great. Eventually the inevitable happened. They started going over to other kids' houses to play or spend the night, and of course there was the television. My husband said that by forbidding TV we would make it so exotic that that would be all they wanted to do. So we bought one."

"How did it go?" asked the mom next to her.

"Well, we stuck it in an insignificant corner of a room we hardly ever go in, so they barely noticed it," she replied. "But what I really want to talk about was this little game we played."

STRATEGY #2: TV GAMES FOR THE ENLIGHTENED

What Lie Are They Telling Us Now?

"Whenever a commercial came on, we played What Lie Are They Telling Us Now? The kids got it right away, even when they were little. Like one time, during a fast-food commercial, my five-year-old son said, 'They're trying to tell us we can go out and buy better food than we can make at home!' We all laughed and jeered as if that was the stupidest thing we ever heard.

"Of course they were very young, but even now that they are older, they pay very little attention to the television. And they don't bug us for every toy they see."

I think this is a wonderfully subversive little game, and I pass it along to you. If you play What Lie Are They Telling Us Now? with your kids, especially during commercials, over time, your daughter will become sharply critical and discriminating. (Your son, too.) Eventually it will become second nature to your kids to question the images, motives, and messages of advertisers.

Would He Do That?

I bring this game to you from my first book, *How to Father a Successful Daughter,* because many parents have said they found it useful and fun. It is productive and worthwhile, and children enjoy it.

Here is how it's played: When a commercial comes on, imagine the characters as the opposite sex. For example, if a woman is writhing around on top of a car and purring into the camera about her "relationship" with this car, imagine that it is a man instead who is writhing and purring. Instantly, it becomes quite obvious that (1) the woman is being used to sell the car, not the attributes of the car itself, and (2) women get put in ridiculous situations to sell products.

This can be done with any form of advertising, not just television commercials. For example, one day, while standing in line at the post office I noticed a poster. On it were four caricatures, three men and a token woman. Above the first man, who appeared to be angry and was waving his fist, appeared the word, "Complaints?" Above the second man, who had a lightbulb glowing above his head, appeared the word "Suggestions?" Above the third man, who wore a pensive, contemplative look, appeared the word "Questions?" Above the woman, who was beaming a smile at the viewer, appeared the word "Compliments?" If you imagine women in the first three roles, as those with the complaints, the bright ideas, and the questions, and a man in the role of beaming compliments, it becomes obvious that women are placed in very limited and constricted roles.

Obviously, sometimes, sex switching won't make a difference in the theme or message of the commercial. But more often than not, it will. Most importantly, this game will teach kids to see through the limited, narrow, and often silly roles into which women and girls are placed by the demands of advertising and sexism.

On rare occasions, this switching of roles has been done by the advertisers themselves. For instance, there is a famous Diet Pepsi commercial during which the women in an office gather at the same time every day to watch a hunky construction worker drink his Diet Pepsi bare-chested.

Fathers in my workshops often object to this commercial, saying things like "Two wrongs don't make a right. I don't want my daughter thinking it's all right for them to objectify a man if it's not all right for a man to objectify a woman." The mothers generally don't object. What do you think?

STRATEGY #3: DECONSTRUCTING DISNEY?

There are other types of cartoons that can carry negative messages besides the television cartoons on Saturday morning. The original feature-length Disney cartoons reissued by the studio to enchant new audiences present a challenge to me as a culture critic because Disney movies are so well loved. I agree that no one can charm like Disney. Yet, like old television reruns on cable, which we will discuss in a moment, the classic Disney movies are rife with old-fashioned, conventional sex roles that were acceptable years ago. Even some of the modern Disney offerings must be viewed with discrimination.

While *Snow White* and *Cinderella,* with their prince-to-the-rescue themes are obvious, many Disney animated films are more subtle but equally oppressive. Take *Lady and the Tramp,* for instance, a truly charming love story that is, unfortunately, replete with stereotypes. Tramp is a stray—independent, footloose, a bon vivant, live-by-his-wits, man-about-town. Lady is a quiet, lovely, well-bred, well-groomed, loving, and obedient pet who takes good care of her humans. He is carefree, spontaneous, and irresponsible. She is dependable, nurturing, and willing to accept responsibility. Lady "civilizes" the reluctant Tramp by making a family man out of him.

Even some of the recent fare, such as *Beauty and the Beast,* sends a stereotypical message that a woman should look beyond the physical characteristics and beastly behavior of her man to see the true, lovable person inside, because through her love and devotion, Beauty can transform the Beast.

How often do we see leading male characters looking beyond physical imperfection to see the beautiful woman inside—except for *The Truth about Cats and Dogs,* which perpetuated another stereotype: smart women are ugly, and beautiful women are dumb. More importantly, however, is this question: should the message be sent to *anyone* to look beyond or put up with beastly behavior? Isn't this just a setup? While there may indeed be a good person inside, many women have suffered persistent abuse because they have bought into the myth that they could transform their mates through love and devotion. When I taught school I learned that some girls seek "outlaw" types because they want adventure. Unfortunately, they also believe they can turn their outlaw into a loving escort through the power of their love.

In *Aladdin,* a highly entertaining and lavish cartoon, a token scene is offered in which Princess Jasmine appears to be an independent young woman longing for her own adventures. In fact, the rest of the movie depicts her passively tagging along with Aladdin on his magic rug and falling in love with him. There is no doubt that *he* is the one for whom adventure waits. She just happens to be along for the ride because she is beautiful enough to have won his love, thereby becoming his chosen companion. We are left to presume that, without him, she would still be sitting by her fountain, singing sad songs and pining for adventure.

These cartoons will begin to shape your daughter's (and your son's) beliefs and attitudes about how females behave (nurturing, caring, passive, and willing to look beyond beastly behavior) and how males behave (irresponsible, beastly, or risk-taking).

Wait until your daughter is a little older to take her to animated features. By the time she is seven, she'll be better able to handle questions, what-ifs, and fantasies about the other ways to view these movies, such as "Wouldn't it be neat if Princess Jasmine had her own flying carpet?" or "What would you do, or where would you go, if you had a flying carpet?" When she begins to use her intellect as a filter to clarify the hidden messages of movies and cartoons, you can try some of the following cartoon discussion questions to get you going.

Lady and the Tramp

1. If you were going to create some adventures for Lady, what would they be?
2. How is Tramp a good father? Do the puppies love him? Does Tramp love them?
3. If Lady left the puppies with their father for a couple of weeks, what might she go and do?
4. What signs of strength does Lady show?
5. Would you rather be Lady or Tramp? Why?

Beauty and the Beast

1. How would the story be different if Beauty were male and Beast were female?
2. Do you think a non-beautiful female can be beautiful on the inside? What might be some beautiful inner characteristics? If she had those traits, would that make her beautiful on the outside too, like the way the beast was transformed into a prince?
3. Which is more important: beauty on the outside or beauty on the inside? Is this true for both girls and boys?
4. What makes a beautiful person? Is beauty different for boys and girls?

Aladdin

1. Where would you go if you had a flying carpet?
2. How many ways would you use a genie if you found one?
3. What would a female genie be like? Describe her powers. Would they be the same or different?

4. What would the story be like if Princess Jasmine had found the genie instead of Aladdin?

5. Where would Princess Jasmine take Aladdin? Could she go there alone?

A Very Special Cartoon

This is a perfect place for me to plug a favorite TV show, which also just happens to be animated: that satiric, subversive, hilarious cartoon series, *The Simpsons.* I believe *The Simpsons* has suffered a bad rap from many parents who have never even watched it and are missing a terrific opportunity to present an excellent role model for their daughters—the character of eight-year-old Lisa Simpson.

I am aware of the concern some parents express over the character of Bart Simpson, and I believe they are justified. I would agree that, although Bart is lovable in his own way, parents might not want their ten-year-old boy emulating that rascal, cute though he may be.

On the other hand, it doesn't take much time to discover that it is the female characters on the show who carry the torch of enlightened thinking. Marge Simpson is a good mother who tries hard to be a positive role model and encourages both her children. Even Marge's two "spinster sisters" do not tolerate male ignorance or dominance and are quite funny. However, it is Lisa Simpson who is truly the smartest, most thoughtful, best-informed, and most enlightened member of the family.

Lisa Simpson gets good grades, plays blues on the saxophone, tries to enlighten her ignorant father, is a vegetarian and an animal rights activist, protests injustice wherever she finds it, stands up for herself against her recalcitrant and attention-seeking older brother and his self-centered friends, and is an altogether smart, ambitious, playful, adventurous, warm, funny, polite, clever, and compassionate little girl. Okay, I admit it. Lisa Simpson is my role model!

In one episode, a parody of the controversy that erupted over the Teen Talk Barbie of a few years ago who said, "Math is tough," Lisa becomes outraged that her new talking Malibu Stacey doll says sexist things like "Don't ask me, I'm just a girl (giggle, giggle)!" Lisa, encouraged by her mother, Marge, marches off to the manufacturer and complains in person, demanding that the doll be changed. Utterly ignored by the corporate hierarchy, Lisa seeks out the creator of the doll, who, it turns out, is also disenchanted with the persona her creation has acquired. Together they design a new doll named Lisa Lionheart. The manufacturer decides to use Lisa's voice for the new talking doll. During a recording session, they give Lisa a script to read in which she must say, "When I marry, I want to keep my own name." Lisa pauses thoughtfully, then suggests a change: "This should probably read, 'If I *choose* to marry, I will keep my own name.'"

In this episode, as in many others, Lisa is smart, takes risks, takes action, and has faith in her ability to influence outcomes. She sees through sham and tells the truth about what she sees. She is one savvy little girl.

Therefore, for its mostly positive images of women and girls, I recommend *The Simpsons* as a good show for girls, starting at age seven or eight. Older boys—say, twelve and over—will also enjoy the show and will probably have acquired enough developmental maturity to see through Bart's escapades and not be tempted to emulate him. Use your judgment here.

STRATEGY #4: SITCOM RERUNS—MORE THAN JUST NOSTALGIA

Beware of the messages embedded in the old sitcoms being rerun on cable television—*The Andy Griffith Show, Bewitched, I Dream of Jeannie, Dick Van Dyke, Leave It to Beaver,* and *Lassie,* among others. These old favorites of the fifties, sixties, and seventies portray traditional, stereotyped sex roles that perpetuate many negative images of femininity. TV has been one of the slowest mediums to respond to changes in sex roles. Perhaps this is so because programming decisions are made primarily by men in suits or because over 80 percent of comedy writers continue to be male.[1]

Today's television sitcoms are much better. (Thank you, Roseanne—a true pioneer who broke the ground.) Sitcom writers have discovered that exposing gender stereotypes and poking fun at gender roles can be an almost limitless source of jokes. Of course, they do this with greater and lesser degrees of sophistication, but for the most part, they do display modern awareness of stereotypes and changing sex roles and use this awareness as a source of comedic inspiration.

If you observe your daughter watching an old rerun and you

notice traditional or negative messages about femininity, act quickly. Speak up. Point them out. Teach her how to question the dramatic or comedic situations. When your daughter is old enough, casually pose the questions below to evaluate the messages being broadcast. You needn't sit down and proceed through them all at once or make it seem like a quiz. Just bring them up every now and then.

- What do the women do? Do they work? Inside the home or outside?
- Are their opinions sought? Do other characters heed their advice?
- Are the women in control of their lives, or do others control their lives?
- Are they powerful or submissive?
- Are they presented with opportunities to show courage and daring?
- Do women and girls have adventures? If so, what kind?
- Are they taken care of by others, or do they take care of themselves?
- Are the women attractive? If not, what is their status?
- Are women and girls funny because they are incompetent, silly, or make bad decisions?

Although I guarantee that the conversations initiated by questions like these will not always evolve according to your expectations or elicit the responses you want to hear, they *will* engage the mind of your daughter—and your sons, too. Questions such as these will activate a girl's intellectual curiosity and increase her aptitude for thoughtful criticism—skills of rational thinking and problem-solving. Even though your daughter will not always say what you want to hear, she will at least be pondering these subjects, which will help to filter out the impact of negative messages. In addition, these discussions will give you the opportunity to find out what kind of gender beliefs, and thus sex-role identification, she is carrying around inside her head.

When your daughter expresses viewpoints that you wish to correct (be careful here), go about it by posing more questions or by saying, "What about…" or "What if…" or "Suppose…" rather than by engaging in an argument. Arguing will only tend to make her more intractable or cause her to assert her position with greater force. Posing questions has the advantage, particularly as she gets older, of keeping her open and inquisitive. With a little practice you will become proficient at asking the kinds of questions that will make your daughter and your son think about the images they see and question the motives and values of those producing the images.

The Pressure Continues: Media Resistance for Ages Eleven to Eighteen

As your daughter matures, the absurd messages and relentless pressure will continue, even escalate. Your daughter will need continuing help in staying resilient and resisting the influences of some of the worst vehicles of negative sex-role stereotypes still in store for her: romance novels, soap operas, rock and rap lyrics, and of course the endless procession of emaciated magazine models who parade across the screens of the collective female psyche.

Let's start with the supermodels, those super-thin, super-fit, super-beautiful anomalies we first mentioned in discussing reflected appraisals.

I wish I could report differently but the truth is, I doubt that, short of a feminist revolution, we can eliminate the deadly consequences to girls of this relentless procession of beautiful, thin, large-breasted, tiny-torsoed, long-legged, thin-nosed, big-eyed, big-haired, pouty-mouthed, usually blond icons of perfection. Can we ameliorate the effects? Of course. Can we eliminate them? I doubt it. It would probably be more effective to foment the revolution instead. But I digress.

Our first problem is that these images are everywhere—TV, movies, posters, newspaper ads, magazines, billboards, any medium where a visual representation is used to capture our attention and hold it. In an increasingly visual society, this problem is not going to go away any time soon. In addition to presenting these images, the media—and particularly advertisers—bombard viewers with what appears to be the payoff of good looks: glamorous lifestyle, sandy beaches, tropical breezes, heaps of adoring males, "love," and what passes as a sort of generic happiness.

The job of adults who care about girls is to begin in every way possible to divest these images of their power. There are a number of ways to do this. One method bears repeating: raise your daughter's awareness of the techniques employed by advertisers to lower female self-esteem in order to get their money. It is as simple and as crass as that.

When you watch television or thumb through magazines with your daughter, ask her the following questions.

STRATEGY #5: WHAT ARE THE SUPERMODELS TELLING US?

- What do the advertisers want us to believe about the woman in this ad?
- What lies is the advertiser telling us in this commercial?
- What diabolical scheme does this ad reveal?
- How are advertisers trying to make you believe you need something more than just your own natural self to attract boys?
- Who are they using to try to make you feel bad about yourself?
- What ridiculous fantasy about women is being perpetrated here?
- What is the symbolism of this ad?
- How is the advertiser trying to lower your self-esteem in this ad?
- What lie does this sponsor want you to believe so that you will go out and spend your money on this product?

When you encounter a magazine ad or a TV commercial featuring an emaciated, waiflike model, say, "Look at that poor girl. They force her to starve herself to make a lot of money. It's not worth it. There are many other ways to make a lot of money." Then perhaps follow with a discussion of all the different ways your daughter can think of to make money. Or say, "They are trying to make you believe that the only way to get guys to notice you is to starve yourself. You can be healthy, active, interesting, funny, and charming. Guys like that as well."

Another effective tactic is to tell your daughter the real-life secrets of the fashion industry—the physical hardships and crushing boredom endured by models. A woman I interviewed who had worked in the fashion business told me the following stories, and I pass them along to you to share with your daughter. The first involved a photo shoot for winter clothes. The shoot took place in August in order to be ready in time for winter magazine deadlines. The second took place in November for the summer line.

"We were at Grant's tomb in August. It's all cement. The temperature was ninety-five degrees, and the humidity was unbearably high as well. The poor models were dressed in cashmere leggings, wool coats, knit hats, and boots. They had to run up some steps, jump in the air and run back over and over and over in that punishing heat. And they had to look happy about it.

"We had to have ice packs available for them when they fainted! If they indicated any discomfort, they were out of there. No complaining was tolerated.

"The same thing happened when they did the shoots for the summer line. There we were out at Coney Island on a wet and windy day in November. The models were dressed in these gauzy little outfits and were freezing to death, but they had to stand around for hours while the photographers got their equipment ready, waited for the right light, or positioned the models and the props.

"Models are treated like horses or some kind of commodity. The only ones who are treated with any respect whatsoever are the supermodels who have attained a whole different level of achievement, and even they are not coddled like people think. What's worse is that, in many cases, it is other women oppressing them. Little old anorexic ladies in Chanel suits treating these girls like pieces of meat."

Arming your daughter with this kind of information about the real world of the fashion industry will help deglamorize it. Don't forget to tell her about the short professional life of models as well. Like dancers, many of them are considered has-beens by age thirty. Make her aware that modeling is a temporary profession only.

Finally, teach your daughter to appreciate the physical evidence of health and vigor by encouraging them to admire all types of female bodies: big-boned and muscular, slender and lithe, round but strong. Also, draw her attention to the beauty of older female bodies that have been well maintained and are healthy, strong, and vigorous so that she sees beauty as a result of health and fitness, not youth and thinness.

STRATEGY #6: ENLIST DAD'S HELP

Be sure to enlist the participation of your daughter's father in the endeavor to keep her self-esteem intact during the onslaught of puberty and the media emphasis on looks, since she will be listening to discern what males approve of, and her father will be one more male whose opinion counts. Since she will almost certainly need reassurance about her maturing body, especially by a male, he should express his approval of her in appropriate ways, saying things like, "You're looking so pretty I'm going to have to keep the boys away with a baseball bat someday!" or "Lookin' good today, honey," when she makes an effort to get dressed up or look good for a special event.

While this may seem like pandering to the forces that place greater value on beauty in girls than on intelligence, it need not be so. He should not stop praising her accomplishments, but he must also talk to her *where she is coming from.* That means recognizing that her culture has placed pressure on her regarding her appearance, and her father can help keep that stress at a minimum by freely giving his approval. Keeping her self-esteem high means letting her know that the young woman she is about to become is attractive.

Her father must studiously guard himself never to tease her about her body, even if it is meant in fun. As you know from having been a teenage girl yourself, she will not interpret it as "all in fun." Most importantly, he must never make subtle remarks about losing weight, for this can trigger panic in his daughter. It can also present a dangerous precedent for eating disorders.

He should openly express approval of female forms that are strong, healthy, vigorous, and active. He can also make critical remarks about the models on television: "She's too skinny," "She looks like a skeleton," "She doesn't look healthy and strong," or "Strong, healthy females are more attractive than victims of starvation." Feel free to coach him.

There will be more advice regarding dads and their influence on beauty issues in Chapter 10, on puberty, but for now just make him aware that his praise of strong, healthy, active females counts heavily as a male opinion and will contribute to a healthy body image for his daughter.

Song Lyrics

Rock-and-roll and rap lyrics and music videos composed and created by men seek to establish and perpetuate male dominance. They venerate it. While this may or may not be conscious on the part of those who write lyrics and create music videos, it is the result. Many lyrics by all-male groups condone and even promote violence against women. A large number of music videos portray women as objects for men to do with as they please. These are dark forces to which your daughter will become increasingly exposed as she matures.

Luckily, the pop music scene is no longer a bastion of male dominance. Many, though not all, new female recording artists offer provocative and even aggressive rebuttals. A female singer who uses her lyrics to resist male dominance or question the purpose of the beauty cult can be an effective role model and an ally in the fight to keep your daughter mastery-oriented. These singers can be particularly potent because so many teenage girls identify with and try to emulate them.

Become familiar with the lyrics of the artists and the bands your daughter listens to. When she gets interested in MTV, watch it with her and use some of the questions that appear in the supermodel section earlier in this chapter.

Rap, in particular, often contains angry lyrics that undermine girls. Give your daughter and her friends the opportunity to make their own angry statement; to be active rather than passive; to exercise their right to judge others, just as they are judged by others; to think of themselves as *other than* a physical object of desire. How can you do this? Read on.

STRATEGY #7: RAPPING

Challenge your daughter and her friends to write some rap lyrics about the boys they know. They could even write a rap song, rehearse it, and perform it at a school talent show. Be sure you check it out first, though, to make sure they haven't used profanity, a staple of rap music. Encourage them to tell it like it is and to have fun by making the drum and rhythm sounds with their mouths and hands like the real rap performers do. They can add dance or a homemade video if they choose.

Danger and Passion: The Romance Novel

> Favel Farrington knew very little about her new husband... who had swept her into marriage with the fierceness of a summer storm.... [T]here was something calculating in him, perhaps a streak of malice. She came to believe later that he fascinated her so quickly because she could not be sure of him and it took her a very long time to discover what sort of man he really was.
>
> (From *Bride of Pendoric,* by Victoria Holt)

Romance novels, which exploit in a dangerous way the restless desire for adventure that arises naturally in teenage girls, become popular with them during adolescence. Although romance novels have evolved over the years to reflect changing social values, mothers need to make certain that teenagers understand the elements in them that an adult would recognize as pure fantasy. One of these elements is the formulaic persona of the leading male character, the one who becomes the heroine's love interest and who must be mysterious, unpredictable, and potentially dangerous. The heroine, unsure whether he can be trusted, is excited by this challenge. This is what makes him desirable and gives him an edge over regular, "boring" men.

Once the meeting has taken place, the heroine must endure a series of challenges that test her belief in him. Often she must look beyond his beastly behavior. He must continue to act in mysterious ways that are difficult to interpret. He must be changeable, and he may even place her in jeopardy. In the end, of course, he turns out to be a good guy after all, but this is dangerous stuff and a counterproductive way for girls to challenge themselves. It is also a variation on the love-as-redemptive-of-another theme that began with *Beauty and the Beast*.

If your daughter likes romance novels, you must read them too. Once you have read one she is currently reading, casually mention you picked up one of her books. Don't be heavy-handed. In a humorous tone, mock the formula—teenagers love to mock things—and point out to her how silly it is to try to satisfy a desire for adventure through taming dangerous men. Here are some suggested comments to get you started.

STRATEGY #8: POKE FUN AT ROMANCE NOVELS

- I picked up the book you've been reading. I can't believe the way they make women seem in those romance novels—as if their only opportunity for adventure in life is to get it through a guy. They must think women are just a bunch of wimps.
- Wouldn't you rather have your own adventures in life? Who wants to have to depend on some guy for excitement and adventure? Make your own. Go climb a mountain or invent something or see the world. Now there's real adventure!
- Can you believe the way those romance novels set women up for danger by making potentially abusive guys seem glamorous and exciting? There's nothing exciting about being hurt, either physically or emotionally.
- Those romance novels are so bogus I can't believe it. In real life, men who seem potentially dangerous (a) usually are, (b) are unlikely to change, and (c) cause pain and suffering, not pleasure. Good guys are the ones who are pleasurable and fun. Bad guys are just a drag.
- Men do not satisfy their desire for adventure through their *relationships.*

Soap Operas and Talk Shows

Soap operas are not slice-of-life dramas. They do not depict the way real people make choices and act in their lives. You know that and I know that, but does your daughter know that? Since most kids have no way of knowing what constitutes realistic behavior among adults, other than their parents, you will need to help your daughter see daytime and prime-time soap operas for what they are— *entertainment only.* Help your daughter to understand that because soap operas must hold the viewers' attention from one episode to the next, they must create unrelenting suspense. They do this by leaving the viewer with an unanswered question at the end of each episode. Furthermore, they rely heavily on continuous crises as well as melodramatic villains, unrealistic heroes, and highly charged sexual situations.

You want your daughter to realize that the characters on soap operas are highly dysfunctional. They behave in ways that are almost exactly the opposite of the behavior of healthy, rational people. To meet the dramatic requirements of the writers who must endlessly prolong the suspense, the characters make terrible, often ridiculous, choices based on emotions unleavened with rational thought. Often they are the worst emotions: jealousy, greed, envy, and paranoia. Furthermore, they frequently resort to the romance-novel formula of making dangerous men seem attractive. Were you to encounter one of these characters in real life, you would probably turn and run in the opposite direction.

STRATEGY #9: EXPOSE THE SOAPS

Mark Twain once said, "Against the assault of laughter, nothing can stand." So stage an assault against the ridiculous notion that soap operas represent realistic adult behavior by mocking, jeering, deriding, and making fun of the characters and situations. If your daughter is old enough to understand sarcasm, it is okay, even appropriate and effective, to employ it. Take advantage of this form of humor loved by adolescents and use it against the ridiculous scenarios and characters of soap operas. Here are some comments to get you started:

- I sure am glad we have these soap opera characters to show us how to behave in life. Otherwise we might be tempted to behave in a rational manner.
- Wouldn't you just love to have a best friend who acted like that?
- Boy, there's a great role model.
- Now, that's what I call rational decision-making.
- Don't you wish you could be as self-centered [or greedy or paranoid] as she is?
- Those writers will do anything to get you to tune in tomorrow!
- It's a good thing this is just entertainment. Otherwise it would insult your intelligence.

Like soap operas, many talk shows inflate their ratings by falsely generating suspense. (At least in a soap opera we know it is fiction.) Also, like soap opera characters, many talk-show guests are downright dysfunctional and even mentally ill. Will this one call that one a name? Swear at him? Shove her? Hit him? Throw a chair? Shoot someone after the show? Obviously, we do not want our children to believe that people on talk shows set the standards for adult behavior.

At the same time, there are a few talk shows that attempt to deal responsibly with *issues,* not personal vendettas or private behavioral dysfunction. When a talk show conscientiously avoids sensationalism most of the time, when it consistently deals with issues by educating and edifying the audience, when it utilizes experts to explain behaviors and raise them to a conceptual level—and not just during the last five minutes of the show—then, perhaps it can be considered acceptable viewing. Unfortunately, this is not usually the case.

If your daughter gets hooked on some sleazy talk show, remind her of realities like ratings and sponsors. Make her aware of the theatrical illusions promoted by producers. Make her aware that producers often encourage guests to argue to make the show more exciting. On one talk show, which shall remain nameless here, before I went on the air, the producers took me aside and told me to "Create some excitement. People just love that." The more knowledge your daughter has, the less likely she is to believe the illusion created when "information" becomes entertainment.

STRATEGY #10: RECOMMEND SHOWS WITH POSITIVE ROLE MODELS

Throughout this book I have made suggestions for giving your daughter positive images of adventurous women as a counterbalance to negative, stereotyped, and helpless images and as a counterbalance to the myriad action heroes boys have as role models. Here are my recommendations of good films and TV shows that have successfully overcome these stereotypes and promoted female role models that are good for your daughter.

Let's begin with some sitcoms that have become part of popular culture. You are probably already familiar with *Roseanne* and *Mur-*

phy Brown and *Dr. Quinn, Medicine Woman*. And don't forget Lisa Simpson.

Three more TV role models worth mentioning are Xena, Warrior Princess, Captain Janeway of *Star Trek: Voyager* as well as some other female *Star Trek* characters, and Sally, lieutenant to the high commander on *3rd Rock from the Sun*.

Xena: Warrior Princess is actually a spin-off of *Hercules: The Legendary Journeys* and was designed precisely to offer girls a hero of their own. The show opens with Xena charging along on her trusty steed while the voice-over intones, "A land in turmoil cried out for a hero. She was Xena, a warrior princess forged in the heat of battle. Her courage would change the world." Xena looks like the classic Amazon. She is big-boned and towers over most of the men she encounters. Her mission is to fight injustice in her world of mythological beasts and villains. Xena has a trusty sidekick, Gabrielle, an orphan she rescued. Although Gabrielle is physically smaller and younger, she proves herself time and again, aiding Xena in her adventures. Gabrielle is an excellent role model for younger girls or girls who are slight in stature. In one episode, Gabrielle turns out to be the heir to the Amazon throne, so the series shows her growing up from a scared orphan into a powerful woman in her own right.

The world of science fiction can also offer role models for girls. Formerly a bastion of scantily clad alien females, more recent science fiction offers images of strong women, including Sarah Connor, who trains herself to be a combat fighter in the *Terminator* movies, to Dana Scully, the medical researcher and FBI agent of *The X-Files*. However, the *Star Trek* series stand out above the rest. *Star Trek* has been at the cutting edge of social trends from its inception, when the original *Star Trek* featured a multiracial crew. Unfortunately, however, the original series ran before the women's movement and so contains many outdated images of women. You'll need to do the same deconstructing work with this series that was necessary with the other older TV series.

Captain Kathryn Janeway of *Star Trek: Voyager* couldn't be a better role model. She is strong and in command while always remaining calm and respectful of the special talents and skills of her crew. Captain Janeway has a more difficult challenge than her male predecessors. Her ship is lost in space, far from the Federation of Planets and support of Starfleet. She must rely on her own resources to guide her ship and crew safely home, a responsibility that includes dealing diplomatically with races who know nothing of the Federation and using necessary force when the ship is threatened.

The other two series also have strong female role models. *Star Trek: The Next Generation* has two female senior crew members, Beverly Crusher, the ship's doctor, who is also a single mother, and Deanna Troi, the ship's counselor. This series also features the wonderful Whoopi Goldberg as Guinan, the resident bartender. *Next Generation* also gave us the first female chief of security, Tasha Yar, who was killed in the line of duty. *Star Trek: Deep Space Nine* has two female senior officers, Lieutenant Dax and Major Kira, formerly a freedom fighter for her people, the Bajorans, when their planet was occupied by a hostile race, and also Keiko O'Brien, a botanist. Female admirals, ambassadors, scientists, and politicians are often presented in featured or cameo roles. Indeed all three of these series show a mix of women, many of whom have families as well as important careers.

Sally on *3rd Rock from the Sun* is valuable as both role model and instructor to your daughter because she exposes sex-role stereotypes in a humorous yet unrelentingly honest and clear-eyed fashion. This is possible because Sally, an alien, is a macho military type, who, in her mission on earth, gets stuck inhabiting a female body. Of course, she has absolutely no idea how she is supposed to behave. She is constantly outraged by the inequities she witnesses in her role as a woman, and she has no qualms about voicing her indignation. "Why do I have to be the one to be the woman?" she shouts at the high commander.

In no way does Sally ever appear helpless. In one episode, for example, she realizes that she is the only family member who will be unable to relax and enjoy herself on Thanksgiving Day, instead being expected to slave away in the kitchen by herself. "Oh, great," she says, "yet another perk of being a woman," and, as a lieutenant, she orders other family members to help her.

In another episode, mistaking her role in an upcoming school bake sale, she whips into shape a crew of homemakers and transforms them into a well-oiled, highly disciplined military machine. She blows whistles, has them doing push-ups and marching in file in the school cafeteria, addresses them as "Men," and has them saluting and yelling "Yes, sir!" Before the bake sale she delivers to her troops a stirring speech that's worthy of a great general like Patton or a legendary coach like Vince Lombardi. Her troops hold the most profitable bake sale in the history of the school. For her role as a character who exposes stereotyped sex roles, Sally is unsurpassed.

The movies I have chosen to recommend have protagonists who are contemporary female warrior characters. The movies are *A Little Princess, The Secret of Roan Inish, Fried Green Tomatoes, Heart Like a Wheel, Thelma and Louise,* and *The Silence of the Lambs.* The first two will be enjoyed by girls ages six to eight or older, the third and fourth can be handled by girls of around nine or older, and the last two should be postponed for viewing by girls over twelve—*The Silence of the Lambs* because of its sheer terror and *Thelma and Louise* because of the graphic and violent rape scene. In all of them, the female lead character is a mastery-oriented risk-taker who rescues another female or a whole group of people. In both *A Little Princess* and *The Secret of Roan Inish* a young girl sets the example. In *Roan Inish* the female child-as-heroine rescues an entire town! In *Heart Like a Wheel,* we see the true story of female risk-taker par excellence, Shirley Muldowney, the race-car driver, her inspiring relationship with her father, and the struggles she endured to become a seventeen-time National Hot Rod Association national champion and three-time world champion. What makes *Fried Green Tomatoes, The Silence of the Lambs,* and *Thelma and Louise* special is the unique element of lead characters who are *female rescuers of other females.* Men do not rush in at the last moment to save the day. The cinematic experiences created for girls by these movies are powerful and moving, and I highly recommend them.

CHAPTER 8

Not for Boys Only

Ten Strategies for Developing the Thinking Skills of Mastery

Kids are a lot smarter than you think. They don't know what they *can't* do.

Nicole, age fourteen

There are two types of thinking skills that promote mastery. The first contributes to resilience and persistence. It is based on the knowledge that learning sometimes entails confusion, and success includes some failures along the way. The second is a set of intellectual capacities that contribute to problem-solving and generate multiple solutions.

Both types of thinking skills are equally important. The first increases motivation; the second generates desired outcomes. This chapter will offer strategies to develop both.

Age Five and Under

You can begin cultivating your daughter's mastery-oriented thinking skills at the very moment of her birth. Although her first needs are physical—hunger, warmth, and sleep—her emotional need for love and safety are just as important, especially in the establishment of a strong and resilient personality. If her physical needs are provided for and the requirements for love and safety are met, then trust in herself, the very cornerstone of self-efficacy, will grow.

While this may seem self-evident, meeting physical needs and responding lovingly to her cries (a positive reinforcement) will send her the message that she can communicate her needs to others and that the external world is safe and responsive. She learns that she has some control over her environment and thus can affect events that concern her. Remember, crying is an infant's only means of communicating her needs to you, so respond positively.

Minding Her Mind

The latest research on brain development indicates that as early as the infant stage, the brain's capacity to develop cognitively, to absorb and process information, and to learn language, math, and music is truly awesome. Furthermore, this astounding capacity is present *from birth* and has already been progressing by age three. Your response to your baby's need for stimulation will have future repercussions on your daughter's capacity to fully develop.

Bear in mind that the windows of opportunity for learning certain types of thinking—logical, mathematical, physical, emotional, linguistic, musical—open and close during certain critical stages.[1] They are as follows:

Physical and motor (with some spatial):	Birth to 5 years
Emotional:	Birth to 2 years
Social:	Birth to 2½ years
Linguistic (first language sounds):	3 months to 3 years
Linguistic (second language vocabulary):	6 months to 9 years
Math and logic (with some spatial):	1 year to 4 years
Music:	3 years to 9 years

As early as possible, take advantage of the phenomenal brain development that occurs in early childhood and read to your daughter, talk to her, and interact with her. Provide a wide variety of stimuli to ignite her brain functions, such as those discussed below. The list of strategies may seem overwhelming, but you do not need to do every one. Pick and choose. Pay attention to which ones your daughter likes best. Have fun!

STRATEGY #1: USING MULTIPLE STIMULI

Children learn through many different avenues—visual, auditory, and kinesthetic (touch)—so provide stimuli in all three areas. This will keep all of her channels of perception open and receptive to learning.

For example, when you set your baby girl on the floor with playthings, be sure you present a variety of kinesthetic stimuli: a cold metal jar lid, a warm, fuzzy sock, a rough pot scrubber (not steel wool), a soft sponge, a smooth ball, or a hard rock. When you choose a mobile for her crib, be sure it has visual stimuli in many colors, shapes, and sizes. Create visual stimuli at floor level by taping colorful pictures from magazines on your lower kitchen cabinets and walls for her to look at when she is sitting on the floor. You can even match a picture with a word. For example, tape up a picture of a dog with the word written under it. Although this may seem a bit much for a baby, it is not unusual for gifted children to teach themselves to read by age three, so help them along. Many parents are taken by surprise when their child spontaneously reads a sentence out loud. Provide auditory stimuli by talking to her in a variety of tones: soft, high, low, funny cartoon voices, or dialects. If you are bilingual or multilingual, by all means speak to her in many languages. Make funny sounds. See if she can mimic them. Whistle and sing to her a variety of songs, not just soft, soothing lullabies but also soul-stirring college fight songs and national anthems. Play her music from Bach and Mozart to rock and roll. The more variety of sensory stimuli she has, the more developed her future abilities will become. But remember to be sensitive to your daughter's reactions. Infants, just like adults, have different thresholds for stimulation. In other words, some infants can become overstimulated. This can stress your baby unnecessarily. Be sensitive to behavior indicating stress: fussing, crying, expressions of fear or panic.

STRATEGY #2: SPORTS, GAMES, PHYSICAL EXERTION, AND THE BRAIN

Increasingly vigorous physical activity will be coupled with the continued need for intellectual stimulation as she matures. In reality, separating these two areas of development—the physical and the intellectual—is a false demarcation. Physical activity and cognitive growth are linked. I mentioned earlier that games and sports serve to prepare the brain for learning certain types of thinking skills. Brain research has shown that when kids are physically active—that is, physically involved with what they are learning as well as in daily exercise—they perform better in school. The physicality of childhood is hardwired to the brain development, so one encourages the other.

For example, research has shown that participating in field sports enables a brain to grasp and understand spatial relationships. Fine motor skills, on the other hand, may aid in the ability to read. Understanding music, which contains mathematical relationships, facilitates the ability to understand and intuit math and vice versa. Reading music, which has a language of its own, is also a cross-brain activity, utilizing both the left and right sides of the brain. Therefore, do not be reluctant to allow your daughter to engage in vigorous physical activity. In addition to its being a natural way to expend energy, it makes a profound contribution to brain development.

STRATEGY #3: ENCOURAGE ARTISTIC EXPRESSION

Do not insist that she always stay inside the lines when coloring. There are times when she should try to stay inside the lines to develop fine motor skills and eye-hand coordination, but also let her break out of the lines to encourage breaking through false boundaries. Stimulate her to draw her own version of the picture or change the one she is coloring in some way.

Encourage her artistic expression in a big way, not just small drawings on tablet-size paper. Put up a large blackboard, dry-erase board, or canvas in her room so that she has a large and expansive area in which to express herself, rather than just in a small, feminine, way. When she gets older, you might even consider allowing her to paint a mural on a wall of her room or in the basement.

Remember that artistic expression need not be limited to drawing. Let her play with different materials—clay, fabric, wood and glue, old jewelry.

Musically, help her hear complex rhythms by tapping them out on your knees with your hands and see if she can mimic you. Buy her a toy drum or a recorder (a wooden precursor to the flute and clarinet). When she's five and six, play orchestra conductor, and show her how to keep time by waving her arms in a rhythmical pattern. If you know how to sing harmony, sing duets together. Teach her harmonic sounds from an early age. By five or six, she can be introduced to musical instruments, either formally through lessons, or informally through instruments like the harmonica and recorder, which she can learn to play on her own.

STRATEGY #4: DEVELOP LANGUAGE FACILITY

Expose her to bilingual or multilingual education by introducing foreign vocabulary whenever possible. If you have a family member who speaks another language, allow time for them to be together and interact, or if there is a family on your block you know and trust that speaks another language, encourage your daughter to make friends with their children in order to hear and eventually learn their language.

Some research shows that the differing structures of various languages contribute to different brain development so that some areas receive more stimulation than others depending on the language spoken. For example, languages that read from right to left, such as Japanese and Hebrew, create different patterns in the brain.

STRATEGY #5: CREATE MATH READINESS

You can begin working with math concepts—counting, understanding size relationships, adding, subtracting, cooking, telling time, and so on—before your daughter enters school. This will make math less threatening when she encounters it, just as reading to her makes reading familiar and less threatening.

Here are a few suggestions for very early exposure to math.[2] Remember, the goal here is not to teach mathematics but to introduce concepts and, by doing so, to familiarize her early on with some of the basic language and principles of math she will encounter later on.

1. Teach her to count. You can start very early. For example, you can say, "One shoe. Two shoes," while getting her dressed in the

morning. Keep to like items—in other words, don't count two shoes and two socks and call it four; this is addition, which is a little too advanced for very young children.

2. When she can count to five or more, you can introduce simple concepts of addition and subtraction. Say, "How many cookies do I have?" Then count them together. "How many cookies do you have?" Again, count them. Then put them together and count them all up and say, "Now how many cookies do we have together?" It is not important she get the right answer. You are only familiarizing her with a concept for the future. Don't create stress for her by insisting she answer correctly. If she gets the right answer, that is a bonus. Do the same with subtraction.

3. You can even introduce the concept of fractions. Make them concrete by dividing a sandwich in half, in fourths, and saying such things as "Here is your half. Here is my half. Here is your quarter. Here is mine." Again, you are only introducing a concept and a certain kind of language: halves and fourths. No need to test her. Then eat the fractions, a great way to get her physically involved in the abstract concept of fractions.

4. When cooking, even four- and five-year-olds can be introduced to the processes involved in multiplication and division. For multiplication, use a cookie sheet or muffin tin to show how four rows times four columns equals sixteen cookies. Next time use a different pattern. Show how four rows times six columns equals twenty-four, or two dozen—yet another concept. Do the same with brownies and fruit. Cut recipes in halves and fourths, for understanding division. (You may have to review multiplication of fractions yourself!) You don't have to call these games multiplication and division. Just expose her to them so she will get an early introduction to the processes and concepts.

5. As early as three, four, and five, children can learn to recognize certain times on a clock—noon, and on-the-hour times such as one o'clock, two o'clock, and three o'clock. It will likely to be too early for them to understand half and quarter hours. Be sure to use a clock that has actual numbers on it rather than some decorative symbol or lines in place of the numbers.

6. Kids like to measure things. Starting at age three, have them help you measure their height and mark it on a wall. Use these lengthening demarcations as a way to introduce the concept of tools of measurement such as the yardstick.

7. Introduce the concept of volume by showing three- to five-year-olds how the amount of water in a tall, thin glass is the same as the amount in a short, fat glass. Ask them which they think will hold more. They are likely to choose the taller one. Let them pour the taller one into the shorter one.

School Age: Six to Twelve and Beyond

As your daughter matures into school age, the real work to retain her mastery begins, for her chances of encountering confusion, ambiguity, and failure now arrive in earnest. With the system in place in most public schools—hierarchical order of performance by grades, learning to compare oneself to others, self-worth based on performance, getting helped or prematurely rescued by teachers, and so on—many opportunities exist for her to devalue herself or to learn helplessness. One of the most dangerous aspects of starting school is the first serious encounter with feeling dumb.

There is also the matter of a new adult in her life—an authority figure who, at least initially, is a complete stranger. Your daughter's first teacher may be a skilled professional and a caring human being who loves children unconditionally, or she may be inexperienced, naive, and distraught or even burned out, overworked, and resentful. Whatever first-teacher fate is dealt your daughter, this teacher will almost certainly have expectations and standards. These may or may not differ from yours. Usually this does not pose a problem for girls, since they tend to be eager to please, adjust well to rules, and generally get better grades in early elementary school than boys do.

What may pose a problem, however, is that the teacher will have between twenty to thirty other little individuals to take care of, all of whom will be clamoring to have their needs met—especially boys, who, as you know from your earlier reading, will be jumping out of their seats, waving their hands, and yelling out in class. If your daughter has had no practice in actively expressing her needs prior to this time, she may be reluctant to begin now, particularly with this new stranger. She may get lost in the shuffle.

Furthermore, as I mentioned earlier, research on the classroom behavior of teachers toward girls and boys is not encouraging. Teachers tend to overlook girls and call on boys instead. They respond least well to female students they regard as aggressive, and they often reward girls with high grades for cooperative behavior. This happens for a variety of reasons, but you must make your daughter aware that if she is not being called on, she must take action, particularly if she is to compete with the boys who will be indulging in attention-getting behavior.

STRATEGY #6: GETTING NOTICED

Your daughter should be coached to understand two things: (1) how to get a teacher's attention, and (2) how to talk to a teacher or other authority figure to get help when she needs it. Training her to do this from an early age is better than doing catch-up remedial work later.

You may have to begin at your first parent-teacher conference by asking the teacher if your daughter is speaking up in class. Be sure to ask even if your daughter is already performing well. If the teacher says no, teach your daughter how to speak up or get noticed when she has something to say. Advise her to wave her hand in the air and jump up and down in her seat, if she has to.

I know that some mothers dislike or disagree with this advice, but remember that the boys are exhibiting this behavior and getting rewarded for it! If you have a problem suggesting this behavior for your daughter, then you must talk with the teacher yourself and ask that he or she call on quieter students more frequently. Unfortunately, this is a type of premature rescuing. A better approach is to advise your daughter to speak to the teacher herself. Coach her in how to be diplomatic but firm. Teach her to say, "Ms. Spangler, I had my hand up all during class, but I never got called on. What would you like me to do to get your attention?" (There, the teacher should get the message.)

If the teacher discourages assertive behavior in girls or subtly punishes them by making sarcastic remarks, it will be time for you to take a stand on behalf of the girls. In other words, although it is rare, some teachers do present a no-win situation for girls: they overlook them if they are quiet and polite but demean or punish them if they speak up, are assertive or loud.

STRATEGY #7: COPING WITH CONFUSION

If your daughter gets behind, becomes lost in the material, or gives wrong answers at school, she may come to the conclusion she is "dumb." To make matters worse, other kids, with their cruel remarks, often exacerbate this problem.

As a mother dedicated to keeping your daughter mastery-oriented, remain alert to opportunities to teach your daughter that *success is a process that includes failure*. Educate her early on by explaining that confusion and mistakes are to be expected as part of the learning process—in other words, they are not her fault.

The table on pages 186–87 presents some typical phrases spoken by children when they encounter difficulty. These are followed by some rejoinders often spoken by parents. You will notice that the responses in the second column often contradict the child's statement. This is usually not a good idea. Though it is tempting to contradict or argue with a child when she expresses negative emotions, remember that in so doing, you are *discounting* the child. By trivializing or refusing to acknowledge a daughter's statements of her perceptions or feelings, you send the message that she cannot accurately identify or adequately express these feelings and perceptions. Thus discounting reinforces learned helplessness. A better approach is to respond in a way that will foster a mastery-oriented attitude even when confusion and difficult feelings arise.

Additional Responses to Avoid Discounting

Often a girl might express doubt that she can handle a situation, a teacher, or a class. Every parent is familiar with such statements as, "What if I get a bad grade?" or "What if the teacher doesn't like it?" In cases such as these, be sure to avoid discounting her fears and to reassure her in the following ways:

1. "You don't have to be good at everything. You are allowed to try new things just to see what they are like."
2. "What do you call a bad grade? What if I told you it was all right just as long as you were giving it all you've got?"
3. "Getting a so-called bad grade doesn't mean you are stupid. You're just learning something new."

4. "You'll never know if you don't try! Why not just try and see?"
5. "Do *you* like it? Do *you* want to learn it?"

For older girls, ages nine to twelve, these responses would be appropriate:

1. "What are some ways to ensure that you will do as well as you can? Let's talk about the possibilities."
2. "Getting your feet wet, keeping your options open, and introducing yourself to new material is more important than always getting a good grade. It's okay."
3. "What would *you* like to get out of this endeavor?"
4. "What would be the worst-case scenario? Could you tolerate that? Why or why not?"
5. "Is there a way to make the worst-case scenario less dramatic, more tolerable? Let's talk about ways to make it more tolerable should the worst thing happen."
6. "Will this subject be good to know in future situations or for future choices?"
7. "The only way to discover if you really like or dislike something is to try it. You might be surprised."

As your daughter matures, you will need more methods of helping her retain mastery in the face of confusion. Coaching older girls requires more sophisticated tools.

One excellent way to help an older girl cope with confusion is to develop her capacity to think analytically. The older she gets, the greater will be her ability to use analytical thinking skills. Below are some possible parental responses to an older child's statement that will aid her in problem-solving

Responses Utilizing Analytical Thinking

For example, when your daughter says, "I don't like the way this turned out" or "This is stupid" or "How can I make this better?" it is an opportunity to help her problem-solve. Try the following responses to engage her thinking:

1. "What, specifically, do you mean by 'stupid'? Describe what it is you don't like or find unacceptable."

2. "How or where, specifically, would you like to make changes? Can you describe what those changes would look like or be like?"

3. "Can you embellish it? That means make it prettier, more colorful, more complicated, more ornate, more elaborate, more complex?"

4. "Can you simplify it? That means make it more streamlined, more modern, less complicated, less colorful, plainer, more primitive?"

5. "What do you want it to look like, be like? What should it be able to do? How does it fall short of that?"

6. "Can you minimize what you don't like about your finished product and maximize what you do like?"

7. "Can you take it apart (cut it into pieces, divide it up, look at the individual parts) and put it back together in a new way?"

8. "Has your teacher explained what he or she wants? Is that what *you* want to do?"

If your daughter says, "I'm confused" or "I don't get this," "Why doesn't this work?" or "I'm so stupid," try these responses:

1. "Let's start with what you *do* understand."

2. "Do you get confused at the same place every time? What is that place?"

3. "Let's see if we can break the problem down to find out what confuses you."

4. "Let's make a list of all the questions you have."

5. "Let's come up with all the reasons why you think it doesn't work. Can any of these be changed? What do you have control of?"

Here are some parental responses for girls ages twelve to fifteen:

1. "Can you see a pattern in the elements that confuse you? Can you determine at what point in solving the problem you become confused?"

2. "What elements contribute to your confusion? Time? Teacher? Resources? Can any of these be altered, changed, or modified in a way that would help you?"

3. "Can you explain or articulate the overriding problem you believe is at the root of your confusion?"
4. "Why don't you brainstorm a list of things you think might help you. We'll look your work over together after you are done to see what can be done."

At first, your daughter may respond to your questions with answers that reveal almost nothing such as "I don't know," or she may toss off flippant remarks such as "If Ms. So-and-So would just drop dead, everything would be great." Be patient. Eventually, your line of questioning, which is designed to aid her analytical thinking, will begin to filter through, and she may come up with answers later—perhaps even several days later. Again, be patient. This is how the brain works. It needs time to assimilate new information and even more time to process it into a new answer or product. Over the years, if you persist, she will learn how to ask these questions of herself.

Retaining Mastery Attitudes in the Face of Confusion

Your Daughter's Statement	A Discounting Response	A Response That Will Foster Mastery
I can't do it.	Here, let me do that for you. (This can also happen without saying anything, such as taking something from her and doing it for her.)	I know what you mean. You have to try a little harder. Math can be difficult. Would you like to know what I do?
I'm dumb.	That's ridiculous. You are not dumb.	I know how you feel. I have felt like that too, but eventually I got it. (Give a personal example.) Sometimes I just need a little extra time. Do you think that would help

Your Daughter's Statement	A Discounting Response	A Response That Will Foster Mastery
		you? There are lots of different things we could try. Let's talk.
I'm scared I'll do bad.	Don't be silly. You have nothing to be scared of.	Yes, learning something new can be scary, but fear doesn't have to stop you. Sometimes it can even help you. Would you like to know how?
Everybody thinks I'm stupid.	They do not. Where did you get a crazy idea like that?	Yes, it feels like that when you're confused. It took me weeks to figure out how to use the new computer at work, but then I found out that everybody was as confused as I was. Remember that: everybody gets confused. If anybody says anything to you, just say, "Haven't you ever been confused?"
The teacher hates me.	Don't be ridiculous. The teacher doesn't hate you.	Well, I'm not sure about that, but remember, everyone is not always going to like you in life. That's okay. Let's sit down together and come up with some ways to deal with the teacher and solve the problem.

STRATEGY #8: LEARNING MASTERY THROUGH ACADEMIC PROJECTS

In the fourth grade, teachers begin to assign work in which the students are given opportunities to exercise choice. For example, a teacher may assign a report entitled "An Explorer," and the student is allowed to choose which explorer she wishes to write about. If the topic is, say, Native Americans, the student can choose which nation of people to study.

Be alert to assignments that promote independence and choice as opportunities for your daughter to gain the experiences she needs to practice mastery behavior and to form images of women as mastery-oriented, successful individuals in their own right. The following pages provide some ideas.

Art, Social Studies, History, and Language Arts

Oral histories are dialogues or monologues, often tape-recorded, in which a person gives historical information based on a firsthand account. Check into your own family for the oral histories and stories of your female ancestors—your great-great-grandmothers who braved the terrors of the push westward or who came to Ellis Island with nothing but their dreams and made a life for themselves. (Talk about risk-takers!) Talking to grandmas, great-grandmas, and even nonrelatives in elder care centers will give your daughter a window on history and show her how women—including her own ancestors—have overcome adversity, stayed resilient, and persisted through difficulties she can only imagine. In addition, an oral history proves an opportunity for her to practice the valuable mastery experience of talking to adults in new ways.

Developing the questions that will get these women talking about their experiences, then listening to them and recounting the history of, say, a grandmother—who may have information provided by *her* grandmother, which would make possible a female family history stretching back five generations—can then be followed by such interesting projects as a female family tree, an annotated picture album, a play, or short stories of female struggle and valor.

Here are a few questions to get your daughter started, but let her come up with as many questions as possible rather than providing them for her. That would be premature rescuing again.

- What was the bravest thing you ever saw a woman do?
- What was the smartest thing you ever saw a woman do?
- What do you think is the most important thing women of the past could teach us today?
- Did you know your grandmother? What was she like?
- How did your mother, or grandmother, handle adversity?
- How did men and women make their living in those days?

The category of "herstory"—the oral histories and personal stories of women's individual lives and accomplishments—can be broadened to include biographical research into the lives of women who either made history or contributed to it. This assignment offers a rich vein of fascinating material and an opportunity for girls to see women as contributors, major players, and risk-takers. Don't forget the so-called bad girls—a label that has been bestowed by the patriarchy upon those women who refused to act in accordance with what was socially sanctioned for females; or the true revolutionaries who changed history by challenging dominant views, like Elizabeth Cady Stanton, Susan B. Anthony, Harriet Beecher Stowe; or the incredibly hardy, resilient, and stalwart women of the frontier who scratched out their existence in the male-dominated Old West.

Also, be aware that the history curricula in some school districts isolates women's history into "Women's History Week." This gives the false impression that the female contribution to history can be covered adequately in one week, while the *real* history, the one lived and written by males, takes up the rest of the year. In this case, women's history is perceived by children as a footnote. In any case, it certainly is trivialized.

A better approach is to weave women's history into the fabric of all history rather than to treat it as an oddity to be studied for only one week out of the year. Check into how your district handles this. Push for changes in the curriculum if women are not featured in every stage of history. Until that happens, when the opportunity for choice is presented by the teacher, provide your daughter with the opportunity to learn about the role of women in history by suggesting some of these assignments.

You might also suggest a project wherein, through the use of either images or words, women are depicted as warriors: brave, courageous, masterful, virtuous, action-oriented, often solitary, striving for lofty goals, and possessing wisdom and clarity. Since so few examples are provided for girls of women acting in this role, you must create the opportunity for them.

Remember that the archetype of the warrior need not be a violent or warlike character. In many cultures and traditions, the warrior is neither. In fact, in both Asian and Native American cultures, a true warrior seeks to avoid violence and to use awareness, clarity, insight, and forethought to replace violence with right action. The warrior in these cultures never acts on the offensive or out of anger and ultimately resorts to violence—without anger—only after all other avenues have been exhausted.

The female warrior project can begin by having your daughter determine what the characteristics of a female warrior might be. She can write her own ideas, talk with others, and interview her friends. Then, using these attributes, she can create a photography exhibit of women and girls she sees walking down the street, interacting with children and adults, driving, hiking, and playing team sports. She can select women who embody, either in their personal style of dress or their mannerisms or their body language, those qualities she has identified as characteristic of an honorable female warrior. If she so chooses, she can write a poem to accompany her photography display. (This could also be a great group project for a Girl Scout troop.)

Finally, remember the female warriors mentioned in the preceding chapter on positive media heroines: Xena, Captain Janeway, and Lisa Simpson as well as the heroines and female rescuers of females in *A Little Princess, The Secret of Roan Inish, Fried Green Tomatoes, Thelma and Louise,* and *The Silence of the Lambs.* Watch these series and movies with your daughter before you begin the project, and discuss the female warrior from the standpoint of these shows. Remember, of course, to exercise judgment concerning the age-appropriateness of the material, limiting the more violent material to older girls.

Math, Science, and Computers

While efforts over the last decade to keep girls in math and science are having some positive effects—the gender gap is closing somewhat in math and science achievement for all students, and girls are enrolling in more math courses than they used to—we still have a long way to go, and we must not relax our vigilance. Prior to about age twelve, most girls still like math and science and do well in them. However, as the material becomes more challenging and, simultaneously, as the opportunity to drop math and science is made available to students, girls drop out.

A 1994 study found that high school girls are much less likely than boys to enroll in courses like physics and calculus. Furthermore, their high school course choices still tend to follow traditional sex-stereotyped patterns.[3] In 1990 a majority of females who took the SAT said they planned to work in the social sciences—or, in the jargon of universities, the "soft sciences."[4] Because they opted out of advanced math and science courses in high school, those courses will be closed to them in college. In science achievement the gender gap is actually *increasing* for students at the top of their class. Even girls with exceptional high school preparation in math and science choose them as careers in disproportionately low numbers.[5] It is essential that we keep our girls enrolled in math, science, and computer and technology courses as long as possible in order to keep their options open. They won't all become rocket scientists, but they will be more competitive for the high-paying, high-demand jobs of the future.

By high school only one girl in seven describes herself as good in math, and girls are much less likely than boys to describe themselves as interested in science.[6] Although nine-year-old girls are interested in science activities, they do not participate in the diverse ways that boys do—that is, in science fairs and science projects. Also, when teachers need help demonstrating a technique in the classroom, eight out of ten times they choose boys to assist them.[7]

Computers, being that peculiar combination of math and machine, are still viewed as a male domain. At home fathers typically teach computing to their sons and link the instruction to future career options. At school, boys monopolize computer labs and give girls a hard time when they try to compete for access to the computers. More boys than girls are sent to computer camps, particularly those camps that cater to older students and are more expensive. One study showed that 60 percent of boys had computers at home while only 18 percent of girls did.[8]

These statistics deserve special attention. Parents and teachers still seem to make a greater effort to provide opportunities for boys to become familiar and comfortable with computers than they do for girls. At the very least these statistics seem to indicate that parents and teachers are not doing enough to turn the situation around. Furthermore, to put an end to the myth that boys are just naturally more interested in computers than girls are, computer use by girls skyrocketed in a school where adults intervened by setting up girls' computer clubs and structured "girls only" time in the computer room.[9]

Remember that when a mother assumes her daughter is not going to enjoy math or perform well because she didn't, or when she excuses her daughter's reluctance to enroll in math, science, and computer classes because "girls don't like those subjects," she may be letting her daughter off the hook too easily. This attitude causes us to overlook the girls who are good in math and enjoy these subjects. How many girls, potentially skilled in mathematics or science, have been lost simply because they were overlooked? Maybe you were one of them. I know I was. Don't let it happen to your daughter.

Encourage interest in math and computers, and stress learning goals over performance goals. Here are some math skills activities to get you started. Have fun!

More Ways to Encourage Mastery in Math (Ages 6–10)

1. Continue to use math activities in daily life. These include measuring things, estimating sizes of things, cooking, gardening—computing the size of your yard and how much fertilizer to buy, for example—and figuring out tips at the restaurant.
2. When she gets old enough, teach her how to play "21," then pinochle and bridge. The requirement to add scores quickly and accurately, make bids, and take tricks, all using a different "language"—cards—is a fun way to develop both math skills and risk-taking skills.
3. Telling time can be used to teach the concept of different bases—for example, our number system uses base 10, while a clock utilizes base 12.
4. Work jigsaw puzzles together. They are a concrete tool that helps with spatial thinking. So are Tinkertoys, Lincoln Logs, and Erector sets.

5. Help her learn to develop her own strategies for working through a problem. Don't say, "This is how you do it," or "Watch how I solve this," but rather, "How do you think this problem should be solved?" or "What strategy would you use to get the right answer?" Furthermore, do not give her tricks for solving problems. Math teachers tell me these tricks often completely bypass the critical thought involved in problem-solving, so even though the tricks may work, they are not serving the overall goal of critical thinking in math.

6. Together, brainstorm and develop alternative strategies for staying afloat while learning potentially difficult material that has caused her problems in the past. Don't become Ms. Answer Person. Hire tutors if necessary. Utilize peer study groups or peer tutors (they are less expensive).

7. Buy your daughter a computer, enroll her in computer programming classes, send her to computer camp, play computer games together.

Encourage your daughter to work on science projects, because the scientific method itself is an excellent teacher of mastery behavior. The cognitive skills required and the difficulties encountered as one tests and retests a hypothesis are processes that encourage problem-solving.

First, the necessity to develop a new hypothesis if, based on the information gleaned from one's research, the theory proved faulty or incorrect is a lesson in persistence since a great deal of time and effort have usually gone into the research effort that produced the information.

Second, as research progresses, modifications in one's methods are usually required. Research is a constant learning process. Making adjustments helps a girl avoid regarding a modification as a failure, because she sees adjustments as part of a larger process that all scientists go through.

Third, strategizing a method of research and then restrategizing or starting over completely with a new procedure based on a new hypothesis is excellent practice for developing alternative methods for reaching a goal—another mastery skill. Finally, the simple process of waiting for results while a research project unfolds teaches patience and persistence.

For these reasons, encourage your daughter to learn *and work with* the scientific method. Formal science projects in a classroom setting with the help of a science teacher offer an excellent way to do this. Also, entering her science project in a science fair is an empowering experience for a girl. She will be in an arena where she'll be competing mostly with boys, and it is prestigious to be asked to participate. The life stories of female scientists and inventors offer another opportunity for girls to become familiar with adult women working in difficult, usually male-dominated arenas where women were not welcomed or were even actively discouraged.

Peer Tutoring

Acting as a tutor to one's peers, mentoring another, or being in a position of authority as the person with the information and the skills to help another, is yet another empowering experience. It may be even more so if your daughter has the opportunity to tutor male classmates. Any girl can participate in this fashion. She need not be a whiz kid to be a peer tutor. She need only know more than the person she is tutoring. She can tutor younger students, for example. As anyone who has ever taught knows, the best way to learn anything is to teach it; therefore every time she tutors another, she reinforces her own mastery of the subject.

Keeping Aspirations High

Another way to nurture mastery cognitively is to keep our daughters' aspirations high. We know from research that during the period between eight and eleven years, girls have their highest aspirations, even higher than when they reach college.[10]

Keep your daughter's aspirations high by encouraging her to express herself in as many ways as possible—verbally, certainly, but also in other ways: in sports, art, music, math, and architecture; in her clothes, her viewpoints, her silliness, and her laughter; with girls, boys, siblings, parents, and teachers; on the Internet, the playground, and the playing field; in the classroom, the orchestra, and the computer room; at school, at church, at home, and at her grandparents' house; and in publications. In other words, to keep her aspirations high, encourage your daughter's visibility in the world.

The more freedom a girl has enjoyed to be who she is, to be seen and heard in her world, to be recognized as an individual with a contribution to make, the harder it will be for her to relinquish this freedom without a fight. It will be harder for her to become a "good girl" in the conventional sense—compliant, polite, quiet, acquiescent, "nice," dependent, self-sacrificing, and decorative— traits deemed "feminine" by our society. Since at puberty the pressure to be feminine and attractive assumes paramount importance and the pursuit of relationships often takes priority to the exclusion of other activities, the more we nurture a girl's aspirations and visibility in a wide variety of venues, the greater her chances for valuing these venues and staying active in them. So don't be afraid to nurture her aspirations, and be willing to dream the big dreams with her. This is an important part of the process.

STRATEGY #9: MAKING THE DREAM BIGGER (A REPRISE)

Remember the mother who was distressed when she realized she had limited aspirations for her daughter within her own mind, the one who went from visualizing her daughter as an investigative reporter to seeing her as managing editor of the newspaper? Bearing that story in mind, you must exercise vigilance in order to avoid imposing your own culturally induced beliefs about female limitations onto your daughter and thus perpetuating self-imposed boundaries on yet another generation.

One technique to keep your daughter's imagination healthy and her aspirations high is to help her see her choices through the widest lens possible. When she says, "I want to be a paleontologist," you can reply, "How neat! Did you know the director of the Natural History Museum is a paleontologist?" If she says, "I want to be an accountant," you can say, "All right! Maybe one day you'll start your own accounting firm."

Even more traditionally "feminine" responses can be opened up in this way. If she says, "I want to be a nurse," you can say, "Great. You know I heard about a surgical nurse, who, due to her experiences in the operating room, invented a new surgical procedure that's now in use by surgeons worldwide." If she says, "I want to be a teacher," you can say, "That's a wonderful goal. I can even see you as principal or headmistress of a school based on your own original theories of learning."

Note that these responses do not in any way discount or discourage your daughter's original dream. You should *not* respond, "Oh, that's not good enough. You could be a managing editor," or "Just a nurse? Why not a doctor?" Your response should enthusiastically reinforce her goal and then upgrade it a notch or two. Do try to balance this somewhat. If you do it all the time, your daughter is likely to begin rolling her eyes and saying things like "Why do you always have to think of something better? What's wrong with my idea?" Therefore, give it a rest before it becomes tedious to your daughter. If she does seem disturbed by your comment, respond with "You're right. I'm sorry, I do admire your ideas. I just want you to be aware of the vast array of choices open to you. You know me—I don't want you to feel limited." Your purpose is not to make your daughter feel that her dreams are inadequate but rather to help her see how one career often leads to another, how a set of goals accomplished can lead to still higher goals, how the process of work and achievement unfolds throughout a lifetime, and most importantly, how high she can allow her aspirations to go.

STRATEGY #10: GETTING THE JUMP ON YOUR DAUGHTER'S FINANCIAL EDUCATION

A sound financial education is critical to your daughter's future economic self-sufficiency. Furthermore, seeing to her financial education is a must to make her a mastery-oriented positive risk-taker with regard to money and income. Developing her financial skills and cognitive understanding of how money works will ensure that she is prepared for life in the twenty-first century. The goal here is to make girls as financially independent and self-reliant as possible. As Wendy Wasserstein reminisced, "My mother always told me: 'Wendy, whether you're rich or poor, it's good to have money.'"

Inasmuch as finances have been an overlooked arena for girls in the past, you yourself may have some difficulty with, or fear around, the subject of money and investments. If so, this would be an ideal mother-daughter mastery project. Your goal is to help your daughter learn how to handle money wisely and to enjoy doing so.

The most important recommendation I can make is to teach your daughter that she must get her money the old-fashioned way—she must *earn* it—so begin early to make the connection between labor and income. By age eight, do not just give her an allowance; insist that it be provided only in exchange for work.

If she gets excited by earning money, has a special event coming up, or wants to buy a particular item, she may be eager to earn extra money and work overtime. Teach her to keep track of her hours, and remunerate her at time-and-a-half wages. Also, if she takes on a big job, one that will involve responsible work over a period of time, such as painting her room or taking care of the neighbors' dog while they are on vacation, sit down with her and negotiate a contract. This will teach her how to think through the responsibilities and time constraints of a particular job, how to appreciate the nuances of contracts, and how to stand up for herself through the negotiation process. Of course, you must then see to it that she meets the requirements set forth in the contract, since that is what an employer would do.

Be sure to allow her to spend some of the money she earns—perhaps fifty or sixty percent (you can negotiate the percentage together). Allowing her to spend some money teaches her to enjoy the process of earning money and the self-esteem and sense of independence that goes with it. In this way, she will associate money and the ability to earn it with reward and pleasure, not just responsibility and stress.

Once she grows accustomed to earning money and the two of you decide how much she should be allowed to spend, she should devote the rest to wealth accumulation—in other words, to saving and investing. As she matures, teach her the concepts of investments and compound interest—how money can be manipulated to multiply—so she understands that she will have more to spend later if she is thrifty now. Show her how interest works and use this as a vehicle to teach her percentages and decimal points. Some kids have difficulty with these ideas as long as they remain abstract concepts but catch on immediately when the concrete object of money is used.

Teach her the difference between saving and investing. Teach her that savings will produce a cushion—a margin of safety—and will keep a cash flow handy. It is indeed prudent to save a certain percentage of one's money for security purposes so the cash will be there when one needs it. At the same time, don't forget to include the second ingredient—investing—and teach her that that portion of her money has the potential to bring greater rewards, even though the risk may be greater. Teach her that investing is less liquid and thus, while earning more money, it is not as quickly available. This combination of saving and investing is the financially sound concept of a diversified portfolio, the don't-put-all-your-eggs-in-one-basket philosophy. In other words, teach her that wealth accumulation has two aspects: saving and investing.

By helping her to invest now, as a child, when it is safe, and by making investing a kind of game, you will help her overcome her fear surrounding money. Let her pick a stock and watch its progress. As she matures, teach her the meanings and definitions of financial terms and how to read the financial pages. Teach her basic financial tenets like the fact that when the stock market goes up, bonds go down and vice versa, and the concepts of appreciation and depreciation, compound interest, supply and demand, and return on net investment.

You don't have to sit down and teach a lesson. Just work this information into normal conversations. Suppose she wants a new bicycle, for example. Ask her, "How will you get the best return on your net investment?" When she says, "What is that?" you can explain it. Tell her to find out which bicycles retain their value the longest and have the highest resale value. Search the Web together for information about bicycles. This would also be an opportunity to explain depreciation, since, unlike a house or real estate, machines and gadgets become less valuable over time, not more. If she wants a puppy, discuss puppy prices. Explain supply and demand. Explain that some breeds are rare and therefore cost more.

Let her start a little business and stake her a loan. Require regular loan payments with interest. Or hire her as your apprentice. Remember that the basic guidelines for your daughter's financial education follow the same precepts and paths as an adult's education in finances: earning, saving, investing, and entrepreneurship.

Suggestions for Your Daughter's Financial Education

1. Include your daughter at bill-paying time. Let her see you make financial decisions and choices. Allow her to record the checks in the check register. When she is older, let her write out the checks before you sign them.

2. Don't just give your daughter money. Be sure to pay her for her labor. Let her experience the connection between labor and income. If she works longer hours than usual, pay her overtime at time-and-a-half.

3. Negotiate a contract for longer jobs with more responsibilities.

4. Hire her as your apprentice.

5. Help her start a little business. Stake her a loan and insist upon monthly loan payments with interest.

6. When there is an opportunity in daily interaction to educate her about financial concerns (a new bicycle, buying a puppy, starting her own savings account), seize it. Make money real to her by teaching her how to make her own money work for her.

7. When she is old enough, start a small investment portfolio over which she has some control. Let her choose some stocks and other investments. Teach her how to read stock exchange information in the newspaper in order to monitor her investments.

8. When she reaches her teens, discuss annuities, mutual funds, the stock and bond markets, and the market indexes such as the Dow-Jones and Standard & Poors. Make it real by explaining how good investments could help fund her first car or her college education.

9. If you are self-employed, or if you itemize your deductions, let her help you organize your records at tax time. This will teach her the value of saving receipts, as well as introductory concepts about business and household deductions. If she does this every year for five years, say from age twelve to seventeen, she will be likely to remember what qualifies as a deduction when she gets older, and she will certainly have an understanding of the concept.

CHAPTER 9

Looking After Herself

Six Strategies for Keeping Her Safe

Safety is an illusion.

> *Beryl Markham, author of* West with the Night

As I was cleaning out the garage the other day, the six-year-old girl next door showed up and asked me what I was doing. Before I knew it she was in the garage with me, poking into piles, pulling stuff out, and interrogating me: "Are you giving this away? What's that? Why are you throwing this out? Can I have this?"

Just as I was about to recruit her to help me sort through a pile, her father arrived, angry and distraught. "Andrea!" he shouted, red-faced and worried, "I have been looking everywhere for you! I didn't know where you were! How many times do I have to tell you? You are not to leave the house without permission! Understand? Don't you ever do this again!"

"But Nicky's not a stranger," she pleaded. "I didn't talk to a stranger."

"I don't care," he responded, too angry to hear her words. "Just go home."

"But, Daddy, I..." she said, tears of humiliation welling up in her eyes.

At that point he interrupted, pointed her in the direction of home, and shouted, "And I mean now!"

After her departure, I apologized to him, saying I hadn't realized he didn't know where Andrea was. I assured him that next time I would insist she ask her parents' permission to come over.

He thanked me, adding, "Well, this isn't the first time. She has taken to gallivanting all around the neighborhood. We've taught her not to talk to strangers, but you know how scary it is."

Yes, I do. I related this story to you because it allows me to raise an important point. Developing your daughter's risk-taking skills while simultaneously trying to keep her safe is a little like living with bees in your head. The two goals seem irreconcilable. On the surface, they are. Unfortunately, there are no answers that will absolutely guarantee your daughter's safety. What answers there are lie once again in the same direction: developing her mastery-oriented behavior—in this case, the mastery behavior of learning to take care of her*self*.

If you think about it, that should be your ultimate goal. After all, you want your daughter to be safe whether or not you happen to be present. You want her to engage her brain in order to keep herself safe in all circumstances. In an effort to feel more in control of the situation, however, most parents want to believe that *they* can keep their children safe. While this desire is understandable, it is not realistic. The period in your daughter's life during which you can keep her safe from harm is very short—practically nonexistent. The instant she is out of your sight, she *could* be in danger. Obviously, you cannot follow her around all the time. Not only is that impossible but it will eventually become downright invasive.

The answer is to teach her to be aware of and think about her *own* safety. In other words, the more knowledgeable your daughter is about ways to keep her*self* safe—without relying on you and others to do so for her, expecting rescue, relying on luck, being overly trusting, or being unaware of signs of danger—the safer she will be. We will begin with the age at which your daughter is mature enough to be curious about her world and mobile enough, either on foot or on wheels, to go exploring.

Early and Late Childhood

Around age five or six, and even younger for some, many children become fascinated by the sights, sounds, and adventures awaiting them in their neighborhood. (Don't you wish you still had that kind of wonder at such simple things?) It is not unusual for them to go blithely off to explore their world, initiating visits with the neighbors or just off on a lark, sans parents and sans even parental knowledge of these wanderings and visitations.

Well, exploring *is* a mastery-oriented behavior. It requires curiosity, confidence, courage, and independence—all positive traits to be encouraged in a girl. I know what you're thinking: it also requires naïveté, and that scares you. At the same time, while confidence is important, parents rightfully fear overconfidence, which, when combined with the innocence (or should I say ignorance?) of childhood, can lead children into trouble, causing them to take risks, the consequences of which they are unprepared for or unaware of. Furthermore, it is inevitable that there will come a time when she changes the rules concerning boundaries. Sometimes she will do so deliberately—when she is with friends, perhaps, and there is peer pressure to ignore the rules. At other times she will do so unconsciously—for example, when she just gets naturally curious and, without thinking, goes too far. Finally, she must "go further" as she matures. It is her developmental job.

Once she is able to separate herself from you and wander off on her own in shopping malls, parks, and her own neighborhood, *your* job is to teach her what a stranger is.

STRATEGY #1: TEACH HER WHAT A STRANGER IS

The most critical step in teaching your daughter to keep herself safe is often overlooked. Most parents teach their children not to talk to strangers. But imagine if I said to you, "Never, never talk to a moig. Never get into a car with a moig. Never go anywhere with a moig. Do you understand?" If you were a young child, you would nod your head to please the adult, but it would not occur to you to ask what a moig is. (Perhaps children do this because they are used to being confused by adult vocabulary.) Therefore, not only must you explain to her that she must never talk to a stranger or go anywhere with one, but you also must explain what a stranger is.

Inform her that a stranger is anyone she does not know, has never met or talked with before. Inform her that if a person is not a relative, a neighbor, or a friend she has met previously through you, she must not talk to that person. Some parents feel more secure carrying this one step further and naming the people who are safe: Grandma and Grandpa, uncles, aunts, next-door neighbors, baby-sitters, and close family friends. Remember to explain that even the friends of next-door neighbors are strangers to her.

Here are some ways to explain to her that she should avoid strangers:

1. You know how you sometimes play "pretend"? Well, some adults do that too. They pretend to be nice or friendly or helpful, but they are not.
2. Since you can't tell if people you don't know—strangers—are nice people, just walk away from them. They may act nice or seem nice, but some of them are just good pretenders.
3. Most people you meet are very nice, but some are not. You can't tell which is which when you don't know them.
4. Don't talk to strangers because some people tell lies.
5. Most people would never hurt you, but some would. It is impossible to know who would and who wouldn't if they are strangers to you.
6. You don't have to be afraid of strangers. Just be smart. Simply leave them alone. Don't talk with them or go with them for any reason.
7. Even if they talk to you and are nice, you don't have to talk back, especially if you are alone.

STRATEGY #2: ROLE-PLAYING FOR SAFETY

Once you feel assured your daughter knows what a stranger is, explain how it is possible to encounter a stranger who appears to be in need. For example, a stranger may present himself as injured, complete with blood, bandages, or a cast. (Remember Ted Bundy?) Teach her that if someone is hurt, the best thing she can do is to go get adult help. Teach her that a stranger may pretend to be looking for a stray puppy, trying to retrieve a ball, asking for directions, or even offering to take the child to see Mommy and Daddy at their request.

Role-playing some scenarios with your daughter will not only help her to understand how to act but will give her practice in doing so. This in turn will make her more mastery-oriented and self-assured if and when she should need to be, and it will help her remember what to do under pressure.

Play "pretend." Pretend you are a stranger. Enact various scenarios that child predators have been known to use, such as "I'm looking for my lost puppy. Will you help me?" or "Your mommy has been hurt, and she asked me to take you to the hospital to see her," or "I am a police officer and you must come with me," or "I have a box of kittens in the car. Would you like to play with one?" Do this role-playing in locations she is likely to be in: walking home from school, at the mall, on the playground, and so on. Both you and your husband can play these roles with her so that she understands a stranger can be a man or a woman and can appear to be friendly, helpful, and kind.

Teach her that no matter how much she wants to play with the kittens, she should walk away from the stranger. Promise to take her wherever the stranger promised to go or to do whatever the stranger promised—to play with some kittens, for example. Let her know that the only adult she is allowed to go with is someone she already knows—a trusted relative or a family friend whom you have given her permission to be with.

Next, since even trusted adults can indulge in inappropriate behavior with children, teach her to say no forcefully to an adult. Again, let her practice. Teach her to be assertive, even aggressive, if need be. Teaching this mastery-oriented behavior to a child is sometimes difficult for parents because they believe children should respect their elders. I agree. They should. On the other hand, it is important that your daughter doesn't feel reluctant or embarrassed to be forceful with an adult who has made an inappropriate request. As she matures, you can explain that an adult worth respecting would never ask her to do something with her body that made her feel embarrassed or afraid or uncomfortable. Let her know that no adult—not even her favorite friend, relative, or teacher—has a right to touch her body in private places or to request that she remove her clothes or do anything else that makes her uncomfortable.

You may have to spell out for her in detail what is acceptable and unacceptable behavior from adults and what she has the right to forcefully refuse. Then, of course, you must teach her to come and inform you immediately, even if the adult has told her she shouldn't.

STRATEGY #3: EMPHASIZE SAFETY OVER DANGER

One word of caution. As you communicate that it is unacceptable to talk to a stranger for any reason, or comply with an adult's wishes that make her uncomfortable, try to avoid scaring your daughter to death. It is not a good idea, as far as cultivating mastery behavior goes, to make her feel like the world is an unsafe place (even though it is). I am thinking of a particular father in one workshop who said, "I tell my daughter if she isn't careful she could wind up dismembered in a plastic bag by the side of the road." Obviously, this is not the kind of terror tactic I had in mind! It only instills fear.

Nor should one harp on danger. Emphasizing safety over danger may seem like too fine a point to draw, but the constant use of the concept of danger can create a fearful or overly timid child. Periodic gentle reminders emphasizing safety rather than danger are sufficient. These reminders are particularly useful when they are appropriate, such as when she walks alone to a friend's house for the first time.

Early to Late Teens

STRATEGY #4: BUILD HER AWARENESS

When your daughter comes home with a request to do something you deem too dangerous, instead of flatly forbidding it by saying, "Absolutely not," use it as an opportunity to increase your daughter's ability to keep herself safe. You might say, for example, "That makes me uncomfortable. How do you plan to keep yourself safe in that circumstance?"

If she replies, "I don't know," say, "Why don't you go off by yourself and think it over. Come back when you have some ideas." If she never returns with ideas, you are off the hook. If she does, you now have a valuable opportunity to accomplish two goals: first, to require her to elaborate on whatever safety measures she devises, and second, to hear whether or not she is really mature enough to handle the request.

With regard to the first goal—elaborating on safety measures—simply reply to each of her suggestions with "Yes, that's good. What else?" When she offers another idea for safety, say "Yes, what else?" Resist the temptation to think up safety precautions for her rather than allowing her to think of them. If you provide all the ideas, such as "What if this?" or "What if that?" then you have taken the bait. *You* are the one thinking about her safety, rather than *her*. This would be counterproductive to your goal of teaching her how to keep her*self* safe.

Regarding the second goal—determining whether she has the awareness and maturity to keep herself relatively safe in a given situation—you will have much more information to use in your decision-making process than if you come up with all the answers. You may still decide not to let her go, but at least your decision will be based on something more concrete than your imagination or your assumptions concerning her awareness.

STRATEGY #5: TAKE A SELF-DEFENSE CLASS

I know from my travels doing workshops in other cities that some local police forces have initiated self-defense programs for children. They are usually taught by self-defense experts, police officers, and child psychologists. They can include awareness-building of inter-personal violence, signs of potential violence, preventive action, and even training in actual physical resistance. Find out if your local police department or recreation center offers a course like this. If not, ask them to organize one, or offer to help them do so.

With a little more maturity, your daughter can be enrolled in a martial arts class. The advantages are numerous, and it's easy to get kids interested because they love the martial arts. Joe Signorelli, who has been a martial arts instructor for twenty-two years, eighteen of them working with children, advises that, although some schools and instructors will accept five-year-olds, he feels they are too young. "It's a cognitive thing," he says. "They don't have the attention span or ability to concentrate and pay attention before about seven or eight."

Call around to find out what martial arts schools are available in your community, and check out their reputations and experience in working with children. Once you are convinced a school is credible, enroll your daughter if she shows an interest. If she doesn't, suggest taking a class together as a mother-daughter mastery project. Not only will your daughter learn the skills and art of self-defense, she will also learn the skills of mastery behavior that are intrinsic in these ancient teachings: discipline, awareness, clarity of mind, skillful action under stress, strength, resilience, and persistence. That's quite a package.

For a teenager, the experience of learning self-defense can become more intense. One of the most effective courses is called Model Mugging. The strength of Model Mugging programs is that they use a technique based on what is known as state-dependent conditioning—in other words, they *use* the fear rather than trying to eliminate it. They take advantage of the adrenaline produced by fear (that would naturally occur during an assault) to empower the individual to act.

"It's about utilizing the high-adrenaline state as a resource of power, rather than freezing and flailing," said Eugenie Morton, the CEO and senior trainer of the Colorado chapter of Model Mugging. "It's about turning the fear state into an ally."

"Why do people say it is so intense?" I questioned her.

"We teach females how to deliver full-contact strikes at maximum force to vulnerable body targets. Since most females have never had the experience of delivering a full-contact strike to another human being, much less at maximum force, it is an intense experience for them.[1] We also use a lot of vocalization, as in screaming and yelling." Many of the martial arts also use vocalization as a means of accessing one's power and strength, or to throw off or threaten an opponent.

"Even though they do not have to rely on strength alone, we recognize that muscle strength is a definite advantage, so we teach females to use their hips and legs, the largest muscles in the body, to defend themselves. This type of training is highly effective for two reasons. First, the largest muscle groups are the easiest to use when you're scared out of your wits. Second, in an assault, a woman usually gets knocked down and winds up on her back anyway. So learning to fight with their legs is a great advantage."

In the basic class, participants learn to defend themselves against a single unarmed assailant, the most common type of assault. Two advanced adult classes are also available. The first teaches defense against an assailant armed with a knife, gun, or club. The last teaches defense against multiple assailants, where three to five model muggers jump on one lone woman.

The Colorado chapter offers a teen training program and a kids' program as well. Not all chapters do, but many do. Check your phone book to find out if your city offers a model mugging program for kids and teens. If not, a girl is often eligible to take the adult course when she is seventeen or eighteen. Sometimes allowances are made based on maturity or other life circumstances and situations.

And Speaking of Life Situations...

A girl may find herself in a dangerous situation no matter what she does. Perhaps her choices were faulty (it can happen to anyone) or she was not given a choice, or perhaps circumstances placed her in a situation of ultimate danger. If she has some training in self-defense at least she has the option to physically resist in a skillful and successful manner.

"Listen to this one," began the mother of a fifteen-year-old girl in one of my workshops. "You're not going to believe it, but it's a true story. It happened to my daughter.

"My daughter Kelly and her friend Karen were picked up at a party by an older girlfriend with whom they had made arrangements earlier that evening. The friend honked for them, and they ran outside and got in the car. After a few minutes they realized that their friend, the driver, had been drinking with her boyfriend and was actually too drunk to be driving. They argued with her, even got physical, but she refused to let either of them drive her car. After she ran a red light and nearly hit another car, Kelly and Karen demanded to be let out.

"It was about eleven o'clock on a Friday night. We live kind of out in the country. It's not a completely rural area, but there are large open spaces of fields and trees with no houses or lights. So here they are, two teenage girls, walking along together on this dark, deserted road when a car pulls up and the driver, a stranger, offers them a ride. Karen, my daughter's friend, wanted to get in the car. It was the middle of winter, she wasn't dressed properly, and she was miserably cold. She also said she thought they would be safer in the car than walking along the road by themselves."

"Uh-oh," murmured a woman in the audience.

"Kelly didn't want to do it. I had always drummed it into her head never to get into a car with a stranger. She pleaded with Karen to keep walking, but Karen opened the car door and got in. Kelly said, 'Mom, what was I supposed to do? I know I shouldn't have gotten into the car, but I was scared to stay out there on that road all by myself.'"

A chill of fear mingled with compassion for her predicament ran up the collective spine of the audience and the instructor. We instantly perceived the terrible situation in which Kelly found herself—in danger either way.

One woman said, "Wow, that is some pretty heavy decision-making for a sixteen-year-old."

Another responded with what the rest of us were thinking, "It would be heavy decision-making even for an adult."

The mother resumed. "The upshot was that a police officer had driven past the two girls, gone a little farther down the road, thought it over, and decided to turn around and check on them. When he got there, they were getting in the stranger's car. Here comes the scary part. It turned out that the guy whose car they were getting into was a convicted felon—a sex offender out prowling for young girls. If the cop hadn't come to check on them at just that moment, who knows what might've happened?"

I bring this story up not to frighten you out of your wits but to be realistic about danger and safety. Because every beating heart is vulnerable to suffering and death, in the final analysis, there is no ultimate safety. Therefore I believe we do our children a favor if we enable them, as early as possible, to defend themselves should they, through no fault of their own, find themselves in a potentially dangerous situation. Even violence awareness and self-defense are no guarantee (there are no guarantees), but at least they are a start.

So don't stick your head in the sand. Be sure your daughter can defend herself, change a tire on a lonely road, spot a potentially dangerous situation, understand the concept of safety in numbers, and state her wishes assertively and convincingly when she must. In short, be sure she has learned the mastery traits of a female warrior.

And don't make your daughter go to self-defense class alone. Enroll together. It's good advice for you too.

STRATEGY #6: TAKE SWIFT ACTION AGAINST SEXUAL ABUSE

The tendency for a mother to be attentive to, even vigilant of her daughter's interactions with men—including fathers, uncles, and brothers—is a natural response to having grown up female herself. Statistics show that many mothers were the unwilling recipients of adult male attention before they felt ready. One estimate is that one-third of all girls experience an unwanted, sexual encounter with an adult male before the age of eighteen. Approximately one-fourth of these incidents occur before puberty.[2] If you suspect, or have evidence of, sexual abuse of your daughter by her father or others, you must take swift and decisive action. You must not make excuses or turn away or pretend you don't know. This is one situation where you must take over. Your daughter cannot handle this one by herself.

Before discussing what action to take, let me say a few cautionary words. The notion of "suspicion of abuse" is a delicate matter. If a man is wrongly accused of sexual abuse, the accusation can, and probably will, ruin his life. Therefore, if you suspect abuse but have no concrete evidence, consult an expert such as a school counselor or social service worker to determine if your suspicion is valid. Be aware that an expert has a professional obligation to follow up in an official capacity, so you might want to call anonymously for the first contact.

By the same token, do not be timid either. If you suspect abuse, it is likely you have some good reason for doing so and should investigate further. The most important thing is to act quickly. Either talk to a professional or remove your daughter from danger. Do not wait. Your daughter's welfare is at stake if abuse is occurring. The emotional and psychological damage done by sexual abuse by men, especially fathers, takes an inestimable toll on a girl's life. You cannot afford to drag your feet or hope it isn't so. Do not let denial become an additional problem.

There are a number of reasons why denial has the potential to become a problem. Exposing sexual abuse by a father has the potential to, is even likely to, destroy a family. At least it will destroy the family as you now know it. But you cannot sacrifice your daughter to keep the family together. First, it is unconscionable to allow the destruction of one family member in order to "save" the others. Second, if he is abusing one daughter, he may have abused or he may in the future abuse other daughters or even sons. Third, "the family as you know it" is not really the family as you know it. Keeping a secret of this magnitude within a family is akin to having termites in the foundation of a building: the entire structure rests on a rotten foundation and will eventually tumble. Ignoring the problem will not solve it, make it go away, or save your family from destruction.

What will be the consequences? It depends. There are short-term, immediate consequences and long-term consequences. Short-term consequences revolve around the decisions of the authorities. Private therapists, doctors, or social service agencies may or may not insist that the father leave the home. They may insist that you prove you can keep your daughter safe from him if he remains in the home. Or they may remove your daughter from your home. Long-term consequences involve therapy, possible legal action, divorce, and financial concerns. Given the magnitude of these consequences, it is easy to see why some mothers pretend they don't know about abuse in order to keep the economic status of the family intact. Nevertheless, you must confront your fears and seek help. It's out there.

PART IV

Teenagers

CHAPTER 10

The Peril of Puberty

The Promise of Romance

I'm just a person trapped inside a woman's body.

Elayne Boosler

"Polly was the last person I ever expected to waltz in and ask for fake nails," said a mother in a workshop. "I mean, this is a girl who never gets out of torn, baggy jeans and flannel shirts. She's a tomboy, is enrolled in advanced math, and likes to play basketball with her brother, so when she announced she wanted fake nails, I was floored.

"When I asked her why, she rippled her fingers in the air and said, 'To make my hands look long and graceful. Mine are so stubby they look like a guy's.'"

"My daughter keeps changing her handwriting," added another mother. "One day there are hearts dotting her *i*'s, the next day happy faces. Then, for about a month it was printing only, very angular and artsy. After that, it was cursive, with girlish flourishes and curlicues."

"At least your daughter is only experimenting with her handwriting. Wait until she dies her hair purple or starts piercing and tattooing herself," said a good-natured mom who could actually laugh as she spoke.

"Or starts wearing seductive clothing," added a fourth mother, in a more serious tone. "I refused to let my daughter out of the house when she waltzed out of her bedroom in a skirt slit so high you could see her underpants. I'm a woman, and I understand she wants to be attractive, but I won't let her leave the house looking like a slut!"

Yes, one of the outstanding characteristics of puberty is that it is a time of experimentation with one's identity, which for a girl involves deciding which model of femininity she wishes to emulate. The wide variety of models available can be confusing. Though today's girls seem to feel less pressure to incorporate "nice and sweet" into their model of femininity than their mothers did, this cultural expectation has not disappeared entirely (varying from region to region), and we know that all girls feel pressure to be sexy, alluring, and attractive.

Acquiring a Feminine Persona: Why Bother?

Prior to puberty, displaying feminine traits was probably not all that important to your daughter, unless it was emphasized by her family. ("Act like a little lady," "Nice girls don't act like that," and "I hope you come out of this tomboy phase" are all comments of mothers reported by girls in mentorship groups.) Just learning about the world was probably far more interesting. With the advent of puberty, however, the cultivation of femininity moves to center stage.

Acquiring a feminine persona is a far more complicated matter than just coping with the new hormones coursing through one's body. Being popular in most schools is linked to one's ability to attract boys. During puberty, girls who acquire boyfriends come under intense scrutiny by other girls: how they look, act, talk, and dress. They become the new standard upon which a girl is judged as acceptable by her peer group.[1]

Add to this new standard of popularity (1) her own awakening body; (2) her newfound power over boys and her natural biological drives; (3) the opportunity to get love and approval from both her peer group and an individual boy, which is especially attractive to girls who feel inadequate or unloved; (4) cultural pressure to couple up; and (5) plain old healthy teenage curiosity—and you have a potent combination of forces. So potent that many girls will be distracted from achievement and preoccupied with acquiring feminine wiles as a tool to attract male attention and gain popularity.

Even if you have done your work diligently over the years and your daughter's self-esteem is strong and her behavior is resilient, at puberty you should not be surprised if your daughter experiments with different models of femininity or if she feels confusion, lack of self-confidence, or fear of inadequacy. She will be adjusting to the intense emotional fluctuations that accompany new hormones. She must cope with a new and as yet unformed sense of self as she works on decoding and developing her new identity as a young woman. She will be encountering for the first time, consciously or unconsciously, the cultural conflict between femininity and achievement and will be experimenting with reconciling the two.

Most importantly, she is preparing to enter, in a serious way, what Dr. Margaret Eisenhart calls the culture of romance. The problem is a one-two punch to a girl's strength and resilience. First, those aspects of femininity tainted with the demand to be deferential, decorative, and attractive can make incorporating femininity *and* staying mastery-oriented quite a challenge. Second, the demands of the culture of romance—its deeply held beliefs and expectations, the realities of the sexual marketplace, and a girl's newly acquired sexual currency—will become the greatest obstacle to both her mastery behavior and her self-esteem.

Unfortunately, we cannot change the historical time in which our daughters live and the confusing messages that come with changing sex roles. We cannot change the culture's ambivalent attitude toward femininity and achievement. We cannot change the culture of romance, which requires girls to be to be sexy and attractive in order to attract a mate. We can, however, with care and forethought, make girls aware of the forces acting upon them, and we can help them understand that they must keep their options open to avoid being oppressed by these lingering historical realities.

The Culture of Romance

To understand the modern culture of romance, as well as the myths embedded in it, let's take a quick look at its historical roots.

The model of modern romance actually began around the twelfth century with the notion of courtly love. This model required a knight to court the object of his affection by displaying tokens of his passion: songs; love poetry; carrying out her wishes by running errands, taking care of unpleasant chores, and rescuing her from dangerous situations; and bestowing gifts, both frivolous trinkets and expensive baubles. In turn, the lady was expected to play it coy for a while in order to challenge her knight. Later she would encourage him by allowing him to become physically closer—holding hands, hugging, kissing, and eventually petting and intercourse. While increasing physical intimacy can be seen as the natural course of events, the implication that the male "buys" the favors of the female complicates the picture substantially.

In today's sexual marketplace your daughter will discover that she possesses sexual currency in the form of her physical attributes, sexiness, and femininity. She will be subjected to a deeply embedded myth within the culture of romance that this currency can buy her happiness. The myth goes something like this: An attractive female, without exerting much effort or working too hard, can acquire wealth, status, intimacy, and safety simply by attracting the attention and favor of a man, particularly the "right" man. If he is a wealthy or powerful man, like Prince Charming, she can be freed from the drudgery of working, of cooking and cleaning, and in a more generic way, of having to cope with the difficulties inherent in life, for her man will be there to free her from these mundane chores and rescue her from difficult situations.

Though this model has undergone some modification over the centuries and has waxed and waned in popularity, for the most part, it remains the same. If you doubt the historical evolution from courtly love to modern romance, I ask you to consider the following.

First, a girl's physical attributes and the inherently attractive qualities of youth figure prominently in her ability to attract a quality mate. After all, it is Cinderella's beauty, not her social standing, brains, personality, self-esteem, or mastery skills that attract Prince Charming. As a girl acquires this sexual currency, it is natural for her to experiment with finding out what it will "get" her. This type of informal power is irresistible due to its sheer potency and simply because she has it!

Second, many a young woman is lured by the deeply embedded myth within the culture of romance: the possibility of not having to work, if she gets married and has children. This is the most insidious and deadly aspect of the culture of romance because it promotes a myth upon which many young women base all of their life choices. They often derail their own achievement and lower their aspirations in order to be successful with men in the sexual and emotional arena. The grain of truth that keeps this myth going is that some girls—a tiny, tiny minority—will actually marry rich men. This is unlikely, of course, and even a rich husband can go bankrupt or abandon his wife for a younger model. Also, in today's economic climate, the upper middle classes are much less financially secure than they were when you were growing up.

Of all the many bright, capable, and privileged young women who enter college with high aspirations and career goals for all the right reasons—namely, the intrinsic value of education and the desire for economic independence and professional opportunities—fewer than a third meet their own expectations for the future. In one study it was found that bright and capable women in coed colleges "ended up with intense involvements in heterosexual romantic relationships, marginalized career identities, and inferior preparation for their likely roles as future breadwinners."[2] We must ask ourselves why so many young women scale down their expectations and enter willingly into situations of economic inferiority that limit their options and make them vulnerable in an unpredictable economy.

According to the authors of that study, the peer systems of girls "promote and propel [them] into a world of romance in which their attractiveness to men counts most. The women [in the study] were subjected to a 'sexual auction block'...where academics commanded only limited attention." Though this study was conducted on college-age women, I can attest from listening to the girls I work with that these pressures begin as soon as girls reach sexual maturity, and their testimony suggests that culturally the pressure on girls may have increased over the last ten years. Much of the current literature on girls implies that the danger years occur during puberty and then end, but this study shows that young women are vulnerable to the myth of romance for many years following puberty, perhaps as long as they remain fertile.

In an eight-week series of group meetings I organized, wherein high school girls and adult women (not their mothers) met weekly to discuss issues of career, education, training, relationships, and life choices, everything went swimmingly until the subject of romance, marriage, children, and the dreaded possibility of divorce came up. When the adult women shared their experiences in relationships with men and emphasized how important it was for the girls to stay economically self-sufficient, the girls reacted with such extreme resistance that the women were shocked.

"We have never had a cross word in our group until the subjects of romance, marriage, children, work, and divorce came up," one woman reported. "The girls hung on our every word, as if pearls of wisdom were dropping from our mouths, until we got to the subject of marrying a financially secure husband, having babies, and living happily ever after."

"In our group there was no problem with the girls' level of aspiration," said another woman. "They wanted to be surgeons, architects, and attorneys. They believed they would have these fabulous careers and would reach their career goals by or before age thirty. Then they would marry a great guy, have children, stay at home for five to ten years, raise their children and take them to soccer games in their sport utility vehicles. Then, when that part of their lives was over, they thought they would be free to resume their fabulous careers."

Another woman added, "When we tried to encourage them to consider staying employed 'just in case,' they became sort of hostile. When we pointed out they would probably need two incomes to afford a decent house in our affluent community, they argued with us. 'We'll live in a small house,' they said. When we suggested that giving their children the advantages they themselves enjoy would probably require two incomes, they said. 'Those things are not important.' When we had the temerity to bring up the great unmentionable—the possibility of divorce—they went ballistic on us. 'You guys are just bitter because you have been divorced. Just because you made mistakes and poor choices doesn't mean we will.'"

While recognizing the noble aspect of this sentiment—the desire for a quality of life emphasizing family, friends, free time, and all the other ineffable aspects of life that money can't buy—gently let your daughter know that she needs to build survival skills to buttress herself against the uncertainties of life. The girls' protestations were a healthy backlash against the perceived mistakes of their parents, just as the career women of the 1970s were attempting to correct the excesses of the 1950s. However, the girls at the workshop were assuming that the world they faced would be the one their mothers faced. As we know, the only constant is change.

Today many women long to stay home and raise their children, but for the majority of women that is simply not a dependable scenario upon which to base life choices. Even if a woman is lucky enough to manage such a position for a time, too many things can go wrong: the death or debilitating illness of a spouse, loss of a husband's income through layoffs or downsizing, and the simple reality that nearly half of all marriages end in divorce. The truth is, staying home to raise one's children is a privilege, not a choice.

While it is true that children bring wondrous gifts into the lives of their mothers, they can also bring hardship, sacrifice, and difficulty. No one knows the fate of a child in terms of medical needs, personality, temperament, or any of a zillion other things that will also affect the life of the mother over the ensuing years. The greater a mother's financial independence, maturity level, degree of autonomy in the world, and control over her own life, the less vulnerable she will be to the stresses that a child can generate and the greater will be her opportunity to enjoy the marvelous gifts a child can bestow. Therefore, a critical component of keeping our girls resilient and well prepared for life's surprises and calamities is to ensure they see themselves as future breadwinners, just as we do our boys. Failing to do so leaves girls unprotected and deeply vulnerable to an uncertain future. Anything less cheats them and their children and leaves them vulnerable to economic dependency.

Perhaps the girls in the group described above failed to see the big picture because of their own class advantages. Most of them came from affluent, highly educated families in white suburban neighborhoods. My experience with working-class girls and those from less privileged families is that they have a different and often more realistic view of the world. In a survey of thirteen- to seventeen-year-olds by Girls Count, a girls' advocacy group in Denver, however, 81 percent said they did not expect to work outside the home once they had children.[3]

Furthermore, we must make girls aware that their income as the female partner must be more than just supplementary. When women enter voluntarily into economic dependence by accepting jobs that yield a low standard of living, they leave themselves far too vulnerable. If circumstances change and their income becomes the sole source for their family, they can be in serious trouble, particularly if they become single mothers. Generally speaking, if your daughter maintains her own source of income adequate to meet the needs of her family, she will be in greater control of her emotional life as well. Most of us know our share of women who are stuck in bad, perhaps even abusive, relationships because they lack the financial wherewithal to leave. This is particularly true when children are involved. When a woman owns her own money and has a viable source of income, she is less vulnerable to mistreatment by a spouse. To protect our daughters, and their children as well, we must teach them that to be economically dependent on a partner is a double-edged sword—a privilege with a price.

"My father harped on economic self-sufficiency all my life," said a mom in a workshop. "He absolutely insisted that all of his girls be educated and financially able to support themselves. I think it was because he watched both of his sisters marry complete flakes who were terrible providers. One sister had no education, no skills, no reliable means of support other than her husband, and she wound up struggling endlessly with periods of poverty and deprivation. The other sister, who was educated and ran her own business, was able to earn a good living, so her life was easier."

To be honest, some of the mothers in my workshops who stay home and raise their children seem to be a little shortsighted on this issue. Those who are fortunate enough to be taken care of by a loving spouse sometimes seem to forget that not all mothers are able to enjoy this status, that their daughters' futures may not be as certain as theirs, and that their status could change in a heartbeat. On occasion a mother will wonder aloud if I think stay-at-home motherhood is a viable option for girls. My answer is an ultimately practical one: It doesn't matter what I think. What matters is that many girls are mesmerized by the myth of romance, believe a man will take care of them, willingly limit their options, surrender their self-reliance, and thus become economically disadvantaged.

As counterpoint to the myth of romance, then, my advice is based not on my personal opinion but rather on the harsh realities of life. We must train our girls to prepare themselves well and protect their economic self-sufficiency first and foremost. Then, if they are lucky enough to have the option to stay home with their children, they can exercise personal choice in the matter.

The Culture of Romance and Its Effect on Mastery and Self-Esteem

The promise that is integral to the culture of romance wreaks havoc on the two most important arenas we have outlined for successful daughters throughout this book: a girl's mastery and her self-esteem. It doesn't take a rocket scientist to figure out that, if being attractive is the key to acquiring security, wealth, safety, and intimacy, many girls are going to lose their motivation to remain mastery-oriented high achievers. After all, if such valuable commodities can be won through the relatively simple act of attracting a man, why bother with all the hardships and difficulties inherent in high-level achievement? Of course, as adults, we know that hardships and difficulties are inherent in relationships as well, but this is not part of the promise. Happily-ever-after is the slow-to-die promise of romance. Furthermore, since mastery behavior is equated with masculinity in our culture, maintaining it becomes a more conflicted process, especially when femininity suddenly appears to be a girl's most valuable asset.

The culture of romance will also inflict serious damage on a girl's self-esteem if she doesn't measure up to this new criterion. Perhaps she does not fit the current standards of ideal feminine beauty. Perhaps she is a late bloomer. Perhaps her intelligence, ability, or mastery behavior scares away potential suitors. Since she won't know her sexual capital until she tries it out, however, she will be unsure whether or not she has the "right stuff." A girl will assess her physical attributes in relationship to the current ideal. She will look at what she can get in return for what she has to offer.

"In my school, the girls who put up with assholes are the ones who know they can't do any better," said a popular fifteen-year-old girl. "A cute girl knows she can get lots of different guys, so she doesn't put up with bad treatment."

"The guys know this, too," added another. "If an average guy manages to go out with a girl who is better-looking than he is, he usually treats her pretty well."

"For example?" I prompted.

"Well, he takes her out, buys her things, pays attention to her, talks nice about her to his friends. He figures if he doesn't, she'll find herself a guy who does."

"Also, a lot of guys know that you might get an ugly or fat girl to go further sexually because she is more desperate for attention," said a third. "It's pretty simple, really."

It's simple all right. Simple and brutal. The model of courtly love has morphed into a treacherous experience for many girls. For those who fall short of the ideal, there can be serious consequences, especially when they lower their expectations of respectful treatment from boys in order to make up for their supposed physical deficits. A girl who willingly endures bad treatment is giving testimony to her lack of confidence in her desirability, her value, her very self-worth. This attitude can increase a girl's vulnerability to the dangers inherent in promiscuity or in a willingness to accept abusive treatment.

Beauty, the Beast

Obviously, the pressure to be attractive is not exerted on teenagers alone. How many of us, if we speak honestly, have not assessed our own worth, our value in the sexual marketplace, and made accommodations to what we discover? How many of us cannot identify with Polly, the teenager who wanted fake nails, in order to acquire a more feminine, graceful silhouette? How many of us cannot sympathize with her attempts to acquire what was not genetically in the cards? How many of us can say we are satisfied with our bodies? After all, is this not the very stuff upon which Madison Avenue has built an empire?

A mother's own beauty issues will play an important role in her daughter's transition into puberty. If a girl witnesses her mother's constant preoccupation with her appearance and weight, how can she be expected to be free of this struggle herself? In addition to the pressure to be thin and fit, many girls tell me their moms add to these pressures with fashion and grooming critiques, particularly mothers of girls who adopt a grunge or granola style of dress (ripped and baggy jeans, oversize flannel shirts, rag socks, clunky boots, straight hair) or the Goth look (for Gothic, those girls who resemble refugees from an Anne Rice novel). Here are some actual statements provided by girls in my workshops, ages thirteen to seventeen, made by their mothers concerning their daughter's appearance.

To Granola or Grunge Girls	To Goth Girls
• You would look so much prettier if you would curl your hair or put on some lipstick or wear something feminine and attractive.	• Why don't you put on something pretty, something more feminine? Guys like girls to look feminine and pretty.
• Why don't you put on some makeup? You would look so much better.	• You look rough. Why not cultivate a softer look?
• You have such a lovely figure. Why do you hide it under baggy clothes?	• You'll never get a guy looking like that.
• If I had your legs, I'd show them off.	• Those big clunky shoes are not attractive. They make your ankles look thick.

"My mother took me to the mall last weekend to try on clothes," volunteered a girl in one of my mentorship groups. "I came out of the dressing room to show her this outfit. She said, 'That looks good on you. It hides all your figure flaws.' It made me feel terrible." Then she added, "My mother actually thought she was being supportive!"

Even though these comments may be well-intentioned, they often do more damage than good. More dangerous still are such "supportive" comments as "Aren't you putting on a little weight?" or "Should you be eating that?" or "How many calories have you consumed today?" or "If you exercised a little, you could take that weight off."

Since the whole issue of femininity and sex appeal is fraught with opportunities for mothers to project *their* own neuroses on their daughters, I humbly submit that distress over your daughter's appearance may be more about your ego than her emotional well-being. If you have always hated some figure flaw in yourself and notice that your daughter has inherited it, say nothing. Do not create in her the same self-hatred you have been trying to conquer all these years.

By the same token, if your daughter has a beautiful body, don't compliment her constantly or convey your envy. "My mother is always telling me how she would love to have my thighs with no cellulite or the firm breasts of youth again. It's embarrasing," said one girl. These kinds of comments only continue to draw attention to her body and can add to her self-consciousness.

Now, what if you have the opposite problem? What if you are not subtly pressuring your daughter to be appealing, attractive, or sexy, but she's doing it (*overdoing* it is perhaps the greater problem) all on her own? She may be dressing more seductively than you are comfortable with or spending vast amounts of time, money, and energy attempting to be beautiful. Is this a problem?

It depends. On the one hand, "vast amounts of time and money" would certainly be a red flag. On the other hand, most girls will experiment with the decorative accoutrements of femininity to one degree or another. Even the ones we would least expect, like Polly with the press-on nails.

"I was completely taken by surprise," said Polly's mom, "but we went to the store and got the nails anyway." There was a long pause.

"Is that the end of the story?" someone asked.

"No," she continued. "It wasn't long before she discovered they were a pain in the neck, popping off when she played basketball with her brother or shifted gears on her bike. She took them off, and I haven't heard anything about them since."

At that point, the women in the room breathed a collective sigh of relief—a response that I found curious, since it contained another kind of judgment. In truth, it is neither the fake nails nor the dress nor the hair that is the problem. The problem is that girls feel judged by their appearance. Some feel judged because they don't look feminine and attractive enough, while others feel judged if they do. Either way, the emphasis on appearance is perpetuated.

Girls will use self-decoration for a variety of reasons. One may use it as a means of self-expression and creativity, an artful statement of her individuality; this girl does not have a problem. Another may use her appearance as a status symbol, a weapon, or a way to get love and approval; she may have a problem. Another girl may simply be bored by attending to her looks and may have other interests to pursue; she doesn't have a problem. Still another may outwardly display a lack of interest in her physical appearance but may be motivated by the fear that she will be unable to meet the standards of beauty even if she tries; she does have a problem.

Appearance remains a complex issue for girls and their mothers. Of course I understand the motivation behind a mother's comments to her daughter concerning appearance. However, as adults we must be careful not to make girls feel self-conscious or inadequate one way or the other. Some mothers become concerned when their daughters seem sublimely unconcerned with feminine sex appeal. These mothers should remember that a healthy indifference or even outright rebellion may be a sign of character strength in a girl. Other mothers become concerned when the opposite is true. These mothers should remember that even a preoccupation with appearance may be nothing more alarming than experimentation with identity that is natural to this phase of life.

Conflict over appearance may be about generational differences concerning the outward display of femininity, or it may be about individual differences in taste between a mother and a daughter. So, even if your daughter looks a little too tomboyish or grungy or feminine or prissy (as one workshop mother called it) for your taste, if she seems happy with herself and has friends, maintains a decent grade point average, participates in school activities, and has lots of interests, do not create a problem where none exists. Use your discernment, but give her the chance to experiment. It's normal.

Suffering to Be Beautiful: Dieting and Femininity

In today's teen culture, the most critical aspects of your daughter's youthful femininity are weight and body type. The anecdotal evidence I have gathered from girls over the last ten years is that, while a pretty face is generally considered good, it is not enough to attract a guy if a girl is overweight. For a teenage girl, being overweight is the death of hope where boys are concerned. With this loss of hope comes the death of self-esteem as well. Today's girls live in fear of fat. This fear is so serious among teenage girls that it can ruin an otherwise happy life.

Even in girls who do not appear to have a bona fide eating disorder, I have witnessed a kind of pride in their conversations about resisting food, almost as if being a borderline anorexic were a badge of honor. Whereas ten or fifteen years ago girls in the hallways of my junior high used to congregate to talk about hair and makeup, girls now form little groups to discuss food and how to resist it. Just listen:

- Food is gross. It makes you fat.
- My sister told me I should try to stay hungry all day.
- I try not to eat at all.
- I only eat an apple and a potato per day. Oh, and nothing on the potato.
- I only drink diet drinks and eat lettuce or celery.
- My parents threatened to ground me again if I didn't eat. So I agreed to take one bite of whatever we have for dinner, but I take tiny bites.
- My friend is so lame. She complains about her weight, but she eats lunch every day at school. I told her she can't get skinny if she's going to eat.
- In response to one girl who says she is unable to starve herself because she gets too hungry, another replied, "My mother says you have to suffer to be beautiful."

I have witnessed junior high and middle school girls throw perfectly good sack lunches in the trash day after day without touching a bite. One girl told me, "I don't look in the sack in case there is something in there that might tempt me. My mother used to sneak things in my lunch that she knew I liked so that I would be tempted to eat. Now I just throw it away without looking."

Without the fuel necessary to keep brain activity functioning at a peak, these girls run the immediate risk of low performance and low grades, not to mention low energy and compromised immune systems. Over longer periods, should they develop full-blown anorexia, they will suffer from low blood pressure, infertility, edema, and hypothermia, not to mention the long-range damage that prolonged starvation causes to the heart, gastrointestinal system, and brain. Still, even when girls know this, they believe that the benefits of being thin far outweigh its consequences, as evidenced by the fact that fully 80 percent of our girls have been on a diet by the time they reach fifth grade![4]

Bulimia is also a very serious and very common problem. Bulimics, who get caught in the binge-purge syndrome and abuse laxatives and diuretics, will suffer physical repercussions. Constant purging can lead to a ruptured esophagus, damage to the pharynx, severe tooth erosion, bladder infections, and, even more seriously, heart and kidney failure.

Because girls with eating disorders typically hide their behavior or lie about it, concrete numbers are hard to come by. One thing we do know is that eating disorders are most likely to be exhibited by high achievers, perfectionists who are demanding of themselves, particularly when it comes to meeting the expectations of society. Since the models, actresses, and beauty queens held up as the ideal of feminine beauty are thinner than 95 percent of American women,[5] part of society's standard of achievement is thinness. Earning good grades, performing well in advanced math and science classes, being accepted by the college or university of one's choice, getting into graduate school, landing a good job, and starting one's own business are still not enough. One must also be thin to be a truly "successful" female in our society.

In urging our girls to be successful, we can inadvertently contribute to a preoccupation with thinness when they reach puberty. A mother must therefore take care not to give the impression that a certain weight or body type must be achieved in order to win her approval or meet her expectations. Society already does enough of that. A mother's job, and a father's as well, is to love unconditionally.

Emotions, Self-Esteem, and Mastery

During puberty a girl must learn to cope with the emotional ups and downs that accompany the new hormones coursing through her body—both the range of fluctuation from high to low and the rapidity with which they occur. We enhance a girl's resilience by teaching her to tolerate anxiety, endure frustration, and allay temporary feelings of inadequacy and self-doubt—in other words, the same components and processes of mastery behavior discussed earlier are now applied to the emotional realm.

To that end, let's take a moment to examine emotions more closely, since the appeal of talk shows and the popular psychological literature of some women's magazines can lead one to faulty conclusions concerning the meaning and importance of emotion.* While emotions can tell us a great deal about an individual's beliefs, how she responds to outside stimuli, and what hormones or chemicals are currently present in her bloodstream, in the end, they tell very little about who she is. Allow me to explain.

The most striking characteristic of emotions is that they are constantly shifting and changing from one minute to the next. In fact, the Latin root word from which the word "emotion" evolved is *movere,* which means "to move." Because emotions are constantly shifting, they are not reliable indicators of one's worth, abilities, talent, potential, or self-esteem. They are poor instruments for decision-making and poor prognosticators of one's future.

All that our emotions really tell us is how we are responding to our current circumstances and how consistent these circumstances are with our hopes, dreams, and desires. For example, when the external world matches our internal desires—that is, when we make the grade, get selected for a good job or a prestigious position, receive recognition from our peers, acquire material things, or attract the attention of a high-status guy—we usually feel good. When external reality does not match our internal desires, however—when we are rejected by a desirable person or overlooked for a good job, when we are criticized or forced to endure material deprivation—we feel bad. Feeling good and feeling bad, sometimes within minutes of each other, is a perfectly normal human response to the swirling, dancing, ever-changing landscape of external reality and internal desire.

You may be objecting here. Perhaps you are even in therapy to explore your emotions. Please remember that as an adult you have a more fully developed emotional life based on years of life experience. Not only are your daughter's turbulent emotions caused in part by her raging hormones, she also simply does not have as much information to use in processing her emotions. For example, if you have a critical boss, you may be able to allay potential distress by

---

*Clinical depression, which is often referred to in the popular parlance as an emotion, is in fact a physiological problem that is treatable. In addition, a depression that is caused by a distressing life event, such as sickness or the death of a loved one, is a normal response to loss, follows a relatively predictable course, has a beginning and an end, and is grief mislabeled as depression.

remembering a supportive boss. You then can control your emotional response to the situation by realizing that perhaps your current boss just isn't a nice person. You might not even realize that you have developed this moderating mechanism, as it may have become second nature. For those who lack this framework, however, emotions can easily spiral out of control and take on a life of their own. This is what your daughter is experiencing.

To take what would, in an adult, be a fleeting or moderated emotion and invest it with meaning is fraught with danger. "I feel bad" becomes "I am bad." Negative emotions in particular, which arise so easily in puberty, must be seen as part of the fabric and texture of life and not something to be "believed." They seem to carry meaning, and when they arise, we believe we are worthless. Positive emotions make us feel we are good or have value. In reality, both are fleeting responses to a passing moment.

The problem is, how often in everyday life does external reality actually match internal desire? Deconstructing emotions by accepting that they are a result of the interplay between desire and reality—and not an indication of who we are, what we are, or what we can be—is cultivating mastery in the emotional realm. It is developing the capacity to look at a negative emotion and say, "Well, either I'm not getting what I want or I'm getting what I don't want, but these circumstances can change"—no conclusions or proclamations or decisions concerning self-worth.

The component of mastery behavior you are seeking to develop in your daughter, then, is this capacity to see *through* emotions, so that they are not the only story available. To continue the process of developing resilience that began in childhood, you must help your daughter understand that identifying herself with a passing negative emotion or a temporary situation is just another "story," another way to construe reality that gives rise to confusion and pain; that a bad day, a negative event, or a temporary setback does not have to lead to a loss of self-esteem. There are several ways to do this.

Emotions are powerful and convincing, so do not trivialize your daughter's feelings. If you do that, she will become even more theatrical to convince you this emotion is "real" even though it is likely to pass quickly. This theatricality often occurs when fathers and teenage daughters interact, because men do not, for the most part, take feelings very seriously, and this causes their daughters to become exceedingly melodramatic. Protestations of "You just don't understand!" accompanied by door-slamming episodes in which she throws herself tragically upon her bed become increasingly frequent.

Instead of trivializing her emotions, say a few comforting words to acknowledge her feelings and give her some comfort, but do not overindulge her or subtly collude with her by searching for their meaning. She will get plenty of that from her girlfriends. Remember that parents are more likely to discuss sad events with girls than with boys, and they use more emotional language with girls.[6]

Instead, keep it simple. When she's feeling better, follow up with a conversation and disseminate the information that emotions arise when people become stressed. Tell her that puberty is a time when she is confronting, for the first time, many of the life skills she will need as a young adult, so she naturally feels emotional and stressed out. Remind her that intense emotions arise as one learns to negotiate one's way through life and through great changes: puberty, starting a new job, entering a new school, going away to college, getting married, moving to a new location, having a baby, even aging and dying. Intense feelings come and go as each new life skill is encountered and learned. My own mother, in response to my tears as a teen, would say, "I know you feel terrible, but you have to take the bad with the good in life. They go together."

Most importantly, do not assume she knows these things. Tell her. By doing so, you teach your daughter how to give emotions their proper place. You teach her that they exist, they are valid, they will be experienced, and they will change.

An emotional display that is related to a failure can be a particularly ripe moment, an opportunity, if you will, to remind her of the nature of the process. By puberty she will have lived long enough to have acquired some of the perspective that comes with the passage of time. Therefore you can remind her of the days when she couldn't read, ride a bike, stay upright on her skates, ski down a mountain, play a tune on her guitar, do long division, or a hundred other things you will come up with. When she feels inadequate or unprepared, tell her that in your experience most of life involves preparing to the best of your ability and faking the rest. Tell her about the times when you have done exactly that:

- Even though I wasn't sure I could handle the situation, I just thought, Well, I'll handle it as it comes, and even if I blow it, there will be more opportunities to do it right in the future.
- I just told myself that humans make mistakes and I'm human!
- Even though I felt unsure, I decided to rise to the challenge when it presented itself.
- It's smart to take one day at a time. Projecting too far into the future is counterproductive.

Teach your daughter a resilient interpretation of and response to the endless and vivid array of life's ups and downs:

- Even though you don't feel so hot today, remember you are still a strong and capable person.
- Even though you are temporarily confused, you are quite capable of understanding and succeeding at math. Confusion just means you haven't arrived there yet.
- Even if you don't do well in the competition, I adore you anyway.
- Even though that particular boy, at that particular time did not ask you out, you are a lovable and adorable person. You have no idea how many other boys wanted to ask you out but were afraid.
- Even this situation, bad as it is, will pass. I promise you, you will feel better.

If she says something self-deprecating, respond with

- That's not how I see you.
- I can see you feel bad about yourself right now, and I understand why. But what *I* see is a person who is temporarily confused, not feeling well, in the midst of learning something new, frustrated about a particular situation, learning about life.

Remember that these comments are reflected appraisals, statements that reflect back to your daughter how you see her. Since reflected appraisals are one of the ways we learn about who we are, they are powerful over time and with repetition. Notice that the above responses tell your daughter she is perfect, whole, lovable, capable, and beautiful, even in the midst of her confusion, failure, doubt, or dismay. When she argues with you—and she will—remain steadfast in your insistence that she is a lovable, competent, and worthy human being. Say, "You are not going to convince me that you are stupid (or fat or ugly). My job, as one who loves you very much, is to tell you the truth about who you are."

This kind of unconditional love, the kind that says you love, respect, and admire her even when she has failed, even when she doesn't love herself, even when she is lost in confusion and fear, will be a powerful (even if not immediate), antidote to her pain because you are showing her how to love herself. It is from you she will first learn this. You may not see the results immediately, but these are seeds you must plant anyway.

Since puberty is the period during which your daughter will be highly vulnerable to negative interpretations of her behavior, you must offer criticism thoughtfully and carefully. Arguing with her simply doesn't work. When she says something self-deprecating, resist responding with comments like "That's ridiculous" or "Where did you get a crazy idea like that?" To be effective with teenagers, you have to outfox them.

Set an example for your daughter. Allow her to witness you correcting your own shortcomings, errors in judgment, and mistakes in behavior without berating, judging, or condemning yourself. In turn, you must correct *her*, without judging, condemning, or berating her. In other words, you must help her make corrections without subtly suggesting there is something wrong with her.

If your criticism is too harsh or does not have the motivation of real love behind it, your daughter may respond by becoming depressed and withdrawn or by acting rebellious and resentful. Teenagers are adept at seeing through parental ego projections and value judgments, and they are easily hurt and angered. They also have more motivation and energy to engage in battle than their parents do.

Girls with an Attitude

Ironically, although the rebellious response is more difficult for the parent, it can indicate a more masterful, resilient attitude in the girl.

Whereas withdrawal and depression are often the result of internalizing failure or blame—the behavior of learned helplessness that can lead to despair—rebellion can indicate a healthy externalization of the problem. Although potentially problematic, it has the potential to be transformed into something positive because anger has a lot of energy behind it.

I recognize the problem if a daughter refuses to take responsibility for the consequences of her actions. This, however, is more likely to be a male response than a female response. Girls tend to internalize, blame themselves, and become depressed. Nevertheless, plenty of teenage girls will develop quite an attitude and an assessment of adults that is contemptuous and disdainful. This can be disconcerting for parents of daughters who seem to have no qualms whatsoever about expressing their contempt. While a son may huff away in anger, refusing to argue, a girl will likely stand her ground and fight with you verbally.

When I mentioned the research that described girls as reluctant to speak the truth, one mother in a workshop blurted out, "What do you mean? My daughter will stand there and argue endlessly to make her point. She is very sarcastic. She rolls her eyes. She sighs. She has a whole repertoire of very effective nonverbal communications that she uses to strengthen her verbal arguments. The last thing she needs is coaching about how to express herself. She does just fine."

The room then burst into what appeared to be a single, coordinated choreographed movement of heads, all nodding in vigorous agreement by mothers raising teenage girls. The movement was so uniform it looked rehearsed. Everyone started laughing.

"Seriously, though," she continued, "what do you mean?"

First, it is important to remember that your daughter's ability and willingness to argue with *you* is founded on a feeling of safety. Just because she can stand her ground with you does not mean she necessarily does so with others. Second, to a certain degree, she is doing her developmental job. She must form an individual identity separate (though connected) and unique from her parents, so, to some extent, this behavior is normal. Third, the hormonal changes experienced by girls will make them volatile until things settle down physiologically. This volatility can last until age seventeen or eighteen, though it is usually associated with early adolescence.

While some adolescent girls will put on a marvelous display of resistance to their mother's advice, the operative word here is "display." If, during her childhood, you modeled and mentored and, most importantly, established a loving relationship with your daughter, she will probably be more receptive to motherly advice than she is willing to let on. My experience with girls suggests that they are less mother-resistant than they would like us to believe.

"Even though I argue a lot with my mom," said a thirteen-year-old, "I go back to my room and think about what she said. Lots of times I take her advice, too. I just don't tell her. This makes me feel a little guilty, especially if we've had a big fight, but I feel that if I tell her, then she'll have too much control over me."

There is a wealth of information in that statement. First, girls often *do* listen to their moms. The research also shows this. Girls are strengthened by close associations with women who have "been there," with advice from the clan. Second, they need time to think over what their mothers have said, and they are likely to do so when not engaged in the heat of battle. Third, adolescent girls need to feel independent and free to make their own choices, liberated from the watchful guidance of their mothers. Of course we know they still need this watchful guidance, so mothers have to outsmart, outfox, and outstrategize their daughters. There are several ways to do this.

Learning to Give Advice That Teenagers Can Hear

Learning how to give advice, guidance, and wise counsel to a teenager, without appearing to control her, is an art form. If you don't learn it, you will become engaged in more battles than is necessary. (A few are inevitable.)

The most likely way to be heard is simply to relate your personal experience. If you think about it, this is where most of your opinions come from anyway. Talk to your teenager scrupulously using the pronoun "I" rather than "you." (Psychologists refer to these as "I-messages.") This may seem nitpicky, but using the pronoun "you" will only sound like a lecture to a teenager. Remembering to us "I" can be especially difficult if your daughter actually asks your opinion. Consider the following:

Mary: Mom, do you think I should take algebra next year?
Mom: Absolutely.

Mary: But I don't like math.

Mom: It doesn't matter whether you like math or not. You should take it.

Mary: But what if I get a bad grade?

Mom: You won't get a bad grade if you study.

Mary: Yes, I will. I hate math, and I get confused.

Mom: You should take it anyway because it is important for your future if you want to get into college.

Mary: Yeah, but a bad grade will ruin my grade point average.

Mom: If you study, you'll be all right.

Mary: You never listen to me. I told you I don't understand math, but all you think about is what I *should* do.

Mom: Why did you ask my opinion if you didn't want to hear it?

In addition to Mary's negative response to the phrase, "You should," you may have noticed that she is also a master of the "Yeah, but" game. Mom, beware! There is a trap for parents in "Yeah, but," and it is a no-win situation for you. Mary is seeking to get Mom to solve her problem, but there's a catch: Mary has asked her advice, wants her mom to solve the problem, but doesn't really want to take the advice from her mom. Here is an alternative.

Mary: Mom, do you think I should take algebra next year?

Mom: Absolutely.

Mary: Yeah, but I don't like math.

Mom: I know what you mean. I felt that way when I had to learn the new programming language at work. But since I didn't have a choice, I learned it anyway. Now I'm glad I did, because I have acquired another career skill. It will make me more competitive for future jobs and more self-reliant in this one in the future.

Mary: Yeah, but I *do* have a choice. I don't have to take algebra.

Mom: I think it only appears you have a choice. To get into college and later to have a chance at the best career opportunities and the freedom to move around, certain skills are going to be necessary. Math is one of them.

Mary: I hate math.

Mom: Yeah, preparing oneself for the future requires a lot of effort.

Mary: What if I get a bad grade?

Mom: Well, that won't be the end of the world. When I was in high school I got a few low grades on the first couple of quizzes in chemistry, but I went to the teacher for extra help, learned how to study chemistry, and eventually began to understand it better. The low quiz scores caused me to get a lower grade the first quarter, but I was able to bring it up during the rest of the year.

Mary: Yeah, but what if I can't? What if I just get more and more confused?

Mom: Well, no decision is carved in stone. A person can always make a new decision. My opinion is that math is so important for future jobs and such that, if I were you, I'd take the risk and see how I do before deciding it wasn't for me. Also, I'll be glad to help you where I can or get you a tutor or whatever you need to help you succeed.

Notice the absence of the phrase "you should" in the above conversation, although there were many opportunities to use it. This is not always easy. You may have to pause and collect your thoughts in order to avoid it. It's okay to pause and say, "Let me think about that for a minute." This is advisable because the typical teenager has her antennae out, ever ready to detect the slightest attempt to control her. Since many teenagers believe adults are always telling them what to do, rather than letting them make their choices, learning to avoid the phrase "you should" is well worth the effort.

In addition, the quickest way to deflect an argument is to agree with your daughter or acknowledge her. This means that no matter what she says, you can respond with an acknowledgment or agreement and then follow with your own point. Avoid using the word "but," as in the following responses:

- "I see your point." Pause. "Have you thought of this?"
- "I hear what you are saying." Pause. "Here is an idea."
- "I can see you feel strongly about that." Pause. "Here is my point of view."
- "That's an interesting way to look at it." Pause. "I think this is a possibility as well."
- "I never thought about it quite like that." Pause. "On the other hand..."

You get the idea. The idea conveyed by the word "but" is implied within what you are saying. However, using the word "but" is an immediate signal to a teenager to argue further, since she will feel you are discounting her points.

Although these techniques will not circumvent every argument, they will send the message that you respect her point of view. This will make her more receptive to yours and less likely to close down in anger. (Besides, it's fun to outsmart your kids!)

In some situations, though, the wisest course is simply to allow the natural consequence to happen. Vigilance and even foresight are required to detect where an encounter is likely to go. If, for example, you see a situation developing much like others in the past, simply refuse to become embroiled. Consider the following:

Fatima: (Pleadingly, from her bedroom.) Mooooommmmm, I can't find my red shirt.

Mom: (Yelling back from the kitchen.) Wear a different one.

Fatima: I don't want to wear a different one.

Mom: Maybe it's in the clothes hamper.

Fatima: I looked. (Becoming increasingly frantic.) Mom, come in here and help me look. I'm already late for school!

Mom: (Standing in the bedroom doorway.) You know, if you would keep your room picked up, this wouldn't happen. Look at this mess! You never put anything away. I don't know how you can stand to sleep in here. I didn't raise you to live like this. This is disgusting.

Fatima: Jeez, you act like I'm a criminal or something.

Mom: Oh, don't exaggerate. Here's your shirt. Oh, my God, look at this. It's wrinkled. You can't wear it like this! Now you have to take the time to iron it. If you had put it away in the first place, you wouldn't have lost it and then you wouldn't have to iron it.

Fatima: Forget it! Leave me alone! I ask for help, but all you ever do is criticize.

Mom: Fine. Don't ask for my help next time.

Fatima: Don't worry, I won't!

Now, this is not a serious enough argument to cause a permanent rift in the mother-daughter relationship. It does, however, reflect a certain tension between mother and daughter that could have been avoided. There was a point in the conversation at which Mom could have given a different response, refused to become involved, and let her daughter fend for herself with the problem she had created. When her daughter said, "Mom, come in here and help me look. I'm already late!" her mother could have replied, "Honey, we have had this argument before. I do not wish to get involved in this again. Every time I do, we just get in an argument. I'd love to help, but you're on your own."

Now, I didn't say this was going to be easy, nor is it psychologically appealing to many women. Some mothers will be sorely tempted—dare I say compelled?—to go in and help, particularly when their daughters plead or resort to the perennial, plaintive wail, "Moooommmm" that you are all so familiar with. It will take fortitude to avoid rescuing her, but one day in the not-so-distant future, you will not be there to find her shirt or iron it for her.

Remembering Puberty: A Way to Help

Most of us would prefer not to think back to our own experience of puberty. The majority of adults do not recall this period with fondness, nor do they number the events of puberty among the most sterling moments of their personal histories. Nevertheless, recalling your puberty and even allowing yourself to reexperience the feelings associated with it will help you empathize with your daughter. So take a moment right now, as an adult, and think back to that time in your life.

Remember worrying that your first period would arrive during school hours, cause an accident, and embarrass you to the extent that you would be unable to return to school—*ever?* Remember checking your breasts nearly every day to determine if they were growing? Remember asking your mother if you could shave your legs? Remember checking for pubic hair? Remember hating the way that pad felt and thinking that you would never play basketball with your brother or have any fun, ever again? Remember worrying about inserting your first tampon? Remember your first bout with cramps? Remember the emotional mood swings?

All of the above have been related by mothers and daughters in workshops. I am sure you will identify with them. I am not going to give much advice here about the physiological and emotional changes of puberty because you've been there, done that. My only advice is to remind you that puberty is happening to girls today earlier than it did for many of their mothers. Before your daughter reaches age ten, you need to tell her everything that will be happening to her body, because some girls will begin to experience puberty by that age.

Also, I think it's a good idea to purchase all the equipment and give it to her ahead of time. Tell her to put it somewhere in her room so it is there for her when she needs it. This will enable her to be self-sufficient if you happen not to be at home when her period arrives. Or, if your daughter wants to handle it by herself before she tells you, she will have the opportunity to do so and will feel independent and in control of the situation.

The Arrival of Boys

Remember the first time a boy showed sexual interest in you? How did it make you feel? Some girls, no doubt, were surprised, some frightened, some flattered, some annoyed, some intrigued, some insulted, some flustered, some intimidated, some thrilled. The vast majority of us felt a combination of clashing emotions, a confusing blend of wonder, fear, and embarrassment mingled with curiosity and anticipation. It is simultaneously exciting and scary to discover in oneself this awesome new power of femininity. Particularly unsettling is the fact that this power is one that a girl does nothing to acquire. By virtue of her youthful hormones she simply has it one day. Like growing, her body does it while she isn't paying attention.

I remember the first time a car full of boys hooted at me on the way home from school. I was about fourteen. My first response was shock. I actually looked around to see who they were shouting at. Then there was a brief moment of realization ("My God, they're hooting at me!"), followed by indignation ("How dare they!"), then wonder ("Is this a good thing or a bad thing?"), then secret pleasure ("Does this mean I'm attractive?"), and finally fear ("Are they going to bother me?").

My conversations with mothers and girls suggest that my reaction was a typical one. Since this type of male attention is such a confusing mishmash of both tribute and insult, a girl often has difficulty gauging her feelings. Sometimes, if she is with other girls the first time it happens, she will take her cues from them—flattered if they are impressed, embarrassed or indignant if they are disapproving.

She might also take her cues from you, if you tell her how you reacted in similar circumstances.

Indeed, with each new experience of herself as an awakening sexual being, she will need time and compassion as she processes all this new information into her value system. Your experiences will be invaluable to her.

The Preoccupation with Boys: How Much Is Too Much?

In my experience, a serious preoccupation with boys can be a threat to a girl's aspirations and performance. It can also be an indication of her lack of self-confidence in academic and social areas, an over-identification of herself as a sexual object, or a need for attention from an adult. It should not go unheeded. If you believe your daughter has become sexually active, jump ahead to the next chapter, which gives some tips in coaching your daughter through love relationships and sexual encounters while keeping her mastery and self-esteem intact.

How do I define a "serious preoccupation"? This is a difficult call because interest in the opposite sex is a normal aspect of the awakening that happens at puberty. Furthermore, let's face it, adolescent girls—like mature women—talk about guys and their relationships with them all the time. Therefore, determining what is a problem and what is normal is a bit of a challenge.

A girl who seems to be getting her self-esteem solely from male attention—one who focuses her energy exclusively on attracting dates while ignoring her development in other areas, who seems to have no interests in activities if boys are not involved, who spends the vast majority of her time with boys to the exclusion of female friends—has a "serious preoccupation" that is detrimental to achievement and performance in other realms.

It's not *wrong* for a girl to get sidetracked by male attention—it is not a moral issue—but a girl who starts to acquire her self-esteem, her confidence, and her identity through the attention of boys has fallen into a trap. This is a particular danger if the girl happens to be a beauty. She is likely to receive so much attention simply because of this one facet of herself that she could be completely swept away by the promise of romance.

A preoccupation with boys will probably not have serious consequences in the life of a twelve- to fifteen-year-old, but if it continues as she enters high school, this obsession could become a threat to her aspirations and achievements. My advice in this circumstance may seem shocking: if you can afford it, send her to an all-girls school. I know this sounds extreme (and expensive), but the evidence of the benefits to girls of single-sex schools is so compelling that you may want to consider one of these schools even if your daughter is not preoccupied with boys.

Studies spanning the last twenty-six years document greater benefits to girls who attend single-sex high schools and colleges than to those who attend coed institutions. They show that girls in single-sex schools have higher self-esteem, are more serious about their studies, display greater intellectual curiosity for a longer period of time, show greater interest in math and science, and achieve more in their future careers. Graduates of girls' schools are two to three times more likely to enter medical school, earn undergraduate and graduate degrees in mathematics and science, work for Fortune 500 companies, and become elected officials at all levels of government.

Why? In girls' schools, adult women faculty members are seen as serious scholars, researchers, thinkers, and authorities. There are more leadership opportunities for girls as well; girls are the jocks, the school leaders, and the best students. In short, the achievements of girls are more visible and are taken more seriously. The atmosphere is more studious at single-sex schools than at coed schools, where social life intrudes on academic life. Since there are no boys, the preoccupation with appearance lessens. Girls devote more time and attention to their academic work than to their looks.

Most girls will probably resist the idea mightily, especially at first. She may believe that she will never have an opportunity to interact with boys again. Even some adults use this outdated argument against girls' schools, saying girls do not learn the social aspects of relating to boys. In reality, there are plenty of opportunities for students at girls' school to interact with boys. Girls' schools typically mingle socially with boys' schools and hold regularly scheduled social events together. The difference is that these events do not take place daily on campus where they would cause a distraction from academics. Reassure your daughter that she can meet boys just about anywhere and that attendance at a girl's school does not preclude meeting and socializing with the opposite sex. Tell her that, upon graduation, girls report feeling very positive about having attended a girls' school, and add that the experience helped them develop assertiveness and a strong sense of identity.[7]

Helping Dad to Be a Positive Influence During His Daughter's Puberty

While a loving and involved father is crucial to your daughter's self-esteem from earliest childhood, her need reaches its zenith during her puberty. The father plays a powerful role in a girl's perception of femininity. Most likely, however, he will be unaware of the scope of his influence. It will be your job to make him aware and to help him be a positive influence.

Typically, men are uncomfortable when they feel out of control, yet a daughter's puberty may be the most out-of-control situation her father will ever experience. His once-adoring little girl suddenly couldn't care less if she pleases him. He is hurt. She may express an outright dislike of his authoritarianism. He may clamp down harder. She may think he is silly. He will be offended. If she dresses seductively, he will be confused. If she refuses to be controlled or manipulated, he may blow up. If all of his attempts to control her meet with resistance and all of his attempts to understand her end in confusion, he may withdraw completely. While withdrawal is preferable to rage (another strong possibility), it will be a stealthy saboteur of her self-esteem.

Since she is a long way from emotional maturity and is still operating with a child's mind in many respects, without worldly experience to draw from she will likely reach all the wrong conclusions. She will experience his withdrawal as emotional abandonment, interpreting it as a sign that she is not lovable or "not okay." Like the children of divorce who often blame themselves when Mommy and Daddy split up, she may blame herself and feel inadequate or unattractive.

Couple her feelings of abandonment with her father's fears of her changing body, his confusion of his new role, his lack of understanding of her emotional outbursts, his distrust and jealousy of the adolescent males who are suddenly hanging around, and, for many fathers, what amounts to actual disapproval of his daughter growing up, and you have a volatile situation, with strong potential for a father to abandon his daughter emotionally just when she needs him the most.

All this is to emphasize how important it is for a father to stay actively involved with his daughter throughout her teen years. Since your daughter's father came to maturity as a male, the subtleties of the female experience will escape him. Help him to understand the following:

- He must not take his daughter's emotional outbursts or snotty attitude personally. It is part of her developmental job to separate from him. Even though it may hurt his feelings, it is a natural process.

- He must not emotionally withdraw from his daughter based on his own fears. Instead, he must learn new ways to express his affection: a warm hug, a pat on the back, or holding her hand if she is upset. Simply by making eye contact with her when she is speaking to him, he can send the message that he is emotionally available and paying attention.

- He should try to curb, or at least avoid acting out, jealous feelings that naturally arise when boys start hanging around. Remember, his impulse to be overprotective arises because he was once a teenage boy himself. He has little room for tolerance, feeling he understands teenage boys only too well. Encourage him to trust his daughter and remember that you both have instilled values in her.

- He should not make her feel guilty or "dirty" about becoming a woman. If he has unresolved sexual issues, he may react negatively to his daughter's physical maturation process. He should not project his problems onto her. She is innocent.

- He should take every opportunity to generously bestow upon his daughter one of his most valuable commodities—male approval. Complimenting her on appearance is not pandering to cultural pressures; it is recognizing that his daughter needs reassurance from a loving father that she is becoming an attractive young woman.

- He must never tease her about her body, even if his intentions are innocent or playful. Sometimes, out of his own embarrassment, a father will tease a girl to alleviate his discomfort. She will interpret it as criticism of her body and be hurt.

- He must not always insist she be a "good girl," for this behavior can be confused with submission and acquiescence to the wishes of others.
- He should build her self-esteem through encouragement and love, not pressure or fault-finding.
- He should examine his own beliefs about women, since those beliefs will be transferred to his daughter as she becomes a woman.
- Finally, he must allow himself to grieve for the loss of his little girl in order to welcome the arrival of the young woman. In this way, he will be more open to the beautiful transformation he will be privileged to see only once per child. Help him to cherish it.

CHAPTER 11

Mastery Revisited

The Older Teenager

The trouble is, you raise a mastery-oriented risk-taker and then you're stuck with a mastery-oriented risk-taker.

Mother of a seventeen-year-old girl

Our scene opens early on a Saturday morning. The house is quiet. Everyone is still sleeping except for Mindy and her mother, Sheila. They discuss their week over steaming tea and toasted bagels in a cocoon of domesticity. Sheila is savoring the womanly intimacy that has been developing between them now that Mindy is eighteen, and gives herself a mental pat on the back for the open, adult way in which they communicate. Suddenly, her daughter drops a bomb.

"Hey, Mom. Remember that guy I went out with about a week ago, the soundman for Bitter Fruit?"

"The good-looking blond?"

"Uh-huh."

"He seems like a nice kid."

"Well, he's opening his own recording studio."

"That's nice."

"Yeah, it's so cool." Pause. "Guess what?"

"What?"

"He's asked me to be his apprentice. He said he would teach me everything he knows about sound."

"I thought you didn't like him." At this point, Sheila feels a vague but unmistakable disquiet building from within.

"I don't. Not as a boyfriend anyway. He's too geeky. But he knows a lot about mixing and recording. I think it would be so cool to learn that technology."

"Doesn't that stuff take a long time to learn?"

"Yeah."

Sheila puts down her bagel. "When would you have the time? You leave for college in less than two months."

Mindy pauses, preparing herself for the chain reaction she is about to ignite. "I've decided to take a break before I go to college."

"What!"

"Only for about a year."

"Mindy, have you lost your mind?"

"I knew I shouldn't tell you. I knew you'd lose it."

"Mindy, there is no future in the music business. Everyone knows it's the most insecure, overglamorized, underpaid business in the world. Musicians struggle and struggle and don't make any real money. Besides, you couldn't pick a riskier line of work if you tried. You're not ready for the pressures you would have to face."

"How do *you* know?"

"Don't use that tone with me."

"No, really, how do you know?"

"I just know."

Mindy rolls her eyes. "Oh, that's a great answer. Kind of like 'Because I told you so.'"

"I don't care if it's a good answer or not. I can't stand by and let you make a big mistake."

"Why not? It wouldn't be the end of the world. I'm only eighteen. There'll be lots of time to make up for mistakes. Anyway, how will I learn if I don't try?"

"That's not the point."

"I think it's the whole point."

"You remember how hard your aunt Judy tried, and look where it got her."

"But she's a singer. I'd be on the technical side."

"So? What's that got to do with it?"

"There will always be a demand for good sound techies, and the technical knowledge would apply in other fields."

"What about college? You took the SATs and everything."

"I'm still going to go to college. I told you, this is just a break. My SAT scores will hold for another year."

"Why don't you study sound technology after college? Get some security under your belt and then take a chance with something unusual."

"You call college security? Look at all the kids who come out of college and wind up working as telemarketers or waiters because they can't find a job in their field. You act like college is some kind of guarantee. Besides, the opportunity is now, not four years from now."

"I'm sorry, Mindy. I cannot support you in this. I want you to forget the whole thing."

"Why do you always encourage me to do what I want and be what I want and then, when I try, you go ballistic?"

"I'm not going ballistic. I just thought you were smarter than this."

"Thanks."

"Mindy, I'm not trying to insult you. I just want you to listen to reason."

"Well, I don't want to listen to reason. I'm young and I want to try new things, and you can't stop me!"

Sigh.

Some things do not change, like the conflicts between teenagers and their parents, with the emphasis on the and-you-can't-stop-me theme. But if we disconnect from the emotional issues for a moment, we discover that this particular exchange contains some significant nuances.

Because Mindy has been raised to be a mastery-oriented risk-taker, the unconventional path is attractive to her. She has become interested in a technical field; this is highly unusual for a girl, and the work could be profitable. She is correct when she says the technical knowledge will carry over into other career fields. Mindy does not seem to be motivated by a potential romantic relationship; she's simply intrigued by what the boy has to teach her. Finally, although many of you will not agree with me, I think Mindy makes a point worth considering when she says that, at eighteen, she has plenty of time to make mistakes and corrections. Of course, her mother is concerned she will never go to college, but there are ways to make it worth her while to do so after the experimental year.

I am more interested in drawing your attention to the mother. Sheila appears to be having some doubts about having raised a mastery-oriented risk-taker. Now that Mindy wants to apply the

attitudes and skills, which Sheila has so carefully cultivated, to something unconventional and risky, Sheila is having, shall we say, second
thoughts?

This is, of course, the great dilemma in raising such a daughter.
She may make decisions that stray from the conventional and take
chances that will cause her hardship and difficulty. On the other
hand, she may become a wildly successful entrepreneur like Steve
Jobs or Steve Wozniak. Who can say? It is the very strength and
resilience a mother has cultivated, coupled with her daughter's
curiosity about life and confidence in her abilities that may lead her
in directions for which a mother is unprepared.

On the other hand, unforeseen decisions and detours in the road
can happen anyway. Mindy could go off to college, meet Mr. Right,
and come home to announce she is dropping out of school to get
married. A mother may well ask herself, "Which makes me more
nervous: raising a budding young entrepreneur who is wildly naive
or raising a hopeful young fiancée who is wildly naive? And why?"

Yes, many older teenage girls, starting at around sixteen or seventeen, regain the strength, curiosity, and sheer chutzpah they exhibited prior to puberty, particularly if a mother has been modeling and
cultivating mastery behavior. Even with an older teenage daughter
who has high self-esteem and mastery skills, however, her maturity
is still new and fragile. Unfortunately, she is not likely to see it that
way, and she will make strong arguments to her mother that she is
now an adult and perfectly capable of handling herself in all situations. Indeed, many seventeen-year-old girls, especially those who
have both a job and a car, appear to function very much like mature
adults. Given the mobility of having wheels and the independence
of having a few bucks in her pocket, a girl may feel like her mother's
equal.

This confident attitude creates conflict in her mother because, on
the one hand, she *wants* her daughter to feel like a capable adult
who can make her own decisions and take care of herself, while, on
the other hand, she feels that her daughter's judgment is still far too
immature. Therefore, the issues surrounding adult decisions such as
curfews, dating, chaperons, jobs, car privileges, and so on will be a
battleground for many other mothers and daughters. Somewhere
between the two extremes of a daughter's desire for independence
and a mother's desire to protect, lies a reality with which they both

can live, if the mother is willing to negotiate, negotiate, negotiate. Let's start with a clear-cut issue.

Balancing Work and School

"Having a job makes me feel mature and responsible," said a sixteen-year-old girl in a recent workshop. "I don't understand why my mother objects to it. You would think she would be happy that I am earning money."

It is easy to see both points of view. A girl wants to earn money but her mother is concerned over academics and stress. Some parents get so focused on their daughter's grades, however, that they overlook the psychological benefits that work can bring. Having a job, earning one's own income, being responsible to a boss, and meeting the rigors of a work schedule are all high-level mastery tasks for a teenager and can deliver a powerful boost to the self-esteem of a timid girl or an underachiever in the academic realm. In addition, for all girls, a job is certainly a healthy preview of the requirements that will be placed upon her as an adult. In addition, having a job can be a highly effective incentive to get an education. Nothing like working at a fast-food joint or as someone's gofer to convince you that education, and the opportunity it brings, is a gift devoutly to be sought!

When it comes to a part-time job for your daughter, your first concern should be your daughter's academic performance, particularly if she has outstanding intellectual potential. Maintaining high grades is *de rigeur* if she is to be accepted at a good university and receive the advanced training required for earning a good living in the twenty-first century. By the same token, school isn't everything, so if she can handle both a job *and* her academic responsibilities, which may be significantly greater if she is in an advanced program, then by all means allow her to work and experience the sense of accomplishment, independence, and mastery that earning one's own money can bring.

Points to Consider When Your Daughter Wants a Job

1. Weigh the benefits to her self-esteem, especially if she has not been a high performer academically or if school has already had

a negative influence on her self-esteem. A job may help correct the damage that has been done.

2. Consider whether the job has increased or will increase her mastery behaviors, including her willingness to take the risk to learn something new, her persistence when confused, and her level of responsibility, resilience, and confidence.

3. Decide if the job is helping or will help her to establish a sense of independence and self-reliance.

4. Consider her work hours and school schedule. Even high-energy teenagers—maybe *especially* high-energy teenagers—get stretched too thin. If she seems overwhelmed, help her to see that work *and* school may be too much and she should cut back her hours, apply for a job with a different schedule, or let the job go for a while.

5. Acknowledge her pluck. Appreciate and praise her for her desire to be more financially independent and for her willingness to work for her money.

Drinking, Drugs, and Driving Contracts

Most parents of teenagers are aware of contracts between parents and teenagers concerning drinking and driving, including drugs or any type of potentially impaired perception that is the result of imbibing a substance. These contracts require both parties to honor their side of the bargain. The teenager agrees to call her parents for a ride home whenever drinking or drugs impairs her ability to get home safely or if her driver is impaired. The parent agrees to pick her up, regardless of the time and place, and not to punish her, as in "How could you have gotten yourself in this situation? I told you not to hang out with those kids," and so on. Berating your teenager for being in this situation may be one of the surest ways to ensure that she will *not* call you the next time she needs help.

I have nothing to add to this "drinking, drugs, and driving contract" except to emphasize that it is a great idea and a potentially life-saving tool. All parents of teenagers should initiate this contract with their kids as soon as their daughters begin riding in cars with other teenagers.

Discussing Alcohol, Drugs, and Sexual Assault

In teen culture, the use of alcohol is often regarded as fun rather than debilitating. Many teenagers associate drunkenness with good times, being cool, and feeling more mature. Since they do not naturally associate it with a lack of judgment or increased vulnerability, parents must make this link clear and increase girls' awareness and mastery behavior in this area. There are right ways and wrong ways to go about this.

First, let me stress the importance of avoiding alcohol or drugs as a morality issue, even if you believe it is. If you make it a moral issue, you may stir up an unnecessary and distracting argument that will wind up being more about parental control and less about her safety, which should be your primary concern. Your daughter is in the process of establishing her own moral and ethical code as separate from yours. This is a mastery-oriented task and a natural part of her developmental process as she becomes independent of her parents. Therefore, any hint that she should unquestioningly accept your moral code may send her off in the direction of arguing about *that* instead of guarding her safety.

Second, do not make her feel as if the problems associated with drinking are somehow the result of a flaw in her character or an inability to act in a mature fashion. Present your arguments as you would to an adult, in a way that indicates that *anyone* who ingests alcohol will begin to exhibit lack of judgment; that anyone who drinks too much will find her effectiveness curtailed and her behavior helpless and immature; that these developments are a result of the action of the drug itself, not a reflection of the individual's moral turpitude or lack of character. If you fail to do this, she may be eager to prove to you that she *is* a responsible young woman who can "handle it." You must make her understand that morality, maturity, and mastery are not the issues. If she drinks, she will increase her chances of a negative life experience.

Third, keep the discussion focused on safety issues, not criticism of her friends, especially if her friends are not really a bad crowd but are just engaging in the typical experimental behavior of teenagers. Otherwise, the issue may become your criticism of her judgment and choice of friends, rather than her safety. You don't want to cause a distracting argument about her friends. It may help you to remember that even we so-called adults get into situations we did not anticipate with people who have exercised bad judgment, so give your daughter a break if she asks for your help.

I want to emphasize the link between drinking and drugs and sexual assault or other forms of violence. While you, as her mother, are certainly aware of this problem, your daughter may not be. The way to protect your daughter is to make her aware of the link, between drinking and the potential for exploitation. Talk with her about her increased vulnerability to predatory males when she is under the influence of any mind-altering drug, including alcohol.

Keep her informed of the statistics on date rape and sexual harassment, especially at fraternity parties or anywhere that drunken young men are gathered in a group. Make her aware that a young man who would not have the audacity to mistreat a girl when he is sober and alone with her can undergo a dangerous personality change with a group of his peers who have been drinking and are challenging his manhood.

Let your daughter know that her mastery skills can serve her only if she maintains an alert consciousness, an ability to judge the situation with clarity, and the will to act at the moment she needs to— all of which are severely impaired by alcohol and drugs. Teach her that her hard-won mastery will not be available to her if alcohol or drugs are impeding her judgment.

Teach your daughter *and* her friends the mastery skill of staying in a group if a situation begins to look threatening. Let her and her friends know that finding oneself a solitary woman in a group of drunken men is unwise. Teach them the "warrior skills" of looking out for one another: how to see a situation developing, how to get a friend out of a bind, how to suggest when a friend has had enough to drink, how to receive the message of "no more alcohol" from one who has your safety at heart, and how to be firm—even physical, if need be—with drunk friends who are determined to argue that they are sober.

The main point is to help your daughter recognize that mastery behavior is not just about achieving goals and getting good grades, but about bringing the same attitude and set of skills into all aspects of her life, including her social and romantic life. In this way, mastery behavior will serve her in whatever life situation she may find herself.

Love Relationships and Mastery Behavior

Love relationships and sexual matters are most definitely appropriate arenas to teach your daughter how to demonstrate mastery-oriented behavior. These matters have tremendous power to derail a girl's motivation to achieve. Witness the many adult women who allow their relationships with men to interrupt, delay, and otherwise butt into their careers. Perhaps the greatest favor we can do for our girls at puberty is to teach them how to have loving relationships with men who do not undermine their self-esteem.

Mastery-oriented behaviors—especially risk-taking, persistence through confusion, and externalization of failure—acquire an entirely different connotation when applied to the realm of love and sex. Discussing these matters effectively so that our daughters do not get confused requires the refinement and skill to communicate the subtleties. Before we delve deeper into the mastery-oriented approach to love and sex, I would like to address the subject of abusive relationships.

Abusive situations teach learned helplessness, as well as "opportunity-blindness." Studies show that learned helplessness is so prevalent among battered women that it has been accepted as a legal defense in cases of battered wives who stay too long in abusive situations and finally wind up killing their husbands to defend themselves. Since people in truly abusive situations are often threatened with death if they act, they come to believe that there is nothing they can do.

If you discover your daughter is involved with a boy who puts her down, yells, controls her actions, or even gets physical, discuss with her the consequences of her involvement with this boy. Acquaint her with the reality that abuse always gets worse, not better. Let her know that if she does not leave this relationship, she will likely be dealing with stronger and stronger doses of it.

It is a good idea to bring these subjects up when your daughter's girlfriends are present, for two reasons. First, they will most likely agree with you, and they'll be concerned about her welfare as well. They may take your side and support you. Second, it will also teach *them* that they do not have to endure bad treatment from boys.

Again, there is a right way and a wrong way to do this. First, assure your daughter that you love and respect her. Second, *do not begin by criticizing the boy.* This will only provoke your daughter into defending him. Instead, discuss your concerns about her safety, well-being, and emotional health. If you hear him put her down, openly discuss your feelings. Say something like "Because I love you and want you to be happy, it makes me sad to hear Jason put you down. I know how bad I would feel if your father said those things to me. How did his comments make you feel?" Or "When Alex yells at you, I get concerned for your confidence and happiness. Is there any way I can help?" Or "If you ever need to talk about the way you feel when Michael tries to control your behavior or puts you down, I'm available."

One mother in a workshop told the following story: "I don't like the way my daughter's boyfriend treats her. He is very controlling, but I had avoided saying anything. Then one day Alison came storming out of her bedroom, slammed the door, and said, 'I just hate it when Rick tells me what to do and talks down to me. Today, when I told him about something that was bothering me, he said I was just PMSing. He just discounted everything I said with that PMS crap. Whenever I try to tell him what's bothering me, he chalks it up to PMS. I wish I knew what to say when he acts like that.'

"Immediately I saw my opportunity, but I tried not to pounce." The mother paused as the audience chuckled. "Then I said, 'I know what you mean. You've got to train these guys right away to let them know you don't like their behavior. Want some suggestions?' She was skeptical, not wanting to take advice from her mother, but at the same time she wanted help. Reluctantly she said, 'Like what?'

"Then together we sat down and brainstormed some retorts she could have ready the next time Rick put her down or told her what to do. It turned out to be not only a real female bonding experience but funny, too. We came up with some hilarious responses. The one she decided to use, since he was always chalking up every problem to PMS was 'You better learn to take it like a man. Real men can handle PMS.' We laughed and laughed. She said, 'I like it because it's so in-his-face.' She said the very thing I was thinking myself!"

Meanness and verbal abuse from boys occur regularly in the hallways of your daughter's school, from middle school through high school, so teach your daughter some comebacks. When the time is right, such as when you hear your daughter and her girlfriends discussing bad treatment from boys, sit down with them in a group and turn it into a game by brainstorming some smart and witty comebacks. Write them down and then have the girls role-play. Usually there is enough "child" left in them to have fun playing the roles of the boys and themselves. Encourage them to exaggerate, be theatrical (walk like the boys, talk like them, and so on), and have fun while they learn how to assert themselves.

SAFE SEX, SMART SEX, NO SEX

I hope this is not an area you have waited to discuss, but have been educating your daughter about all along. Still, teenagers need supplemental advice that goes beyond the standard talks about love and mutual respect with a sexual partner. If she has become sexually active, the life-threatening issues of sexuality transmitted diseases and pregnancy are now added to the issue of love and trust.

Of course, the safest sex is no sex, and many mothers will prefer this line of instruction. Nothing wrong with this approach, particularly if it is based on your religious views. However, after hearing many girls speak out in small groups where their mothers were not present, I wish to caution you that believing your daughter will not have sex *may* be an act of denial that could have serious consequences, since many girls do become sexually active by age seventeen. Even in an open, trusting relationship, most girls are reluctant to discuss their budding sex lives with their mothers. (Did *you*?) Therefore, they rely mostly on their peers for information.

To ensure that your daughter is getting the right information, you have to be the one to give it to her. She already knows about menstruation, how her plumbing works, how babies are made, and the importance of love and respect, but have you discussed more difficult areas like pleasure, responsiveness, and a male's responsibility in female arousal?

Now, here comes the part where *I* get nervous. Why? Because I am about to discuss your daughter's desire, capacity, and right to enjoy her sexuality. While most mothers have no difficulty discussing menstruation, birth control, and the biology of reproduction with their daughters, many have a more difficult time discussing sexual issues such as pleasure. However, if we make our daughters aware that they have a right to demand sexual pleasure, and not just to give it, we increase the level of mastery that they take with them into their adult sex lives.

This is an issue I call smart sex. It has to do with truth-telling, giving your daughter information about her body that will enable her to enjoy her sexuality, and making her aware that her partner has a responsibility to please her. I am confident that you will be happy with my advice because it comes with a built-in reason for your daughter to postpone intercourse!

Inform your daughter that the longer she waits to have intercourse, the more she will learn about her own body, about what she likes and she doesn't like, what she responds to and what turns her off. If she allows herself to be rushed into intercourse, she may never learn about her own sexual pleasure. Waiting gives your daughter a chance to discover other sources of sexual pleasure, and best of all, it teaches her boyfriend the same thing!

This is an excellent lesson for her to take with her into adulthood. The longer a male must wait for intercourse, the more likely he is to experiment with other ways to make his partner more receptive. A strategy all women should practice, instead of faking orgasms, is making the men in our lives more attentive, creative, and alert to our sexual needs. By waiting, your daughter will learn to take her time with each new man she encounters romantically. At the same time, he will be coerced into learning more about her body. So it's no longer "good girls don't" but rather "smart girls wait." That is a mastery-oriented female attitude toward sex.

Waiting teaches a boy to slow down and pay attention to his partner and her needs, and he will take this lesson with him into manhood. The girl gets the chance to find out if a guy's intentions are honorable. Then the opportunity develops for a real relationship *before* sex rather than after it. In this way, girls benefit sexually as well as emotionally, because postponing intercourse develops trust and establishes bonds.

If you are having some trouble with the idea of discussing these issues frankly and forthrightly with your daughter, remember that you are preparing her for the challenges of a personal life as an adult, with all that entails—complete with sexual partners and "spousal types." As she progresses through the stages of emotional and sexual involvement, there will arise unforeseen circumstances and subtleties that are part of the trials and tribulations of romantic involvement *as an adult*. Bringing a mastery attitude and a concomitant set of skills to these issues will be to her benefit.

Therefore, having frank discussions with her ahead of time, *before* she is emotionally involved, in which you present unforeseen circumstances for her consideration, will contribute to her sense of mastery and her ability to use it in all situations, including the romantic ones. The list below will get you started. Use your judgment. Tailor your discussions to the age and maturity of your daughter.

Sex and Relationship Questions to Discuss with Your Daughter

1. What if you experiment once, have sex, and then decide you don't want to keep having sex? How will you handle this with your boyfriend, who will probably think that sex is going to continue?
2. What if your boyfriend's attitude toward you changes after you have sex with him? How will you handle this?
3. Do you imagine your first sexual encounter should be romantic and spontaneous, or do you want to be the one who decides where and when? Do you want to be in control, plan ahead, and be prepared?
4. Suppose a boy says he will drop you if you don't have sex with him.
5. What is your motive for wanting to have sex?
6. What if your boyfriend discovers he likes you as a friend only? Will you continue to have sex with him? Will you stop?
7. What if your boyfriend is enjoying a sexual relationship with you but you are not enjoying it? How would you handle this?
8. Suppose you discover that he is dating other girls. Would you continue to have sex?

That Was Then, This Is Now

Not so long ago—immediately following the sixties, in fact—many women denied that they were feminists, so successful was the establishment at depicting feminists as a ragtag bunch of angry, unattractive, recalcitrant, militant, masculine, misfit women who were unsuccessful at attracting men or were uncaring, non-nurturing mothers. Given that depiction, it is no wonder that some women distanced themselves from the label.

Today I am happy to report there has been a shift in our young women of high school and college age. The best way to describe this shift is to quote the girls I have been interviewing over the last five years, for it is in their statements regarding feminism that we see this subtle but distinct change. Five years ago, for example, young women of high school and college age were saying, "I'm not a feminist, but..." and then they would proceed to lay out an entire feminist agenda complete with a pro-choice stance, equal pay, family leave, subsidized day care, and so on. They just refused to call themselves feminists. Today's high school and college girls say "I *am* a feminist, but..." willingly aligning themselves with a feminist philosophy and recognizing its potential to benefit their lives, but making distinctions where they have personal disagreements with the overall philosophy.

Indeed, research shows that girls have been strengthened by the feminist rhetoric of the last twenty-five years. Classic parenting books, like *Growing Up Free* by Letty Pogrebin, have given mothers the tools they need to correct the negative impact of gender stereotyping, enabled them to create nonsexist home environments for both girls and boys, and given fathers a new perspective on their critical role as active parents. Consequently, girls now believe that the momentum of history is behind them, that women cannot be stopped. Of course, they tend to take for granted the progress in women's rights that their mothers and other forebears struggled to achieve. Frequently they see the privileges and choices they now enjoy as a given, as opportunities that cannot be taken away. Their mothers, of course, are a little less sure of this.

Ultimately, this perception that women cannot be stopped is a good one. Our girls will be indignant when their rights are threatened or their choices limited. They will be resilient in the struggle for the equality of women, in which they, and even their children, will be the vanguard. This perception will give them the hope and courage necessary to continue the collective effort.

Finally, the subtle difference between "I'm not a feminist but..." and "I am a feminist but..." is both provocative and potent—the willingness to name the collective needs, voices, and visions of women as a group versus the willingness to rely on the traditional patriarchy to protect one's rights. The difference between aligning oneself with the mentality of sisterhood and entrusting one's future to the mentality of the status quo is the difference between independence and dependence, between the way things were and the way they can be.

See to it, through your modeling and mentoring, that your daughter is resilient and persistent, that she acquires the skills of a mastery-oriented risk-taker with high self-esteem. It will make the difference that leads her to a better life. Do it not only for your daughter but for her daughter as well. Do it for your mother who was once a daughter. Do it for your grandmothers, your aunts, your sisters, your friends. Finally, do it for all the daughters who will one day be mothers.

Notes

CHAPTER 1: ACHIEVEMENT BEHAVIOR

1. The research and findings on adolescent girls and the crisis of puberty has been documented and discussed in many books over the last ten years. Interested readers are referred to the works listed in Suggested Reading, on page 273.

2. David and Myra Sadker, *Failing at Fairness: How America's Schools Cheat Girls* (New York: Scribner, 1994).

3. U.S. Department of Labor Women's Bureau, *1993 Handbook on Women Workers: Trends and Issues* (Washington, D.C.: U.S. Department of Labor, 1994), p. 34.

4. E. S. Belansky, "The Impact of Mothers and Peers on Adolescents' Gender Role Traditionality and Plans for the Future," paper presented at the biennial meeting of the Society for Research in Child Development (New Orleans, March 1993).

5. Sadker and Sadker, *Failing at Fairness,* p. 72. Despite more than three decades of second-wave feminism and the supposed leap of consciousness that has occurred concerning gender and stereotypes, girls and boys in school are still subjected in their textbooks to males, but not females, as achievers, leaders, inventors, risk-takers, and action-oriented participants in society.

6. This was a classroom classic when I was a teacher ten years ago. Since then I have observed many classroom interactions, and I can vouch for the fact that very little has changed.

7. Jean H. Block, "Another Look at Sex Differentiation in the Socialization Behaviors of Mothers and Fathers," in J. A. Sherman and F. L. Den-

mark, eds., *Psychology of Women: Future Directions of Research* (New York: Psychological Dimensions, 1979), p. 25.

8. Michael Siegal, "Are Sons and Daughters Treated More Differently by Fathers Than by Mothers?" *Developmental Review* 7 (1987): 183–209.

9. Doris Yee and Jacquelynne Eccles, "Parent Perceptions and Attributions for Children's Math Achievement," *Sex Roles,* 19, no. 5–6 (1988): 317–34; Max Lummis and Harold Stevenson, "Gender Differences in Beliefs and Achievement: A Cross-Cultural Study," *Developmental Psychology* 26, no. 2 (1990): 254–63.

10. Janet Kuebli and Robyn Fivush, "Gender Differences in Parent-Child Conversations about Past Emotions," *Sex Roles* 27, no. 11–12 (1992): 683–98.

11. Andrée Pomerlau, Daniel Bolduc, Gerard Malcuit, and Louise Cossette, "Pink or Blue: Environmental Gender Stereotypes in the First Two Years of Life," *Sex Roles* 22, no. 5–6 (1990): 359–68. The first study of this kind was conducted in 1975 when researchers analyzed the content of children's rooms and found stereotypical toys and games. Fifteen years later, when this study was done, very little had changed.

12. Sadker and Sadker, *Failing at Fairness,* p. 138.

13. Greenberg-Lake Analysis Group, *Shortchanging Girls, Shortchanging America: A Nationwide Poll to Assess Self-esteem, Educational Experiences, Interest in Math and Science, and Career Aspirations of Girls and Boys Ages 9–15;* R. Caporrimo, "Gender, Confidence, Math: Why Aren't the Girls 'Where the Boys Are'?" paper presented at the American Psychological Association (Boston, August 1990).

14. A. Sullivan, E. Snee, and K. Weinger, *High Hopes, Long Odds* (Indianapolis: Indiana Youth Institute, 1994). As cited in "Synopsis of Research on Girls," copyright © 1995 Ms. Foundation for Women.

15. Greenberg-Lake, *Shortchanging Girls,* pp. 7–8.

16. Sadker and Sadker, *Failing at Fairness,* pp. 139–40.

CHAPTER 2: THE LEARNING PARADOX

1. Betty Allgood-Merton, Peter Lewinsohn, and Hyman Hops, "Sex Differences and Adolescent Depression," *Journal of Abnormal Psychology* 99, no. 1 (Feb. 1990): 55–63; Herman Brutsaert, "Changing Sources of Self-Esteem among Girls and Boys in Secondary Schools," *Urban Education* 24, no. 4 (Jan. 1990): 432–39; Sheila Williams, and Rob McGee, "Adolescents' Self-Perceptions of Their Strengths," *Journal of Youth and Adolescence* 20, no. 3 (June 1991): 325–37. These articles are a small sample of a vast body of literature on girls and their declining self-esteem beginning around puberty. Interested readers are referred to Suggested Reading for further research.

2. Scores of studies spanning the years from 1977 to 1992 reflect the find-

ings summarized in this section. For the sake of expediency, I have condensed and clustered the studies and provided the conclusions of researchers in the field. The actual studies themselves appear in Suggested Reading. Interested readers are referred to the articles and books in this section. Wherever a specific finding is referred to in the text, the pertinent article will be cited.

3. A. H. Stein and M. M. Bailey, "The Socialization of Achievement Orientation in Females," *Psychological Bulletin* 80 (1973): 345–66.

4. Carol S. Dweck and B. G. Licht, "Learned Helplessness and Intellectual Achievement," in M. P. Seligman and J. Garber, eds., *Human Helplessness: Theory and Research* (New York: Academic Press, 1980), pp. 197–221.

5. Deborah J. Stipek and J. Heidi Gralinski, "Gender Differences in Children's Achievement-Related Beliefs and Emotional Responses to Success and Failure in Mathematics," *Journal of Educational Psychology* 83 (1991): 361–71.

6. B. G. Licht and Carol S. Dweck, "Determinants of Academic Achievement: The Interaction of Children's Achievement Orientations with Skill Area," *Developmental Psychology* 20 (1984): 628–36. Also see D. J. Stipek and J. Hoffman, "Development of Children's Performance-Related Judgments," *Child Development* 51 (1980): 912–14.

7. Stipek and Gralinski, p. 369.

8. P. L. Casserly, "Factors Affecting Female Participation in Advanced Placement Programs in Mathematics, Chemistry and Physics," in L. H. Fox, L. Brody, and D. Tobin, eds., *Women and the Mathematical Mystique* (Baltimore: Johns Hopkins University Press, 1980), pp. 138–63. Research shows that the decision to take algebra in the eighth grade is a critical choice. If a girl feels unsure of herself or is not developmentally ready for algebra in the eighth grade, we should persuade her to postpone it for another year or get a tutor, but *not* omit it entirely.

CHAPTER 3: CAUSES AND EFFECTS

1. Nathaniel Branden, *Six Pillars of Self-Esteem* (New York: Bantam, 1994), pp. 3–4.

2. Sedek Grzegorz and Miroslaw Kofta, "When Cognitive Exertion Does Not Yield Cognitive Gain: Toward an Informational Explanation of Learned Helplessness," *Journal of Personality and Social Psychology* 58, no. 4 (1990): 729–43.

3. Many studies have shown that girls' underperformance in math is the result of teaching methods that cater to male learning styles, lack of encouragement from adults, and internalization of failure. The interested reader is referred to Katherine Hanson, "Teaching Mathematics Effectively and Equitably to Females," *Trends and Issues* 17 (1992): 1–34; Deborah J. Stipek and J. Heidi Gralinski, "Gender Differences in Children's

Achievement-Related Beliefs and Emotional Responses to Success and Failure in Mathematics," *Journal of Educational Psychology* 83, no. 3 (1991): 361–71; Cynthia Tocci and George Engelhard, "Achievement, Parental Support, and Gender Differences in Attitudes toward Mathematics," *Journal of Educational Research* 84, no. 5 (May–June 1991): 280–86; J. S. Hyde, E. Fennema, and S. J. Lamon, "Gender Differences in Mathematics Performance: A Meta-Analysis," *Psychological Bulletin* 107 (1990): 139–55; Paula Olszewski-Kubilius, et al., "Predictors in Achievement in Mathematics for Gifted Males and Females," *Gifted Child Quarterly* 34, no. 2 (Spring 1990): 64–71.

4. David and Myra Sadker, *Failing at Fairness* (New York: Scribner, 1994), pp. 73–76.

5. M. Franklin, *Add-Ventures for Girls: Building Math Confidence, Elementary Teachers' Guide,* and *Add-Ventures for Girls: Building Math Confidence, Junior High Teachers' Guide* (Reno: Research and Educational Planning Center, Nevada University, 1990), Hanson, "Teaching Mathematics," pp. 1–34.

6. Delores Gold, Gail Crombie, and Sally Noble, "Relations between Teachers' Judgments of Girls' and Boys' Compliance and Intellectual Competence," *Sex Roles* 16, no. 7–8 (April 1987): 351–58.

7. L. Grant, "Race and the Schooling of Young Girls," in Julia Wrigley, ed., *Education and Gender Equality* (London: Falmer Press, 1992), pp. 91–114.

8. A report of the AAUW's 1993 investigation, researched by Louis Harris and Associates, entitled *Hostile Hallways: The AAUW Survey on Sexual Harassment in America's Schools,* concluded that sexual harassment was rampant in schools. While both boys and girls reported problems, girls were the more frequent targets: 65 percent to 42 percent for boys. For minority girls, it is even worse: 42 percent of African-American girls and 40 percent of Hispanic girls report harassment by sixth grade or earlier as compared to 31 percent of white girls.

Other studies also confirm sexual harassment in the schools. In 1992, when *Seventeen* asked its readers whether they had been subjected to unwanted sexual behavior, either physical or verbal, they received thousands of written responses describing bra snapping, poking with pencils and other instruments, having their clothing yanked at or pulled down, touching, pinching, cornering, forced kissing, public comments and jokes about their bodies, and graffiti depicting them having sexual intercourse or oral sex.

When I taught English in the public schools I was appalled at the student graffiti aimed at degrading girls and using sex as the vehicle. Many of the drawings and sayings included the names of specific girls and were violent in nature. My contacts in the schools inform me that nothing has changed and that the situation may in fact be worse.

9. Jill McLean Taylor, "Cultural Stories: Hispanic and Portuguese Daughters and Mothers," in Bonnie Leadbeater and Niobe Way, eds. *Urban*

Adolescent Girls: Resisting Stereotypes (New York: Teachers College Press, 1995).

10. Elizabeth Debold, Marie Wilson, and Idelisse Malave, *Mother/Daughter Revolution* (Reading, Mass.: Addison-Wesley, 1993), p. 16.

11. Greenberg-Lake Analysis Group, pp. 8–9 (see Chap. 1, n. 13).

12. Jean H. Block, "Another Look at Sex Differentiation in the Socialization Behaviors of Mothers and Fathers," in J. A. Sherman and F. L. Denmark, eds., *Psychology of Women: Future Directions of Research* (New York: Psychological Dimensions, 1979), p. 25.

CHAPTER 5: MOTHERS AS MENTORS

1. Research and theories on a changing view of self are taken from a body of work known as symbolic interactionism. Interested individuals can refer to the classic works of George Herbert Mead for an in-depth discussion on the relationship of self and society.

2. This discussion on the formation of self-concept is based on Morris Rosenberg, *Conceiving the Self* (New York: Basic Books, 1979).

3. Robert Rosenthal and Lenore Jacobsen, *Pygmalion in the Classroom: Teacher Expectations and Pupils' Intellectual Development* (New York: Holt, Rhinehart and Winston, 1974); M. Gail Jones and Jack Wheatley, "Gender Differences in Teacher-Student Interactions in Science Classrooms," *Journal of Research in Science Teaching* 27, no. 9 (1990): 861–74; Cynthia Tocci and George Engelhard, "Achievement, Parental Support and Gender Differences in Attitudes toward Mathematics," *Journal of Educational Research* 84, no. 5 (May-June 1991): 280–86; Paula Olszewski-Kubilius et al., "Predictors in Achievement in Mathematics for Gifted Males and Females," *Gifted Child Quarterly* 34, no. 2 (Spring 1990): 64–71.

4. Ann B. Miser and Nancy Sebring, Evaluation Report. Unpublished manuscript, June 1996.

5. *Working Woman,* February 1996.

6. Carol Kleiman, "Women at Work," *Chicago Tribune,* March 12, 1996. Statistic corroborated by Dr. Douglas Orr, Economics Department, University of Washington at Spokane.

7. U.S. Department of Labor Women's Bureau, *1993 Handbook on Women Workers: Trends and Issues* (Washington, D.C.: U.S. Department of Labor, 1994), p. 34.

8. Kathleen Galotti, Steven Kozberg, and Maria Farmer, "Gender and Developmental Differences in Adolescents' Conceptions of Moral Reasoning," *Journal of Youth and Adolescence* 18, no. 5 (1989): 475–88; Zella Luria, "A Methodological Critique," *Signs: Journal of Women in Culture and Society* 11 (Winter 1986): 316–21; Eleanor Maccoby, "Gender and Relationships," *American Psychologist* 45, no. 4 (1990): 513–20; J. Tsalikis and M. Ortiz Buonafina, "Ethical Beliefs, Differences of Males and Females," *Journal of Business Ethics* 9 (1990): 509–17.

9. Nancy Eisenber and Randy Lennon, "Sex Differences in Empathy and Related Capacities," *Psychological Bulletin* 94 (1983): 100–131. From the authors of the article, which is a summary of numerous studies to measure empathy in both children and adults, comes this conclusion: "There is little evidence for the conclusion that the (self-described) sex difference in empathy...is due to an innate mechanism or predisposition."

10. Maccoby, "Gender and Relationships," 513–20; Linda Carli, "Gender, Language, and Influence," *Journal of Personality and Social Psychology* 59, no. 5 (1990): 941–51. Carli's study, conducted with college students and using language to measure female assertiveness, came to a similar conclusion: that women were more assertive in a same-sex situation and less so when males were present.

11. Sadker and Sadker, *Failing at Fairness*, p. 93.

12. Naomi Wolf, *The Beauty Myth: How Images of Beauty Are Used Against Women* (New York: Doubleday, 1991), p. 4. Interested readers are encouraged to read this incredible analysis of the beauty industry and how it has been used to oppress women both personally and professionally.

13. Daniel Shepardson and Edward Pizzini, "Gender Bias in Female Elementary Teachers' Perceptions of the Scientific Ability of Students," *Science Education* 76, no. 2 (1992): 147–53; Meredith Kimball, "A New Perspective on Women's Math Achievement," *Psychological Bulletin* 105, no. 2 (1989): 198–214.

14. Sadker and Sadker, *Failing at Fairness*, p. 96.

15. Delores Gold, Gail Crombie, and Sally Noble, "Relations between Teachers' Judgments of Girls' and Boys' Compliance and Intellectual Competence," *Sex Roles* 16, no. 7–8 (April 1987): 351–58.

16. Sadker and Sadker, *Failing at Fairness*, pp. 156–59.

17. Ibid. Although I have already quoted this book extensively, I would like to take the opportunity here to encourage all parents to read this enlightening, chilling, and well-researched indictment of American schools and their treatment of girls.

18. Ibid., p. 196.

19. Ibid.

20. Alice Baumgartner Papageorgiou, "My Daddy Might Have Loved Me: Students' Perceptions of Differences between Being Male and Being Female," unpublished manuscript, Institute for Equality in Education, University of Colorado at Denver, 1982.

21. Sadker and Sadker, *Failing at Fairness*, 84.

22. Ibid., p. 85.

23. Ibid., pp. 197–225.

24. Kyle Pruett, "Nurturing Dads and the Kids Who Love Them," *Child* magazine, June-July 1995, p. 115. Mothers were shown to be effective

teachers too, but dads tended to sneak teaching in within the context of play.

CHAPTER 6: BUT I ACTED LIKE SUCH A *GIRL*

1. Nicky Marone, *How to Father a Successful Daughter* (New York: Ballantine Books, 1988), pp. 74–80.
2. Ross D. Parke and D. B. Sawin, "The Family in Early Infancy: Social Interactional and Attitudinal Analyses," in F. A. Pederson, ed., *The Father-Infant Relationship: Observational Studies in the Family Setting,* (New York: Praeger, 1980).
3. Kyle Pruett, "Nurturing Dads and the Kids Who Love Them," *Child* magazine, June-July 1995, p. 117.
4. Andrée Pomerlau et al., "Pink or Blue," 338–359 (see Chap. 1, n. 11). In *Failing at Fairness,* David and Myra Sadker tell the story of one father who refused to let his son play with a walkie-talkie he received as a gift because it was pink!
5. Timothy W. Gallwey, *The Inner Game of Tennis* (New York: Random House, 1986).
6. Betty Edwards, *Drawing on the Right Side of the Brain* (Los Angeles: Tarcher, 1979).
7. Marone, *How to Father a Successful Daughter,* pp. 198–202.

CHAPTER 7: MASTERING THE MEDIA

1. Mindy Bingham, and Sandy Stryker with Susan Allstetter Neufeldt, *Things Will Be Different for My Daughter* (New York: Penguin Books, 1995), p. 219. This was recently confirmed by screenwriting agent Carolyn Hodges of the Carolyn Hodges Agency.

CHAPTER 8: NOT FOR BOYS ONLY

1. Sharon Begley, "Your Child's Brain," *Newsweek,* February 19, 1996, pp. 54–62.
2. These ideas as well as those appearing later in this chapter are based on ideas presented in Peggy Kaye, *Games for Math* (New York: Pantheon, 1988).
3. Amy Sullivan, Ellen Snee, and Katie Weinger, *High Hopes, Long Odds* (Indianapolis: Indiana Youth Institute, 1994).
4. National Science Foundation, *Women and Minorities in Science and Engineering* (Washington, D.C.: National Science Foundation, 1990).
5. Susan McGee Bailey, "Women and K–12 Science and Mathematics Education," testimony before the Subcommittee on Energy, U.S. House of Representatives, Washington, D.C., June 28, 1994; and Wellesley Col-

lege Center for Research on Women, *How Schools Shortchange Girls,* pp. 24–32.

6. Greenberg-Lake, p. 10 (see Chap. 1, n. 13).
7. Bailey, pp. 24–32.
8. Robert D. Hess and Irene T. Miura, "Gender Differences in Enrollment in Computer Camps and Classes," *Sex Roles,* 13, no. 200–201 (1985): 193–203; Marlaine E. Lockheed, "Women, Girls and Computers: A First Look at the Evidence," *Sex Roles,* 13, no. 117 (1985); Carole Nelson and J. Allen Watson, "The Computer Gender Gap: Children's Attitudes, Performance and Socialization," *Journal of Educational Technology Systems* 19, no. 4 (1990–91): 345–53; June Mark, "Beyond Equal Access: Gender Equity in Learning with Computers," (Women's Educational Equity Act Publishing Center, June 1992), pp. 1–8. As cited in Sadker and Sadker, p. 122.
9. Sadker and Sadker, p. 123.
10. Telephone interview with Dr. Kristen Yount, associate professor of sociology at North Kentucky University, November 14, 1996.

CHAPTER 9: LOOKING AFTER HERSELF

1. The individuals chosen to be model muggers are highly trained individuals. First, there is a rigorous screening process involving, among other things, psychological testing. In addition, the individual must be a black belt martial artist. Once past the screening procedures, they get into "the suit"—an elaborate outfit of protective gear including helmet and protective cups. They must then undergo another six months of training before they are allowed to make contact with an actual class.

   "Our muggers were trained not to end the assault until at least one solid knockout strike has been given and received," said Bill Kipp, a model mugger and trainer himself. "Often we make our students deliver two or three and even up to six solid strikes before we quit. We know that we do not serve them by giving up, since an assailant would not, and they may be fighting for their lives. We have been told by graduates who were actually mugged that their assailants were easier to knock out than we were. When we hear that, we know we have done our job."
2. Elizabeth Debold, Marie Wilson, and Idelisse Malave, *Mother/Daughter Revolution* (New York, Addison-Wesley, 1993), p. 37. Statistics vary widely for a number of reasons. The way the researcher chooses to define abuse can change the numbers significantly.

CHAPTER 10: THE PERIL OF PUBERTY

1. Margaret Eisenhart, "The Culture of Romance and the Myth of Gender Neutrality." Keynote address, YWCA Mother-Daughter Brunch, Boulder, Colorado, January 25, 1997.

2. Dorothy C. Holland and Margaret A. Eisenhart, *Educated in Romance: Women, Achievement and College Culture* (Chicago: University of Chicago Press, 1990), p. 4.

3. Elizabeth Debold, Marie Wilson, and Idelisse Malave, *Mother/Daughter Revolution* (New York, Addison-Wesley, 1993), p. 74.

4. Naomi Wolf, *The Beauty Myth: How Images of Beauty Are Used Against Women* (New York: Doubleday, 1991), p. 215.

5. Mindy Bingham, and Sandy Stryker with Susan Allstetter Neufeldt, *Things Will Be Different for My Daughter* (New York: Penguin Books, 1995), p. 293.

6. Janet Kuebli and Robyn Fivush, "Gender Differences in Parent-Child Conversations about Past Emotions," *Sex Roles* 27, no. 11–12 (1992): 683–98.

7. Schulman Yankelovich, *Girls' Schools Alumnae: Accomplished, Distinguished, Community-Minded* (National Coalition of Girls Schools, 1990). As cited in Sadker and Sadker, p. 233.

Suggested Reading

Bingham, Mindy, and Sandy Stryker. *Things Will Be Different for My Daughter.* New York: Penguin, 1995.

Brown, Lyn Mikel, and Carol Gilligan. *Meeting at the Crossroads.* New York: Ballantine, 1992.

Carlip, Hillary. *Girl Power: Young Women Speak Out!* New York: Warner Books, 1995.

Chernin, Kim. *The Hungry Self: Women, Eating and Identity.* New York: Times Books, 1985.

Debold, Elizabeth, Marie Wilson, and Idelisse Malave. *Mother/Daughter Revolution: From Betrayal to Power.* Reading, Mass.: Addison-Wesley, 1993.

Eagle, Carol J., and Carol Colman. *All That She Can Be.* New York: Simon & Schuster, 1993.

Faludi, Susan. *Backlash: The Undeclared War Against American Women.* New York: Crown, 1991.

Gilligan, Carol. *In a Different Voice.* Cambridge, Mass.: Harvard University Press, 1982.

Goleman, Daniel. *Emotional Intelligence.* New York: Bantam, 1995.

Holland, Dorothy C., and Margaret A. Eisenhart. *Educated in Romance: Women, Achievement and College Education.* Chicago: University of Chicago Press, 1990.

Kaye, Peggy. *Games for Math: Playful Ways to Help Your Child Learn Math from Kindergarten to Third Grade.* New York: Pantheon, 1987.

Mackoff, Barbara. *Growing a Girl: Seven Strategies for Raising a Strong and Spirited Daughter.* New York: Dell, 1996.

Marone, Nicky. *How to Father a Successful Daughter.* New York: McGraw-Hill, 1988.

Marone, Nicky. *What's Stopping You? Overcome Learned Helplessness and Do What You Never Dreamed Possible.* New York: Simon & Schuster, 1992.

Orbach, Susie. *Fat Is a Feminist Issue II.* New York: Berkley, 1986.

Pipher, Mary. *Reviving Ophelia: Saving the Selves of Adolescent Girls.* New York: Ballantine, 1994.

Pogrebin, Letty. *Growing Up Free.* New York: McGraw-Hill, 1980.

Rosenberg, Morris. *Conceiving the Self.* New York: Basic Books, 1979.

Sadker, David and Myra. *Failing at Fairness: How America's Schools Cheat Girls.* New York: Scribner, 1994.

Seligman, Martin. *Learned Optimism.* New York: Random House, 1991.

Skolnick, Joan, Carol Langbort, and Lucille Day. *How to Encourage Girls in Math and Science.* Englewood Cliffs, N.J.: Prentice-Hall, 1982.

Solinger, Rickie. *Wake Up Little Susie: Single Pregnancy and Race before* Roe v. Wade. New York: Routledge, 1992.

Tavris, Carol: *The Mismeasure of Woman.* New York: Simon & Schuster, 1992.

Wolf, Naomi. *The Beauty Myth: How Images of Beauty Are Used Against Women.* New York: Doubleday, 1991.

Index

Index